D0992884

Stonewall Inn Editions
Michael Denneny, General Editor

Buddies by Ethan Mordden
Joseph and the Old Man by Christopher Davis
Blackbird by Larry Duplechan
Gay Priest by Malcolm Boyd
Privates by Gene Horowitz
Taking Care of Mrs. Carroll by Paul Monette
Conversations with My Elders by Boze Hadleigh
Epidemic of Courage by Lon Nungesser
One Last Waltz by Ethan Mordden
Gay Spirit by Mark Thompson, ed.
As If After Sex by Joseph Torchia
The Mayor of Castro Street by Randy Shilts
Nocturnes for the King of Naples by Edmund White
Alienated Affections by Seymour Kleinberg
Sunday's Child by Edward Phillips
God of Ecstasy by Arthur Evans
Valley of the Shadow by Christopher Davis
Love Alone by Paul Monette
The Boys and Their Baby by Larry Wolff
On Being Gay by Brian McNaught
Parisian Lives by Samuel M. Steward
Living the Spirit by Will Roscoe, ed.
Everybody Loves You by Ethan Mordden
Untold Decades by Robert Patrick
Gay & Lesbian Poetry in Our Time by Carl Morse & Joan Larkin
Reports from the Holocaust by Larry Kramer
Personal Dispatches by John Preston, ed.
Tangled Up in Blue by Larry Duplechan
How to Go to the Movies by Quentin Crisp
Just Say No by Larry Kramer
The Prospect of Detachment by Lindsley Cameron
The Body and Its Dangers and Other Stories by Allen Barnett
Dancing on Tisha B'av by Lev Raphael
Arena of Masculinity by Brian Pronger
Boys Like Us by Peter McGehee
Don't Be Afraid Anymore by Reverend Troy D. Perry with Thomas L.P. Swicegood

If I read a book and it makes my whole body so cold no fire can ever warm me, I know it is poetry. If I feel physically as if the top of my head were taken off, I know this is poetry. These are the only ways I know it.

—EMILY DICKINSON

This is what you shall do: Love the earth and sun and the animals, despise riches, give alms to every one that asks, stand up for the stupid and crazy, devote your income and labor to others, hate tyrants, argue not concerning God, have patience and indulgence toward the people, take off your hat to nothing known or unknown or to any man or number of men, go freely with powerful uneducated persons and with the young and with the mothers of families, read these leaves in the open air every season of every year of your life, re-examine all you have been told at school or church or in any book, dismiss whatever insults your own soul, and your very flesh shall be a great poem and have the richest fluency not only in its words but in the silent lines of its lips and face and between the lashes of your eyes and in every motion and joint of your body.

—WALT WHITMAN

GAY

&

LESBIAN

POETRY

IN OUR TIME

AN ANTHOLOGY

EDITED BY

CARL MORSE & JOAN LARKIN

ST. MARTIN'S PRESS

NEW YORK

3/96

Pages 393–398 constitute an extension of this copyright page.

Library of Congress Cataloging-in-Publication Data

Gay & lesbian poetry in our time : an anthology / edited by Carl Morse
    and Joan Larkin.
        p.   cm.
    ISBN 0-312-02213-1
    1. Homosexuality—Poetry.   2. American poetry—20th century.
    3. Gays' writings, American.   4. Lesbians' writings, American.
    5. Lesbianism—Poetry.   I. Morse, Carl.   II. Larkin, Joan.
    PS595.H65G39   1988
    811'.54'080353—dc19   88-11546
                                                                        CIP

ISBN 0-312-03836-4 (pbk.)

Design by Robert Bull Design

Contents

Introduction

A CONVERSATION
WITH CARL MORSE AND JOAN LARKIN

JL: One thing people always ask me is: Why a *gay* anthology? Even some of our contributors brought it up.

CM: I remember right here in this living room at a party I mentioned to a straight woman editor I knew only slightly that we were doing this book, and she got really angry. She said, "Why does there have to be a *separate* book for gay people?" At the time I felt she was blaming us and said, "Well, it isn't *our* fault." Later I found out that this woman's son was dying of AIDS, and that she was unable to tell anyone.

JL: This came up all the time in the 70s when the first anthologies of poetry exclusively by women were coming out. Just this morning I read Rukeyser's preface to Louise Bernikow's anthology *The World Split Open.* * She quotes a male publisher: "'If they are any good, they can stand up in an anthology with men.' What will such a book be, a kind of wastebasket?"

CM: And of course the title comes from Rukeyser's lines: "What would happen if a woman told the truth about her life? / The world would split open."[1] That's what Gore Vidal says would happen if Americans were ever told the truth about *anything*—like death, or sex, or money.

JL: So what did you tell this woman?

CM: I just said that very few people would publish this work. I'd say that seventy percent of what we've got here is virtually unavailable to straight readers.

---

* An asterisk indicates citation of a work in the Bibliography.

[1] Muriel Rukeyser: "Käthe Kollwitz," in *The Collected Poems of Muriel Rukeyser*, McGraw-Hill, 1978.

JL: Unless they read lesbian and gay magazines.

CM: Fat chance. Several editors didn't even acknowledge our letter of inquiry.

JL: And the ones we heard from . . .

CM: "Our list is full until the end of recordable time," etc. (*laughter*)

JL: And we both know the major woman poet whose publisher dropped her when the lesbian content got too heavy for them.

CM: I don't think I ever told you about my favorite . . .

JL: Who was . . . ?

CM: Is. A very well-placed editor, critic, and very famous—and quintessentially minor—poet. He read my poems and wrote: "Homosexuality doesn't seem to have made you very happy."

JL: You're kidding.

CM: That was for openers. I can hardly wait for *The Collected Letters:* "Dear James Baldwin: Being Black doesn't seem to have made you very happy." "Dear Anne Frank: Being Jewish doesn't seem to have made you very happy." "Dear Sylvia Plath: Being a woman . . . ." (*laughter*) Well, it's not an ideal world, and someday perhaps there'll be integrated as well as separate anthologies.

JL: Of course, we do see several of these poets in straight contexts—in isolation. But all kinds of sparks result when you get us all together in one place.

CM: And misperceptions about some of us get corrected. As the book took shape, it was very exciting to see how uncoded and uncloseted some of the "establishment" poets are, once you really pay attention. Even familiar poems took on a different life.

JL: And began to speak to one another.

CM: Anyway, God knows it's the first time we've all been caught between the same covers. (*laughter*)

JL: In fact, until now a lot of us wouldn't have been caught dead anywhere together.

CM: Yet the other thing that became clear was that there's *always* been a lot of underground speaking going on between lesbians and gay men. Do you remember when we read at A Different Light bookstore, and Marilyn Hacker mentioned being influenced in the 60s by Duncan and Spicer? And Woolf and Stein and H.D. and Djuna Barnes have had a very deep effect on many gay men. Actually, gay men and lesbians—however quietly—have been giving each other support and permission for years, and continue to do so with every new poem and every new book.

JL: Isn't that what got you started on your lesbian/gay reading series? Open Lines, I mean.[2]

CM: Well, I really got started in Maine in the late 70s. The Midcoast Gay Men's group had a little fold-up traveling library. We met in different safe houses, and Bo Bergström always brought the library. One night I found "The Effeminist Manifesto"[3]—which startled me, to say the least. In fact, I still defy anyone to read it and not be changed. Then, in 1980, I lost my home and business to my local nest of brown-shirts—and the only thing I could find that helped me explain what had happened to me was the women's literature on rape. And I started devouring feminist writing—which was the first stuff that ever made real sense of my life. "Jesus—we always knew it was all lies! Why didn't somebody tell us before?" That's what a closeted teacher friend of thirty-five years wrote me recently. He'd just stumbled across Rich's *On Lies, Secrets, and Silence.**

JL: But which writers did *you* read first?

CM: Well, *your* anthology, of course.

JL: *Lesbian Poetry.*[4]

CM: Yes—where I first read Grahn and Lorde and Parker and you and practically everybody. And then Robin Morgan's *Going Too Far.** I really connected with her rage. And then *Conditions Five**— the Black Women's Issue—and *This Bridge Called My Back,** and *Nice Jewish Girls**—each of them more mind-blowing than the last on sex, race, class, and being gay. I also read magazines like *Heresies**—the Racism Issue and that splendid Sex Issue.

JL: They did a lesbian issue, too. At that point lesbian writing and publishing had been geometrically expanding and blossoming for six or seven years.

---

[2] In 1982, 1983, and 1984, Carl Morse, with the support of the Reverend Paul Abels of Washington Square Methodist Church, New York City, organized and produced Open Lines, a national poetry reading series for gay, lesbian, and profeminist people. Open Lines presented twenty-nine poets plus readings by the Blackheart Collective, the contributors to *Seditious Delicious** magazine, and the Asian Lesbians of the East Coast collective. This book is an extension of the original aims and goals of that reading series.

[3] Steven Dansky, John Knoebel, and Kenneth Pitchford: "The Effeminist Manifesto," in *Double-F: A Magazine of Effeminism,* No. 2 (Winter/Spring, 1973); collected in *A Book of Readings for Men Against Sexism,* edited by Jon Snodgrass, Times Change Press, Albion, California, 1977.

[4] *Lesbian Poetry: An Anthology:* edited by Elly Bulkin and Joan Larkin. Persephone Press, Watertown, Mass., 1981. Now distributed by Gay Presses of New York. Earlier, in 1975, Larkin and Bulkin edited *Amazon Poetry: An Anthology,* which was published by Out & Out Books, a women's independent publishing company.

CM: When did it really start?

JL: Well, the best account of that is Elly Bulkin's essay in *Lesbian Poetry*. [5] Actually, the first all-women's press—The Women's Press Collective—was founded in Oakland, California, in 1970. My own passion for lesbian writing began in the early 70s. One night I heard Martha Shelley's "Lesbian Nation" program on WBAI, and I've never been the same since. It was probably in 1973 that I found Fran Winant's "Poem To My New Jacket." [6] Later, she retitled it "Dyke Jacket." It was brave. Then I discovered *Amazon Quarterly.* * It came in a plain brown wrapper—thank God! And then I heard Audre Lorde, Alta, Judy Grahn, and Susan Griffin read in person. I was electrified. Their poems spoke directly to my hidden life, my real life. In '74, I met Irena Klepfisz and other lesbian poets at Alison Colbert's Focus II coffeehouse series. Together with three other women, Irena, Alison, Jan Clausen, and I formed a lesbian poets' support group. Then, in 1975, Elly Bulkin suggested that she and I collaborate on *Amazon Poetry.* We didn't use the word *lesbian* on the cover; but we printed it on the title page. As far as I know, that was the first place Adrienne Rich, May Swenson, and a lot of other women published in a lesbian context.

CM: At the same time gay men's poetry was mushrooming. The best summary of it all is Rudy Kikel's essay in *Gay Sunshine* * magazine's tenth-anniversary issue. [7] In 1969, Paul Mariah founded ManRoot Magazine * and ManRoot Press, which continues to this day to offer a fine list of gay men's writing. Winston Leyland began publishing *Gay Sunshine* magazine in 1970, and then his Gay Sunshine Press published the two best anthologies of gay men's poetry—*Angels of the Lyre* * in 1975 and *Orgasms of Light* * in 1977. Another important anthology had appeared even earlier, in 1973—Ian Young's *The Male Muse.* * The Boston Gay Liberation Front generated both the radical magazine *Fag Rag* (1971–) *—"the most loathsome publication in the English language," according to William Loeb, the virulent New Hampshire newspaper mogul—and a publishing operation, Good Gay Poets, which, since 1972, has issued an impor-

---

[5] There are two other indispensable accounts of lesbian poetry: Jan Clausen's *A Movement of Poets* (Long Haul Press, N.Y., 1982); and Judy Grahn's *The Highest Apple: Sappho and the Lesbian Poetic Tradition* (Spinsters, Ink, San Francisco, 1985).

[6] Originally published in the anthology *Mountain Moving Day*, edited by Elaine Gill (Crossing Press, 1973), this poem became the title poem of Fran Winant's collection *Dyke Jacket* (Violet Press, N.Y., 1976).

[7] Rudy Kikel: "After Whitman and Auden: Gay Male Sensibility in Poetry Since 1945," *Gay Sunshine*, No. 44/45, Autumn/Winter 1980.

tant series of poetry books by lesbians and gay men. In 1974, *RFD: A Country Journal for Gay Men Everywhere** got started in Iowa, and—now based in North Carolina—is still going strong. And that same year, Andrew Bifrost created his elegantly edited and produced *Mouth of the Dragon: A Poetry Journal of Male Love.* * Founded by Charles Ortleb, with Paul Baron and Michael Denneny, *Christopher Street**—still the most prestigious gay male literary magazine—made its debut in May 1976. And then Felice Picano founded The Sea Horse Press in 1977 and, in 1980, issued the landmark collection *A True Likeness: Lesbian & Gay Writing Today.* * You and three other women have poems in that book. Were you reading many gay men's poems then?

JL: Not really. In fact, in the mid-70s, with rare exceptions I didn't talk to men unless I absolutely had to.

CM: Well, I sure remember when I started putting together Open Lines in '81 being terrified at calling up lesbians out of the blue.

JL: When you called me, I thought: "What does this man want?" But I wasn't a separatist, really—and I managed to live through the phone call. *(laughter)*

CM: Well, the first year of Open Lines readings, I felt I was getting a lot of "What's he up to?" looks from the women. The second year I began to imagine I was getting a few friendly looks. *(JL laughs.)* And the third year, a few women came up to me afterwards and said, "Okay, we get it."

JL: I really didn't believe at that point that there was any poetry by men that had things to tell me that I didn't already know. And I had this stereotype of gay men's writing as—you know—oversexed.

CM: And you were partly right. After lifetimes—centuries—of incredible hypocrisy and silence, gay men could suddenly talk about sex. And did we ever! Of course, people like Barney Rosset with Grove Press started breaking things up in the 50s—the erotophobia, I mean—publishing and fighting in the courts for *Lady Chatterley's Lover* and Genet and de Sade and Rechy. God, remember when we were still smuggling *Tropic of Cancer* in from France. I didn't even *like* Henry Miller.

JL: The gay men's poetry I saw didn't seem like much of an advance over Henry Miller. Objectification bothers me, no matter who's doing it. Also, gay men were men—meaning part of the patriarchy, gynephobic.

CM: Many are. All too often, we remain our parents' children. There are plenty of gay people, including lesbians, still buying into straight power trips.

JL: I really didn't let go of my prejudice until we were deeply engaged in the process of reading for this book. I've found much that—still—disturbs me. But I was surprised at how much in gay men's writing I identify with—that, as the Quakers say, "speaks to my condition."

CM: Which is exactly why I started the Open Lines readings, and then this book. My men friends didn't know the women's writing, and my women friends didn't know the men's writing. Nor did they want to—which I found very painful. I'd love to see some analysis—really serious study—of the almost systematic ways that gay men and lesbians are denied—and deny each other—access to one another. Of course, it is not good news to the folks in charge when gay men and lesbians get together. And worse when gay and straight people do. Did I tell you that, except for the one time I read, not a single straight friend of mine ever turned up at an Open Lines reading in three whole years? I think it was Shaw who said indifference kills a lot more people than physical violence. But which of the men's poems particularly "speak to your condition"?

JL: David Bergman's "Blueberry Man" is one poem that touches me. I've always identified with outsiders. Every neighborhood I ever lived in had a "witch"—someone the adults warned us against—someone to be scared of or make fun of. In this poem, it's a male figure that's feared and yet attractive. I'm also knocked out by Essex Hemphill's "To Some Supposed Brothers." The only poems I'd ever seen before expressing this point of view were by women. And Frank Bidart's poems show real empathy with female experience. They have strong women characters.

CM: And he works so close to the edge.

JL: Lots of these poems are so funny! It's the shared humor that makes a bridge. The outrageousness of Jim Everhard's "Curing Homosexuality." The poignance of Ed Field's "Unwanted." Lines like Harold Norse's "Women pretended he was a table." *(laughter)*

CM: I love Susan Griffin's advice to the man who asked what he could do about women's liberation: "Wear a dress. / Wear a dress that you made yourself . . . ." And Jane Barnes's poem "How to Dress Like a Scary Dyke" breaks me up.

JL: Thom Gunn is another poet whose work I simply didn't know. He writes out of such wholeness. In "The Cherry Tree" poem you feel that's a woman's body he's talking about—from inside.

CM: And that's news—which is what any poem of interest is—*news.*

JL: Yes. And not all of it good. We've both lost people we love to AIDS. A poem like Michael Lassell's "How to Watch Your Brother Die" gives me the means and terms to explore my own grief.

CM: We've never managed to read it aloud without crying. And

now a few women have written elegies for people dead of AIDS—
like Honor Moore's poem for J. J. Mitchell. I remember when she
read it at John Glines's Gay Arts Festival. I was with several gay
men, and we were all deeply moved. It was the first inkling we had
that anyone besides us cared that gay men were dying. You know
what Charley Shively said to me last month: "Well, maybe the les-
bians will have to do it all by themselves."

JL: Another "bad news" poet whose talent startles me is Charles
Ortleb. His report is so radical and spare.

CM: And funny, too. But there are other kinds of news. There's a
real Renaissance of black gay men's writing going on—like nothing
else since the 1920s.

JL: Men *and* women of color.

CM: Yes, indeed.

JL: Audre Lorde and Pat Parker really transformed things. And
Barbara Smith notes, in 1977, the existence of "at least one black
lesbian writers' collective, Jemima, in New York [who] do public
readings and have available a collection of their poems."[8] *Azalea*, a
literary magazine for Third World lesbians, started that same year.

CM: In 1981, after discussion with a number of other black gay
men, Isaac Jackson founded a writers' group called Blackheart Col-
lective. They did three wonderful issues of *Blackheart** magazine,
including a Prison Issue. In 1986, several Blackheart Collective
members and a number of other writers formed a support group
called Other Countries, with a journal of the same name.* And, of
course, other groups in the gay community—including Latina and
Native American and Asian women—have similarly empowered
themselves by forming mutual support groups and writers' collec-
tives, and by publishing magazines and books.* I've heard there's a
gay male Hispanic magazine in the Southwest. One woman I know
is forming a writers' group of lesbians of Italian origin.

JL: I'm also glad that we're presenting important new writers—
like Mark Ameen. "Dying Beast" is such an unflinching meditation
on death. The voice is so exposed.

CM: And Melinda Goodman. It's like being there. And unlike
Stein's Oakland, there's plenty of there there.

[8] Barbara Smith: "Toward a Black Feminist Criticism," in *Conditions: Two*, Vol. 1,
No. 2 (October 1977); collected in *All the Women Are White, All the Blacks Are
Men, But Some of Us Are Brave: Black Women's Studies*, edited by Gloria T. Hull,
Patricia Bell Scott, and Barbara Smith, The Feminist Press, 1982. In 1981, Audre
Lorde, with Barbara Smith, Cherríe Moraga, and others, co-founded Kitchen
Table: Women of Color Press, the creation of which is a landmark in the history of
publishing.

JL: I think we should say that we've been equally concerned about the effect of this book on straight readers.

CM: Yes, I urgently want to expose straight people to these poems. Primarily because I think that anyone who reads them has a good chance of being changed—or at least given pause. And also because I think they're in for a treat. But I also keep seeing the gay kid—maybe their kid—at the bookrack in a Greyhound bus station—as scared as I was in my teens—finding this book. I profoundly share Harry Hay's determination that "no young person among us need ever take his first step out into the dark alone and afraid again."[9]

JL: The permissions given by the poems in this book—to experience—to validate one's own deepest feelings, reactions, relationships . . .

CM: One's sanity. We have time and again chosen the poem that gives "the inside story"—the poem that gives the experience itself, not a report about the experience.

JL: That's good poetry.

CM: Yes. And some of these experiences require recasting of the language—since no one has ever talked about them before—and these poets have done a lot of that. Gay and lesbian poetry refreshes the language. So much of this writing gets away from "polarity vocabularies."

JL: Meaning?

CM: Well, those either/or vocabularies and formulations so imbedded in Western writing. Good and evil. Light and dark. Love and hate. Male and female. I've often said I want at least 121 different words to describe gender. Because there are at least that many ways of having, practicing, or experiencing gender. Polarity vocabularies permit us only three ways—hetero, homo, bi. These poets describe dozens of places on the gender spectrum.

JL: And cut across gender boundaries in all directions.

CM: And class lines, too. We're the only people who meet absolutely everybody—top to bottom, and vice-versa. (*laughter*)

JL: Which isn't to say there isn't classism in the gay community.

CM: Or racism. Or ageism. Plenty. Books like this one are only a step, a sign. Most of the work—hard, brutally hard work—is private

[9] The concluding sentence of the New Member Welcoming Ritual of the first modern-day gay liberation movement in the United States—the original Mattachine Society (1950 to April 1953). Quoted by Jim Kepner in his introduction to the "Western Homophile Conference Keynote Address" by Henry (Harry) Hay; printed in *The Ladder*, June/July 1970. *The Ladder* (1956-72) was the journal of DOB (Daughters of Bilitis, founded 1955), the first successful lesbian liberation organization in the United States.

as well as public and remains to be done. When you consider gay people's talent for moving across all kinds of boundaries, it makes me wonder about the first question straight people always asked when I mentioned this book: "Will it be all *gay* content?"

JL: Meaning all sex—erotic poetry?

CM: Presumably.

JL: Well, everyone knows we never stir from our beds. We spend all day in there. We don't have to earn a living. We don't grow old. We don't get ill. We don't bring up children. We don't do housework. Don't serve in the military. Don't have to resolve our conflicts with our families or our bosses or the IRS.

CM: Or have a relationship to nature or God. And sex is exactly what they mean. They're obsessed with it. God, the question is so innately homophobic—right up there with that all-time favorite: "Which one of you is the woman?" As if they couldn't learn anything from "gay content." Do they ask Gabriel García Márquez if his next book will have all Hispanic content? Sex is vitally important to us—as a number of poems in this book evidence—but we are *not* definable, as the majority culture would so conveniently have it, exclusively by the ways we make love.

JL: I'm reminded that Adrienne Rich objected to being heterosexualized years ago in an interview with Elly Bulkin. Some straight friends had told Rich how "universal" the *Twenty-One Love Poems* were, after reading them with their lovers. I'll quote her:

> I found myself angered . . . at having my work essentially assimilated and stripped of its meaning, "integrated" into heterosexual romance. That kind of "acceptance" of the book seems to me a refusal of its deepest implications. The longing to simplify . . . to assimilate lesbian existence by saying that "relationship" is really all the same, love is always difficult—I see that as a denial, a kind of resistance, a refusal to read and hear what I've actually written, to acknowledge what I am.[10]

CM: The point is, although lesbians and gay men are not separate, *we are distinct*—and, often, we simply see things differently. The most exciting development in the recent history of gay people is the burgeoning evidence that we have always had a distinct identity and culture. And we are just now learning from people like Harry Hay* and Judy Grahn* and Mark Thompson* and Mitch Walker* and Gloria Anzaldúa* and Walter L. Williams* that our vision and our customs and our culture are as old as humankind. Hay, in a

---

[10] *Conditions: Two,* "An Interview with Adrienne Rich: Part II," Vol. 1, No. 2, October 1977.

crucial essay in 1980, describes "the key to the enormous and particular contribution that Gay People may have to make to our beloved Humankind" as "subject-SUBJECT Consciousness."[11] But let me quote Judy Grahn:

> The Gay culture I have set about to describe is old, extremely old, and it is continuous. The continuity is a result of characteristics that members teach each other so the characteristics repeat era after era. I have found that Gay culture has its traditionalists, its core group, that it is worldwide, and that it has tribal and spiritual roots . . . we also help society retain some of its oldest values and customs by keeping them and using them in our own subculture . . . What we perhaps have at the core is an uncanny ability to identify with what we are not, to die as one form and return as another.[12]

No, we are not just-like-straights-except-for-one-thing. We are different because—often from an early age—many of us experience and see the world differently. Again, *not separately, but distinctly.* And because we have a different way of seeing—both "the inside story" *and* "the outside story"—we have, as Williams and Grahn report, been used and valued in many societies as mediators through which disparate, even warring, elements of the society understand one another and manage to coexist—sometimes, indeed, to survive. Boy George was complimenting Americans on their wisdom when he said, "America has always loved a good drag queen." Yes, we have often served as priests (a very healthy percentage of the clergy of organized churches is gay)—as shamans, as advisors, as medicine people in our tribes.

JL: Or—often—in our present culture, as artists. That the arts are vigorously gay is a well-known fact.

CM: Yes. As artists—which is the same or parallel function—the interpretive, the mediating, the shamanic role.

JL: Healers.

CM: That too. Definitely. Of course when I touch on this, my straight friends bristle and say, "Well, you gay people aren't any

---

[11] Harry Hay: "Towards the New Frontiers of Fairy Vision . . . subject-SUBJECT Consciousness." *RFD: A Country Journal for Gay Men Everywhere*, Issue #24, Summer 1980. A shortened version of this essay appears in the collection *New Men, New Minds: Breaking Male Tradition*, edited by Franklin Abbott, The Crossing Press, 1987. An organizer of the original Mattachine Society in the years 1948–50, Harry Hay is widely acknowledged as the founder of the modern homophile liberation movement in America.

[12] Judy Grahn: *Another Mother Tongue: Gay Words, Gay Worlds*, Beacon Press, Boston, 1984—p. xiv, Preface; p. 269; p. 274.

more talented or any better than anybody else." Which is never what one has actually said. There is such a defensiveness about any claim on the part of gay people that they might be making some particular and beneficial contribution—that we might add something without being in competition. Time and again, we see how swiftly straight society coopts anything gay it likes—with the composer, painter, philosopher, writer—be it Gershwin, Da Vinci, Santayana, Cather—forever relegated to some asexual limbo or, worse, explained as some sort of "lost" heterosexual. All those wives and children invented for Whitman—and all that "male inspiration" for Emily Dickinson—by the Gordon Liddys and Oliver Norths of academe.[13]

JL: It's often the gay writer who's taking risks first for the entire culture. We're really good at that. From early childhood, many of us are faced with situations . . . we are forced to deal with . . .

CM: To look around. The gay child who does not look around does not survive.

JL: One of the daring things we do is write poems. Finding some way to tell the truth is part of staying sane. That's why our poems are often risky. And disturbing.

CM: Well, we've often talked, as we worked, about our concern that we had too many poems about violence, rape, abuse, victims. But what we kept coming to was that these events are often the actualities of gay people's lives. Our lives *are* violent—that is, we are all too often on the receiving end of the most violent culture ever seen on the face of the earth. The people we're worried about seem to connect the violence with gay people, and not—God forbid—themselves. It's the old "blame the victim" number. Only straight people claim to be surprised when "nice kids" maim or kill one of us. Remember the police sergeant in Bangor, Maine, who said of the teenagers who threw Charlie Howard off a bridge as he screamed, "I can't swim!": "It's not like they were ax murderers. These people come from respectable families who own property in the city of Bangor."[14]

JL: Let's hope everyone looks at the love poems.

---

[13] For a chapter and verse account of the deliberate suppression, alteration, and obfuscation of the evidence of gay presence in literature from the Renaissance to our day, see Rictor Norton's elegant essay "Ganymede Raped—The Critic As Censor" in Ian Young's bibliography *The Male Homosexual in Literature*, as well as Louie Crew and Norton's invaluable account of "The Homophobic Imagination" in *College English*, Vol. 36, No. 3.

[14] *Boston Globe*, July 13, 1984.

CM: And the ones that connect with nature and animals and things of the spirit.

JL: And healing and recovery.

CM: Of course, our institutions—the schools especially—attempt to protect us from poetry. Poems should be pretty and harmless. "Whose woods these are I think I know."

JL: "I never saw a Moor— / I never saw the Sea—" —the most innocuous lines Dickinson ever wrote.

CM: And, above all, poetry *mustn't* be political. I've noticed, however, that if one does not resist people who insist that poetry is not political, one ends up having to live with *their* politics and *their* poetry rather than one's own. As Plato damn well knew, poetry is a highly political and dangerous business—corrupts young minds, for one thing.

JL: Not to mention adult minds. *(laughter)*

CM: Gay people's poetry does not confirm the status quo—private or public. It is not consoling.

JL: I love Audre Lorde's way of putting it: "Poetry is not a luxury."[15]

CM: But it is—as Cheryl Clarke wrote to us—"such necessary bread."

JL: It's the safe and irrelevant stuff that gets rewarded. I haven't seen anybody die of a *New Yorker* poem all week.

CM: It takes a mandarin education to read a lot of it. Whereas the poetry people need comes from so many different sources. Working class—every possible ethnic and cultural group. We have a lot of poems here that I call the Poetry of Evidence and of Witness— which is as necessary to the tribe as poetry written in the language of high art—although we've got plenty of that here, too. For the majority culture, there are only two or three *right* kinds of poems—even as there are only two or three ways to have gender—or good—or evil. And what we need is 121 different kinds of all of these. Kipling wrote a poem called "In the Neolithic Age," the refrain of which goes:

> There are nine and sixty ways of constructing tribal lays,
> And—every—single—one—of—them—is—right!

JL: Do we have that many different ways in this book?

CM: I think we have as many ways as we have poets and poems.

---

[15] Audre Lorde's essay "Poetry Is Not a Luxury" is collected in *Sister Outsider: Essays and Speeches* by Audre Lorde (The Crossing Press, 1984).

A Note to the Reader

We are profoundly grateful to those writers who have allowed us to print their poems for a modest honorarium or no fee at all. Sharing is a tradition in our community, and it has been honored here. The unprecedented scope and inclusiveness of this book were made possible only through the generosity of these writers.

Several poets appear here for the first time in a gay context. This is a brave thing, and for many, still a very risky one. One contributor lost several clients in her business when she came out in print. Another writer's decision to appear here hinged on our publication date's being later than her review-of-tenure date. At least one lesbian writer works under an assumed name to make her living. Another woman decided—after years of publishing her poems under a pseudonym in order not to jeopardize custody rights to her son—to print her work under her own name for the first time in this book. We are especially moved by the decision of two poets who have been lovers for many years to choose to "come out together" in these pages.

The chief aim of this book is the reduction of fear, and every writer here contributes to that. Several women of color cited fear of being cut off and written off by their communities as a consideration in deciding whether or not to be in this book. Two of the men, both white, not granting permission cited, in one instance, "ghettoization" as the objection, and in the other, fear of "deconstruction" of his work according to the sole fact of his sexuality. Efforts to obtain poems by Lorraine Hansberry were not successful. We also wanted to include, but were not able to obtain permission for, the following poems by Elizabeth Bishop: "Invitation to Miss Marianne Moore," "In the Waiting Room," and "The Shampoo." Finally we were unable to obtain a response from the Estate of Adrian Stanford, whose poems were published in *Black and Queer* by Good Gay Poets Press, Boston, in 1977, or to locate Jamiel Daud Hassin, whose poem "Freddi" appears in *Black Men/White Men: A Gay Anthology.* *

The amount of activity and talent for poetry in the gay and lesbian community is remarkable, even overwhelming. We regret that physical limitations prevented inclusion in this book of every gay and lesbian poet whose work deserves support.

Reading aloud, as we did, day after day, in preparing this book not only changed our perception of what poetry is, but also changed our relationship with one another—toward the side of trust. We urge the readers of this anthology to read these poems aloud—even to themselves—but even better with another person or with a group of people, preferably mixed. Sharing these poems in that way is the best way we know of releasing their gifts.

Finally, we are pleased that there is not one poem in this book about poetry instead of life.

Acknowledgments

A book of this kind can exist only because of the energy of many, many people. We particularly want to thank the following friends and supporters of *Gay & Lesbian Poetry in Our Time.*

The original Open Lines reading series, on which the book is based, would not have been possible without the support and enthusiasm of the Reverend Paul Abels, then pastor of Washington Square Church, New York, and of Charles Bergner, trustee and arts advisor. During the course of the Open Lines readings, Mark Ameen, David Armstrong, Charles Bergner, Louis Carrillo, Richard Foltz, and Peter Prins faithfully and energetically served as "crew"—stuffing and mailing flyers, setting up chairs, running the book table, and handling the sound and recording equipment. At the Riverside Church, New York, where readings were also held during the first year of Open Lines, Ronald Johnson and Margarita Suarez of Maranatha—Riversiders for Lesbian/Gay Concerns—provided similar services.

At different stages in the preparation of the manuscript, a number of people lent us substantive help, advice, and encouragement. We are especially grateful to Mark Ameen, Malaga Baldi, Greg Baysans of *The James White Review*, Frank Bidart, Peter Carey, Louis Carrillo, Cheryl Clarke, C. M. Donald, Bru Dye, Bea Gates, Jewelle Gomez, Thom Gunn, Richard Howard, Martin Humphries, June Jordan, Arthur McLean, Christian McEwen, Eileen Myles, Joan Nestle of the Lesbian Herstory Archives, Juanita Ramos, Will Roscoe, Assotto Saint, Charley Shively, Alan Siegler, Michael J. Smith, and Carolyn Trager.

Randel Ryals contributed a superb proofreading of the galleys. We are also grateful to the many photographers who contributed individual photographs of authors without fee; and we are particularly grateful to Robert Giard, Jill Krementz, Becket Logan, Colleen McKay and Brian Quinby, who contributed several examples of their work.

Finally, we wish to thank Darlene Dobrin at St. Martin's Press, whose calm and good cheer helped us through the production process, and Michael Denneny, our editor, who shared our vision of this book and made it an actuality.

GAY

&

LESBIAN

POETRY

IN OUR TIME

Dorothy Allison

Born in 1949 in Greenville, South Carolina, Dorothy Allison is an expatriate Southern lesbian writer whose work has appeared in *Conditions, The Village Voice, Southern Exposure, The Advocate, New York Native, Quest: A Feminist Quarterly, Off Our Backs, On Our Backs, Womanews, Bad Attitude,* and several anthologies, including *Lesbian Poetry* and *Lesbian Fiction* (Persephone 1981, 1983). Her book of poetry is titled *The Women Who Hate Me* (Long Haul Press, 1983, reprinted by Firebrand). *River of Names,* a collection of short fiction, is forthcoming (Firebrand, 1988), and she is now working on an anthology of erotic fiction and essays and "a semi-biographical novel," *A Bastard Out of Carolina.*

TO THE BONE

That summer I did not go crazy,
spoke instead to my mama who insisted
our people do not go crazy.
We make instead that sudden evening
silence that follows the shotgun blast.
We stand up alone twenty years after
like a scarecrow in a field
pie-eyed, toothless, naming
our enemies and outliving them.
That summer I talked to death
like an old friend, a husky voice
whispering up from my cunt, echoing
around my knees, laughing.
That summer I did not go crazy
but I wore
             very close
very close
             to the bone.

THE WOMEN WHO HATE ME

1

The women who do not know me.

The women who, not knowing me, hate me
mark my life, rise in my dreams and shake their loose hair
throw out their thin wrists, narrow their already sharp eyes
say   "Who do you think you are?"

"Lazy, useless, cuntsucking, scared, stupid
What you scared of anyway?"
Their eyes, their hands, their voices
Terrifying.

The women who hate me cut me
as men can't.   Men don't count.
I can handle men. Never expected better
of any man   anyway.
                              But the women,
shallow-cheeked young girls the world was made for
safe little girls who think nothing of bravado
who never got over by playing it tough.

What do they know of my fear?

What do they know of the women in my body?
My weakening hips, sharp good teeth
angry nightmares, scarred cheeks,
fat thighs, fat everything.

"Don't smile too wide. You look like a fool."
"Don't want too much. You an't gonna get it."
An't   gonna   get   it.
Goddamn.

Say Goddamn and kick somebody's ass
that I am not even half what I should be,
full of terrified angry bravado
                              BRAVADO.

DOROTHY ALLISON

The women who hate me
don't know
can't imagine
life-saving, precious bravado.

2

God on their right shoulder
righteousness on their left,
the women who hate me never use words
like hate,   speak instead of nature
of the spirit not housed in the flesh
as if my body, a temple of sin,
didn't mirror their own.

Their measured careful words echo
earlier coarser stuff,   say

"What do you think you're doing?"
"Who do you think you are?"

"Whitetrash
no-count
bastard
mean-eyed
garbage-mouth
cuntsucker
cuntsucker
no good to anybody, never did diddlyshit anyway."

"You figured out yet who you an't gonna be?"

The women who hate me hate
their insistent desires, their fat lusts
swallowed and hidden, disciplined to nothing
narrowed to bone and dry hot dreams.
The women who hate me deny
hunger and appetite,
the cream delight
of a scream
that arches the thighs and fills
the mouth with singing.

Something hides here
a secret thing shameful and complicated.
Something hides in a tight mouth
a life too easily rendered
a childhood of inappropriate longing
a girl's desire to grow into a man
a boyish desire to stretch and sweat.

Every three years I discover again
that   No   I knew nothing before.
Everything must be dragged out,
looked over again. The unexamined life
is the lie, but still
must I every time deny
everything I knew before?

My older sister tells me flatly
she don't care who I take to my bed
what I do there.   Tells me finally
she sees no difference between
her husbands, my lovers. Behind it all
we are too much the same to deny.

My little sister thinks my older crazy
thinks me sick
more shameful to be queer than crazy
as if her years hustling ass,
her pitiful junky whiteboy
saved through methadone and marriage, all that
asslicking interspersed with asskicking
all those pragmatic family skills we share mean nothing
measured against the little difference
of who and what I am.

My little sister too
is one of the women who hate me.

I measure it differently, what's shared,
what's denied, what no one wants recognized.
My first lover's skill at mystery,
how one day she was there, the next gone;
the woman with whom I lived for eight years
but slept with less than one;
the lover who tied me to the foot of her bed
when I didn't really want that
but didn't really know
what else I could get.

What else can I get?
Must I rewrite my life
edit it down to a parable where everything
turns out for the best?

But then what would I do with the lovers
too powerful to disappear,   the women
too hard to melt to soft stuff?
Now that I know that soft stuff
was never where I wanted to put my hand.

6

The women who hate me
hate too my older sister
with her many children, her weakness for
good whiskey, country music, bad men.
She says the thing "women's lib" has given her
is a sense she don't have to stay too long
though she does
still she does
much too long.

7

I am not so sure anymore of the difference.
I do not believe anymore in the natural superiority
of the lesbian, the difference between my sisters and me.

Fact is, for all I tell my sisters
I turned out terrific at it myself:
sucking cunt, stroking ego, provoking
manipulating, comforting and keeping.
Plotting my life around mothering
other women's desperation
the way my sisters
build their lives
around their men.
Til I found myself   sitting at the kitchen table
shattered glass, blood in my lap and her
the good one with her stern insistence
just standing there wanting me
to explain it to her,   save her from being
alone with herself.

Or that other one
another baby-butch wounded girl
                How can any of us forget how wounded
                any of us   have to be   to get that hard?
Never to forget that working class says nothing
does not say who she was   how she was
fucking me helpless.   Her hand on my arm
raising lust to my throat,   that lust
everyone says does not happen
though it goes on happening
all the time.

How can I speak of her, us together?
Her touch drawing heat from my crotch to my face
her face, terrifying, wonderful.
Me saying, *"Yeah, goddamn it, yeah,*
put it to me, ease me, fuck me, anything . . ."
til the one thing I refused
then back up against a wall
her rage ugly in the muscles of her neck
her fist swinging up to make a wind,
a wind blowing back to my mama's cheek
past my stepfather's arm

I ask myself over and over how I
came to be standing in such a wind?
How I came to be held up like my mama

DOROTHY ALLISON

with my jeans, my shoes locked in a drawer
and the woman I loved breathing on me
    "You bitch.   You damned fool."

    "You want to try it?"
    "You want to walk to Brooklyn
        barefooted?"
    "You want to try it
        mothernaked?"

Which meant,   of course,   I had to decide
how naked   I was willing to go   where.

Do I forget all that?
Deny all that?
Pretend I am not
my mama's daughter
my sisters' mirror.
Pretend I have not
at least as much lust
in my life   as pain?

Where then will I find the country
where women never wrong women
where we will sit knee to knee
finally listening
to the whole
naked truth
of our lives?

WHEN I DRINK I BECOME THE JOY OF
FAGGOTS

When I drink I become
                the joy of faggots.
I try not to drink too often.
When I was younger I couldn't drink at all.

I have grown into this joy
this sense that the night is full of possibilities
conversation an art that can be perfected
with gesture and ease and a glass in the hand.

When I was young I said I would be a writer
   with no sense what it could mean
   how hard it would be.
My friends talked sympathetically
of another friend from Texas
who had driven to Florida in an antique car
who was known for how charmingly he could weep.

A Writer, a Poet, he would drink and talk to me
of how all the men at school wanted to fuck him
of his desire to leave them at the pavement edge
knowing they would remember and want always
his car,   his tears,   his ass,   his poems.

Sensitive,
everyone was sure he was sensitive.
He told me how when his roommate stood
silent over his bed,
he reached up, slapped him,
slapped him again.

"He wanted me, you know."
I knew.

His roommate used to talk of how he resisted it
the desire, the burn for a beautiful boy.
A scholar of greek and latin and buggery
when he drank he became foolish
his moustache hanging damp.

"I wanted him, you know."
I knew.

In the middle of the night I dream
old friends and lechery.
Since I do not drink, I burn.
Is this what everybody knew that I didn't?
how desire and denial roll in the glass?
how the fire, the fire consumes?

She had hands with fingers like tapers
lean legs, dark hair, a car.
Everywhere I saw that car

      DOROTHY ALLISON

just the briefest flash of her
hair, legs, fingers and gone.
Sensitive,
God, she knew she was sensitive
and when I stood over her
she slapped me with the delight of a boy.

"I wanted her, you know."
They knew.

Their poems were published everywhere.
I made a small fire of mine on the beach.

There is a small fire in a glass of whiskey
a backfire that counters the fire inside
like the fire in the eyes of an angry woman
who suspects that inside her hides a faggot
standing silent over someone's bed
holding still for the blows the sensitive give.

Mark Ameen

Mark Ameen was born in 1958 in Lowell, Massachusetts. In 1979, he followed
an experimental theater company to New York City, where he continues to
act and to perform his own work. The chapbook *Aye, My Dear, I Worry About
That* (Harmony Books, New York) appeared in 1982, and was followed by the
full-length collection *A Circle of Sirens* (SeaHorse Press, 1985)—Book One of
"The Trilogy of the Buried Body." *Those of You Who Are Dying Are Very
Gifted*—Book Two—from which "Monologue of a Dying Beast" and two son-
nets are printed here, is presently on offer. A selection of Ameen's poems
appears in *Three New York Poets* (GMP, London, 1987). Ameen is now work-
ing on a new book, *Night Manager*.

SONNET NO 21

On a very hot Independence Day
This elongated Manhattan summer,
The boy of hard darkness, the mad sashay,
Decides that life is no longer a bummer.
While his sweat pours down on Avenue B
And his heart can be claimed by no other
He says, "Oh, young self, do you not yet see?
You've a calling, you're every man's brother."
And so you must wait and attend to life,
Exposing brick and greeting thy neighbor.
No need to spend thought on this living's strife—
The world itself does you the favor.

It's a time when personal panic fades:
This is the very first summer of AIDS.

SONNET NO 22

I don't think that I believe in 'gay life'
Although I know how to dance in a crowd.
But when the coroner inserts his hot knife
I think they will discover I was proud.
I don't think that I believe in 'straight life'
Although I was a junkie with the rest.
In my intestine they'll recover my wife,
Whom forever has put me to the test.
I have thought that I believe in 'my life'
But the credo is tenuous at most.
I think I believe only in 'high life'
And in my life I've tried to play the host.

Anyway, Death gets all the attention
In this womb we're not allowed to mention.

MARK AMEEN

MONOLOGUE OF A DYING BEAST

A LOVER'S COMPLAINT

I

Shall I embrace my disease
and claim it as "the gift of love"
like gonorrhea? Or consider it
earthly penance for the sins of sleaze
and beg further absolution of heaven above?
No, No, No on both counts. Instead,
I shall go out as I came in,
breathless and alone;
O, O, O that tugging in my head . . .
Will I never be granted a home?
My friend, you who have granted
precious little to any other,
for your own is hugely protected and fragile,
you have nonetheless seduced me into speech—
and I will curse you forever more.
For you have made mine a life with a little love,
a lucky streak,
and now I'm clinging while there is for me
no hope of the shore.

This gasping apprehension of
a room's unknown atmosphere
will never again relinquish its hold;
and my only claim to the empire we all sit in
is that I never ever did what I was told.
Still, like the dumbest of marine manueverers,
I shot up for air synchronous with a general collapse,
and the damages for this tragic affair
will be dumped in my lap
as I undergo the last synapse.
And I will dedicate it to you,
with all the drama I possess.
I will call this your poem, your
Death of Love, Love of Death.
The laughter of the other plane I now caress,
'til I myself am lost, become the hidden breath.
The Master Machine is not my invention

and it is never at rest.
Clenched fists at the start, later my best.

Oh where, Oh why, in the search for love,
did the love of search take command?
I am a killer in my stiff black glove
and my victim is giving me a hand.

Every muscle in my body
has become enamored of
the dull ache which is going around.
I am going around.
I am dizzy and so very very sick.
. . . and so much more than I ever imagined.
And nobody I have loved has ever been satisfied.
And that's not true.
And *I* have never been satisfied.
I am too much to bear and I am boring me.
Oh, Daddy, A Dull Ache.

There was a boy. And he would never cry out loud.
But he knew that he must be missing something.
Everybody said leave it alone.
That hurt because something had to be going on.
Everybody said there's nothing go to sleep.
That hurt because he knew the air must be alive.
That hurting is referred to as "the way it is,"
and it shouldn't hurt this much to inhale.
So, sometimes when I do give in and close my eyes,
my heart remembers and I fail to breathe.

Everything came down to a seeming choice in the empire.
Like whether to avoid the ones redundant of
the suffocation one was forced to support as a child—
this is "the grandiose woe of retreat"—
or become stronger than those repeating little murders
and meet them face to face in front of their landscape—
"the incomplete joy of advance"—
which is to become an actor, like they are, and to forget,
or somewhat of a warrior which is worse
because enemies become equals and raise a glass.
I have been an actor and a real one avoids
the Everyday as performance

and the coming home nightly to a collapse.
As to the glory of combat:
I can't envision myself
a tight-end in the Superbowl of Life,
affirming a slippery grid of sales.
There are a few things I refuse to bruise my knees about.
If I wasn't free to not like them then,
then freedom must mean not allowing them now.
This is not bitter fruit; this is Markie's harvest.
So I guess I can claim at least
to have chosen to plow my own field.
And maybe it killed me. At least.
When I perform I wear makeup.
Which is not the same as drag.

If everybody were to walk off the job
we'd have to kill a few people to get our food.
Many of us would be killed as well.
We'd then compose a huge gear in the machine
and change the world from our invisible angle.
This is called the pleasure in dying.
Do not confuse it with falling in love.
I am a tender beast and I am tired of being punished.

A black man on Halloween bought drinks for everybody
and sang out,
"God gave me this and then said, 'Deal with it.'"
He was talking about his cock.
I decided his method was ingenious.
He told everybody that he loved them
and they accepted. Yet it took money,
and they were all wearing masks.

The good thing about us is we believe in Holiday.
And we fuck and suck in all kinds of light.

II

Those of us who publicize pride,
whose only postures are those
by which we might be noticed,
whose only way of being in a room
is the way that will attract the most attention,

we are constantly deploying from zero,
or a new investment in an old invisibility
we never get rid of,
and we are condemned as self-involved
and feared as self-sufficient,
dismissed as self-indulgent
and embraced as self-defeating.
And we fuck and suck in all kinds of light.

Suzy McNamara used to put cigarettes out on my hands.
The power of the machine compels thee.
One evening I was sledding on a luncheon tray,
and the site, called Nun's Hill,
had been completely iced over
owing to a partial thaw kissed by a thorough freeze.
It was a double hill.
The first gathered speed
and the second acted as a ski-jump
and we called it that even though we were on sleds.
A luncheon tray was faster than a sled,
the jumps higher so they left bruises
on our behinds. Joanie Martel snuck up
as I was perched atop Nun's Hill
waiting for the coast to clear
and pushed me backwards.
Mostly buried beneath snowdrifts
and introduced by the shield of ice,
a stairway was built into the side of the hill.
Its bannister was an iron railing.
I picked up speed and then I crashed.
Thrown onto my stomach
I kicked my legs from the knee down.
I lived five minutes from Nun's Hill.
It took them forty to walk me home.
My sister had been sent for
and she helped me in the house.
My mother beat me into the wall with a broomstick.
When the color had completely cleared
from my already pallid face
and she saw my eyes roll
under fluttering lids
she carried me to her bed
and made me feel loved

as we awaited the ambulance.

I did not find my mother erotic,
which many will pretend was my original tragedy,
although I myself consider refusal more heroic
than poking out one's eyes.
So when my people ask me to beat them into pleasure,
which is often enough
because I look sad and angry and ethnic,
I fear only that I might be tempted to
pay her back by turning them into women
and then hitting them for it,
and so many of them don't need any help.
While there are a lot of people
I find it hard to be nice to
it doesn't satisfy me.
I do my best not to make them disappear
but there is so much about them I'm no longer willing to
    understand
and with equal discretion I fail to return their calls.
This may be a mastery I ought to own up to:
I keep strutting right past the sphinx
and losing all the beautifully riddled men.
I must be a new kind of animal—
the seldom rewarded tender beast
tired of being punished—
and it's really my father
who needs to be slapped and kissed.
But as to killing him off,
that's one for the books.

I have decided upon him
and he is ready
and so I embrace
a feeling father
I don't even have to invent:
we used to hold hands
until I fell asleep dreaming of his fur.
He's the one who touched me with
the tingle only hidden fingertips possess,
the one in whose grip resides
a latent lasting caress,
and it remains laced with latency

so I'm pretty hot stuff.
Always remember, never forget,
damage is the house from which
we place our bet. The cause of
your suffering is the source of
your pride. Endure life on earth
without thickening your hide.
Clutch and release,
gurgle and gawk,
Oh Daddy, Oh Daddy,
I want your cock.

If I see one more queer entertaining everybody
I'll kill him. And if I hear one more woman
describe him as "funny" I'll die all over again.
You wouldn't treat me this way if I weren't in a wheelchair.

I was too old to be in a crib,
but there I was,
and please don't try to make something out of it,
and the crib was in their bedroom.
He has a hairy arm.
My little limb stretches through the bars of my bed
and he catches it in his perfect palm.
He squeezes; we shine until sleep;
him in his white cotton underwear,
me in my careful crib.
Clutch and release, gurgle and gawk.
This is why they birthed me with asthma,
so that my crib would be placed in your bedroom
and I'd be in it 'til far too old.
Daddy, Daddy you bastard, I'm you.
And like something to fight about,
these are the bars of your bed.
The crack of the door is just enough,
and you're driving him crazy,
he knows your stuff,
but you're behind the door, like a memory.
It feeds you, this upset, and him, too.
People come and go how much can he do?
Oh Daddy, Oh Daddy, I want your cock.
But Mommy will come in and call us both simple names.
He pulls down the front of his sweatpants,
his jockstrap is dripping and true.

MARK AMEEN

He's rubbing himself through the mist
and everyone knows it's for you.
Daddy, I'll never be through.
He's coming right up to the crack
and pointing himself at me too.
We're in our little room,
the door is almost shut,
and these are the bars of our bed.
There is a locked-up feeling
that makes whatever approaches
seem to be a man. Everybody's
crawling around with flashlights in their foreheads
looking for this feeling.
Daddy, when I meet somebody
I think I might be able to like,
I try to remember to touch his hand
before turning him into something handy.
I am a two-fisted dandy
and I'm opening my door for you.
With big fingers and a quivering grip,
thick-wristed and randy,
and light electric hair
on all of its surface,
these are the paws of the prole
and they may never play the piano.
They are on a lot of winos and merchants,
the traveling salesmen in bathrooms
in all our hidden hometowns
where we are absently attending our roots.
When that fat-fingered hand
shoots into the stall
and clutches your thigh
and cups your balls
with some of the abandoned man's highly charged love,
you will remember the streak of lightning
you are saving in your stomach.
If it exists inside your body
then it was meant for this world
and such is the single chore:
To allow your fathers and uncles
a life with a little love.
Not to mention their sons. And hers. And yours.
The power of the machine compels thee.

MARK AMEEN   17

You may believe that you have heard this
a thousand times before
and I will say it again
at least as many more:
"I love you. You are alive now."
. . . and so much more than I ever imagined.
I have a benign infatuation
but it has been bringing me a lot of pain.

III

There is a house in which
the gross and indecent longs for its body.
Even here, where the light of the homosexual
has become the plight of the homosexual.
And how dare you have the snip to stand there;
you're just so much more frightened than even I,
and that is going to take some getting used to.
Now I ain't sayin' you ain't pretty . . .
but it takes more than a clenched fist to make a man sing.
I want a full-piece jug band blowin' my lips off.
I want the eye of the apple.
And so out of my crusty puddle
may there spring up
something of history and definition.
How the light changes with the assurance
that the tugging wasn't only in your head.
It's all over
when did it start
and you did the right thing all along.

The end is the machine.
And so I go . . .
because if I don't
I'll never stop trying to . . .
because then I thrive in an office
where I don't have to worry about
dying or being gay. I am at last.
A-chug-a-chug-a.
The end is the machine-breath.
There, in the acid grip of removal,
the only place where life in a body can be beautiful

as it is disappearing or coming to be,
there is the place where
the history of definition
is no longer the definition of history,
or is at last;
where nobody's trying to make a parable of their past
for they are surrounded and nobody clings after that.
A-chug-a-chug-a.
The end is the machine-breath calling.
Even this the beginning of dying,
the collaborative manipulation of the same strings
we've here been trying so hard to fiddle with,
is more a release than a responsibility,
unlike any movement we have managed to play out on our own.
A-chug-a-chug-a.
The end is the machine-breath calling me into surrender.
And that's the ticket.
And that's as far as I can get
and I can only stay there for a moment . . . You see,
I am too young to be dying.
You are a hateful and petty people
and I'd better let you know
while I still have a permanent hard-on.
Amen, brothers.
And goodnight, ladies.
And I want to tell you now that
I never baited anybody and I am being murdered.
And who has time for that?

You may have noticed that there are two machines,
and if you haven't had time to notice even that,
then you are *really* too young to be dying
and you should blow something up before you go.
Preferably the triplex of the man
who made you into a houseboy.
And don't ever believe it
when they come back and tell you
you were just standing there
"asking without asking" for such a hand,
which is just what they say
when they rescue other countries
in order to suck other lands.
And now you've got the disease.

And by the time you've figured it out,
you're too old to be a translucent victim
and you spend a few dark-years
in a full-length mirror working on your grip,
until, suddenly,
the other glove fits.
This is the history of those weaned on opportunity
in what is cruelly and hilariously projected as
a "youth culture." It is the pressurized support system
for the other machine.

The real machine, the primary gears,
the cool breath calling
pulling you out of your muscles,
is a temptation to a purple I'll try to avoid.
A-chug-a-chug-a.
It is not without devices, it is crafty
and lies in ambush,
but when you get there
you'll know everywhere you've been.
And it will sneak up on you
in detective-novel fashion,
dropping enough clues to keep you
embarrassed but convinced.
You might tell yourself that it was all
a sleight-of-hand,
some dismissible magic of your own invention,
but it's more likely
somebody else will tell you that.
And I am telling you now to nod
and squint your eyes as though considering it
and say, "Yes, yes, yes indeed,
I think you must be right,"
while in your heart you remain
a traitor to the human condition.

All this, that is, if you decide
only to visit and then come back.
And the only other thing to do is to die.
And it is glorious.
I myself don't know for sure if I am yet
and so I must apologize for leading us both on.
So far I have always decided to come back

MARK AMEEN

to the leanness of three dimensions,
except, if you want the truth,
just now I don't know.
The worst thing denied is the dying person's pride.
How much will it cost to really look at his eyes?
The end is . . .
the beginning on high-heels.
I can't die; I'm still scared of you who look
so much like me. Listen,
do you think those of us who have been punctured
and have learned to love our hook
can get together,
over there,
where we are hanging just out of reach of these rooms,
and do something,
pull some strings and watch our traces
stand up in a circle around our children?
We won't be calling them children.

O, Master and Magnet within Me,
dangling before me my birthright,
consciousness of a position within the machine,
I take joy in detriment,
I applaud effervescent introductions,
and I have traveled just the other side of this room,
to be wielded by your perfect power—
and I came back because I feared I wasn't well enough.
To think that I am still too nervous to die
because I have been so mad as to publicize
the payment exacted for being awake.
You are smooth.
I am a parking lot.
I must lubricate my hook every day.

The inverted mechanism of the empire
attempts to replicate this night-breath
that hovers,
over our room,
our bed,
our relaxed, warm hands,
planting a tick in the lid of my lover,
the tender beast descending—
though he floats his furry limbs alongside me

he, too, owns a rhythm no one else can see—,
feeding our manly fear of suction,
the whirlpool never-ending—
The Machine Breath—
and it fails miserably
because nothing invented by men
is smart enough yet to breathe.
And men are not much smarter.
They are not born asthmatic
but they grow into it
and they never stop bawling.
They have a few pleasant disguises
but the bottom line is the misguided reduction
of suction to seduction
and the funneling of fear
away from the whisper of the moonlit sea
toward the broken-record mystery of dailiness,
as if there were something humiliating
about waking without an alarm,
as if the consistence with which we shape our dream
fixes the limits of our aberrant charm.
Yes this the earth-man's marketplace,
the other-machine,
the song of which resonates
in the bowels of bulldozers,
stings by omission,
is significant only for the bloody condiments
it suddenly refuses to characteristically reduce,
like the number of lower-back spasms
within a typist's pool, or the
calculated misunderstanding of the color black.
It is for me too oblique an investment.
And yet, the return,
the return: I come back.
Just now I don't know.
I have been here.

Here's to my throat, here's to my hands.
Here's to my ass, here's to my lips.
Here's to my asshole, here's to my eyes.
Here's to my tits, here's to my thighs.
Here's to my sweat, here's to my stride.
Here's to my fingers with nothing to hide.

MARK AMEEN

Here's to my cock, my marrow, my slit.
Here's to my balls, my sinew, my sunshine.
Here's to my hair and my smell and my skin.
Here's to my feet.
I have been a man.
I am out.

Those of you who are dying are very gifted.
. . . and so much more than I ever imagined.
We all love you very much.

Antler

Antler was born in 1946 in Wisconsin and, aside from West Coast sojourns and other travels, continues to live there. Acclaimed by Allen Ginsberg as "the most enlightening & magnanimous American poem I've seen of '60s & '70s decades," his book-length poem *Factory* was published by City Lights in 1980. *Last Words*, his selected poems of 1967–83, was published by Ballantine in 1986. In 1985 he won the Whitman Award of the Walt Whitman Association of Camden, New Jersey. In 1987 he won the Witter Bynner Prize awarded annually to "an outstanding younger poet" by the American Academy and Institute of Arts and Letters. He tries to spend at least a month in the wilderness each fall and each spring.

WHAT EVERY BOY KNOWS

Every boy knows what it's like
          when he's really alone,
When it's safe to jack off with a passion,
When it's safe to take off his clothes
          and prance around
And parade his lubricating cock
          before every mirror in the house,

Safe to cry out and talk dirty
        while jerking it,
Really scream "I'm coming!"
        when he comes,
Really stand on his head
        and jack off in his face
        if he wants,
Yes, every boy knows
        when it's safe.

At the country picnic the 12 year old boy
        wanders off by himself in the woods,
        he knows the perfect spot.
On his study-hall break to the library
        the 13 year old stops in the empty john,
        just enough time for a quickie.
The 14 year old boyscout waits till he's sure
        everyone in the tent is sleeping,
        quietly, slowly he plays with his dream.
The 15 year old runs home from school,
        half-way he's already hard,
His heart is pounding
        when he opens the frontdoor,
He knows he's got a full hour
        before his sister or parents return,
Enough time to give himself
        a real workout in the bathtub.
The 16 year old wakes up in the snowy night,
        he watches himself with a flashlight
        magically masturbate under the comforter.
The 17 year old puts *Leaves of Grass* aside,
        leans back on the chair with his feet on the wall
        in the basement at home where he studies,
He likes poetry, but right now
        he needs a good handjob
        before he can continue . . .
No one can see me now, the boy chuckles to himself,
And I'm not fool enough anymore to think God
        is watching me horrified
        and will sentence me to hell.
If God doesn't love to watch boys jack off
        as much as boys love to watch themselves jack off
        he does not exist.

The 18 year old boy licks his lips
    as he jacks off in the hayloft,
If anyone saw me they'd think I was nuts
    he thinks as he squirms and groans,
His devilish lasciviousness to make love to himself
    makes the monkeys at the zoo seem prudes,
There's no posture, no expression on his face,
    no possible method of touch he won't try
    to make it feel more Wow.
The voluptuous 19 year old knows
    he's got the whole beach to himself today,
He basks naked in the sun till baked,
    then floating on the bosom of the lake
    gives himself the best handjob of his life.
The 20 year old mountainclimber still digs the thrill
    of doing it on top of a mountain alone,
He never tells anyone about it, it's a secret
    he keeps to himself,
He still smiles remembering the first time
    he jacked off from a cliff,
Ecstatic boyhood semen spurting and spurting
    tumbling thousands of feet
    into the wild valley below. . . .

Gloria Anzaldúa

Gloria Evangelina Anzaldúa was born in 1946 in Raymondville, Texas, and grew up along the Texas-Mexico border. A Chicana lesbian-feminist poet and fiction writer, she is a co-editor of *This Bridge Called My Back: Writings by Radical Women of Color* (Persephone, 1981). Her recent book, half prose and half poetry, titled *Borderlands/La Frontera: The New Mestiza* (Spinsters/Aunt Lute, 1987), is her historical, mythical, and personal account of life among conflicting cultures and subcultures. She gives lectures and workshops around the country, and has taught at Vermont College, San Francisco State University, and the University of Texas.

WE CALL THEM GREASERS

I found them here when I came.
They were growing corn in their small *ranchos*
raising cattle, horses
smelling of woodsmoke and sweat.
They knew their betters:
took off their hats
placed them over their hearts,
lowered their eyes in my presence.

Weren't interested in bettering themselves,
why they didn't even own the land but shared it.
Wasn't hard to drive them off,
cowards, they were, no backbone.
I showed 'em a piece of paper with some writing
tole 'em they owed taxes
had to pay right away or be gone by *mañana*.
By the time me and my men had waved
that same piece of paper to all the families
it was all frayed at the ends.

Some loaded their chickens children wives and pigs
into rickety wagons, pans and tools dangling
clanging from all sides.
Couldn't take their cattle—
during the night my boys had frightened them off.
Oh, there were a few troublemakers
who claimed we were the intruders.
Some even had land grants
and appealed to the courts.
It was a laughing stock
them not even knowing English.
Still some refused to budge,
even after we burned them out.
And the women—well I remember one in particular.

She lay under me whimpering.
I plowed into her hard
kept thrusting and thrusting
felt him watching from the mesquite tree
heard him keening like a wild animal
in that instant I felt such contempt for her

round face and beady black eyes like an Indian's.
Afterwards I sat on her face until
her arms stopped flailing,
didn't want to waste a bullet on her.
The boys wouldn't look me in the eyes.
I walked up to where I had tied her man to the tree
and spat in his face. Lynch him, I told the boys.

INTERFACE

(for Frances Doughty)

She'd always been there
   occupying the same room.
It was only when I looked
     at the edges of things
my eyes going wide watering,
     objects blurring.
Where before there'd only been empty space
     I sensed layers and layers,
felt the air in the room thicken.
     Behind my eyelids a white flash
a thin noise.
     That's when I could see her.

     Once I accidently ran my arm
through her body
     felt heat on one side of my face.
     She wasn't solid.
The shock pushed me against the wall.
A torrent of days swept past me
     before I tried to "see" her again.
She had never wanted to be flesh she told me
     until she met me.
At first it was hard to stay
     on the border between
the physical world
     and hers.
It was only there at the interface
     that we could see each other.
See? We wanted to touch.
     I wished I could become

pulsing color, pure sound, bodiless as she.
            It was impossible, she said
            for humans to become noumenal.

What does it feel like, she asked
            to inhabit flesh,
wear blood like threads
            constantly running?
I would lie on the bed talking
            she would hover over me.
Did I say talk?
            We did not use words.
I pushed my thoughts toward her.
            Her "voice" was a breath of air
stirring my hair
            filling my head.
Once Lupe my roommate
            walked right through her
dangling the car keys.
            I felt Leyla shiver.
I named her Leyla,
            a pure sound.

I don't know when I noticed
            that she'd begun to glow,
to look more substantial
            than the blurred furniture.
It was then I felt a slight touch,
            her hand—a tendril of fog—
on the sheets where she'd lain
            a slight crease, a dampness,
a smell between candles and skin.
            You're changing, I told her.
            A yearning deluged me—
her yearning.
            That's when I knew
she wanted to be flesh.
            She stayed insubstantial day after day
            so I tried to blur
my borders, to float, become pure sound.
            But my body seemed heavier,
more inert.

I remember when she changed.
I could hear the far away slough of traffic
            on the Brooklyn-Queens Expressway,
the people downstairs were playing salsa.
            We lay enclosed   by margins, hems,
where only we existed.
            She was stroking   stroking my arms
my legs, marveling at their solidity,
            the warmth of my flesh, its smell.
Then I touched her.
            Fog, she felt like dense fog,
the color of smoke.
            She glowed, my hands paled then gleamed
as I moved them over her.
            Smoke-fog pressing against my eyelids
my mouth, ears, nostrils, navel.
            A cool tendril pressing between my legs
entering.
Her finger, I thought
but it went on and on.
            At the same time
an iciness touched my anus,   '
            and she was in
and in and in
            my mouth opening
I wasn't scared just astonished
            rain drummed against my spine
            turned to steam as it rushed through my veins
light flickered over me from toe to crown.
            Looking down my body I saw
            her forearm, elbow and hand
sticking out of my stomach
            saw her hand slide in.
I wanted no food no water nothing
            just her—pure light sound inside me.
My roommate thought I was
            having an affair.
I was "radiant," she said.
            Leyla had begun to swell
I started hurting a little.
            When I started cramping
she pushed out
            her fingers, forearm, shoulder.

GLORIA ANZALDÚA   29

Then she stood before me,
  fragile skin, sinews tender as baby birds
  and as transparent.
She who had never eaten
  began to hunger.
I held a cup of milk to her mouth,
  put her hand on my throat
made swallowing motions.
  I spooned mashed banana into her bird mouth,
hid the baby food under the bed.
  One day my roommate asked
who was staying in my room,
  she'd heard movements.
A friend recovering from a contagious
  skin disease, I said.
She ran out saying, I'm going to the Cape
  indefinitely. See you.
  We had the house to ourselves.
I taught her how to clean herself,
  to flush.
She would stand before the mirror
  watching her ears, long and diaphanous,
begin to get smaller, thicker.
  She spent a lot of time at the window.
Once I caught her imitating
the shuffle of the baglady.
  No, like this, I told her.
Head up, shoulders back.
  I brought in the TV.
This is how humans love, hate, I said.
  Once we sat on the stoop
watching a neighbor sweep the sidewalk.
  Hello, he yelled, hello, I yelled back,
eh-oh, she whispered.
  Watch my lips, Ley-la.
Say it, Ley-la.
  Good. I love you.
Ah uff oo, she said.
  Soon Leyla could pass,
go for milk at the bodega, count change.
  But no matter how passionately we made
love

it was never like before
she'd taken on skin and bone.

Do you ever want to go back, I asked her.
No, it's slower here and I like that.
I hate summers in NYC, I told her,
wish it was winter already.
The temperature dropped 10 degrees 20
and when a chill wind began to blow in Brooklyn
I told her to stop
messing with the cycles that affected others.
I watched what I said
and let Leyla run the place.
She had snow in the livingroom
and a tree in the bathtub.
Nights I lit the illegal fireplace.
Once when reaching toward a high shelf,
I wished I was taller.
When my head touched the ceiling
I had to yell at her to stop,
reverse.
How do you do it, I asked her.
You do it, too, she said,
my species just does it faster,
instantly, merely by thinking it.

The first time she rode the subway
I had to drag her out.
I suppose it was the noise,
the colors flashing by, the odd people
that held her open-mouthed gaze.
I had to do a gig in L.A.,
speak at a conference, was short on cash,
but she wanted to come.
She walked past the flight attendants
didn't even have to hide in the lavatory.
She laughed at my amazement, said
humans only saw what they were told to see.
Last Christmas I took her home to Texas.
Mom liked her.
Is she a lez, my brothers asked.
I said, No, just an alien.
Leyla laughed.

Photograph © 1988 by Jill Krementz

W. H. Auden

Wystan Hugh Auden (1907–1973) was born in York, England, came to the United States in 1939, and became an American citizen in 1946. One of the twentieth century's best writers, and to a telling degree its political and intellectual conscience, Auden reconnected the center of English poetry to engaged speech and life. The influence of his style is felt wherever English verse is written. Auden's life and loves, including his long-term relationship with poet Chester Kallman, are fully set forth in several recent biographies. Auden's poetry is found in *Collected Shorter Poems*, *Collected Longer Poems*, and *Selected Poetry*. His essays are gathered in two volumes—*The Dyer's Hand* and *Forewords and Afterwords*.

"LAY YOUR SLEEPING HEAD, MY LOVE"

Lay your sleeping head, my love,
Human on my faithless arm;
Time and fevers burn away
Individual beauty from
Thoughtful children, and the grave
Proves the child ephemeral:
But in my arms till break of day
Let the living creature lie,
Mortal, guilty, but to me
The entirely beautiful.

Soul and body have no bounds:
To lovers as they lie upon
Her tolerant enchanted slope
In their ordinary swoon,
Grave the vision Venus sends
Of supernatural sympathy,
Universal love and hope;

While an abstract insight wakes
Among the glaciers and the rocks
The hermit's sensual ecstasy.

Certainty, fidelity
On the stroke of midnight pass
Like vibrations of a bell,
And fashionable madmen raise
Their pedantic boring cry:
Every farthing of the cost,
All the dreaded cards foretell,
Shall be paid, but from this night
Not a whisper, not a thought,
Not a kiss nor look be lost.

Beauty, midnight, vision dies:
Let the winds of dawn that blow
Softly round your dreaming head
Such a day of sweetness show
Eye and knocking heart may bless,
Find the mortal world enough;
Noons of dryness see you fed
By the involuntary powers,
Nights of insult let you pass
Watched by every human love.

A LULLABY

The din of work is subdued,
another day has westered
and mantling darkness arrived.
Peace! Peace! Devoid your portrait
of its vexations and rest.
Your daily round is done with,
you've gotten the garbage out,
answered some tiresome letters
and paid a bill by return,
all *frettolosamente*.
Now you have licence to lie,
naked, curled like a shrimplet,
jacent in bed, and enjoy
its cosy micro-climate:
Sing, Big Baby, sing lullay.

W. H. AUDEN   33

The old Greeks got it all wrong:
Narcissus is an oldie,
tamed by time, released at last
from lust for other bodies,
rational and reconciled.
For many years you envied
the hirsute, the he-man type.
No longer: now you fondle
your almost feminine flesh
with mettled satisfaction,
imagining that you are
sinless and all-sufficient,
snug in the den of yourself,
Madonna and *Bambino:*
Sing, Big Baby, sing lullay.

Let your last thinks all be thanks:
praise your parents who gave you
a Super-Ego of strength
that saves you so much bother,
digit friends and dear them all,
then pay fair attribution
to your age, to having been
born when you were. In boyhood
you were permitted to meet
beautiful old contraptions,
soon to be banished from earth,
saddle-tank loks, beam-engines
and over-shot waterwheels.
Yes, love, you have been lucky:
Sing, Big Baby, sing lullay.

Now for oblivion: let
the belly-mind take over
down below the diaphragm,
the domain of the Mothers,
They who guard the Sacred Gates,
without whose wordless warnings
soon the verbalising I
becomes a vicious despot,
lewd, incapable of love,
disdainful, status-hungry.
Should dreams haunt you, heed them not,

W. H. AUDEN

for all, both sweet and horrid,
are jokes in dubious taste,
too jejune to have truck with.
Sleep, Big Baby, sleep your fill.

FROM "IN TIME OF WAR"

Some of our dead are famous, but they would not care:
Evil is always personal and spectacular,
But goodness needs the evidence of all our lives,

And, even to exist, it must be shared as truth,
As freedom or as happiness. (For what is happiness
If not to witness joy upon the features of another?)

They did not live to be remembered specially as noble,
Like those who cultivated only cucumbers and melons
To prove that they were rich; and when we praise their names,

They shake their heads in warning, chiding us to give
Our gratitude to the Invisible College of the Humble,
Who through the ages have accomplished everything essential.

And stretch around our struggle as the normal landscape,
And mingle, fluent with our living, like the winds and waters,
The dust of all the dead that reddens every sunset;

Giving us courage to confront our enemies,
Not only on the Grand Canal, or in Madrid,
Across the campus of a university city,

But aid us everywhere, that in the lovers' bedroom,
The white laboratory, the school, the public meeting,
The enemies of life may be more passionately attacked.

Tommi Avicolli

Tommi Avicolli (born 1951 in Philadelphia) is a performance artist and local news editor for the *Philadelphia Gay News*. A poetry collection *Magic Doesn't Live Here Anymore* (An Androgyne Collective Publication, Philadelphia, 1976) was followed by *Boy Dreams* (self-published, 1983). His "Memoirs of a Sissy" appears in the book *Men Freeing Men* (New Atlantis Press, 1985). Avicolli performs regularly with Avalanche, a gay/lesbian performance art troupe he founded. "The Rape Poem" is a regular part of the troupe's performances.

THE RAPE POEM

Once an ex-con told me
i was pretty,
he said if i were in prison i'd be
somebody's "woman"
i'd have to obey him and be faithful
to him,
if i got caught screwing with someone
else,
i'd be slit with a knife or a
razor blade,
slit until the blood from my
faggot ass
met the blood from my throat,
bled until the redness became a
poem and then a song
until a mute nation heard
but they haven't heard and sometimes
i realize they can't hear at all

yesterday i put on my faggot gown
and went mourning for the
faggots and dykes

burnt in the ovens that burped
and no one heard,
the ovens that digested so
many bones and pink triangles
and once when i was young
a nazi tried to rape me in an
alley
but i bit his tongue and the
blood
dripped swastikas
all over europe

rape,
rape as in genet, the rape of
humiliation
the humiliation of walking past
a corner and being taunted and
called "sweetie" and "faggot"
and when you answer back of
having bottles filled with beer
and rocks thrown at you
because you have somehow
violated their manhood

rape
as in alan's bedroom
when that boy from up the street
broke in with a knife, out of
breath, whispering "suck me off
or i'll slit your throat"
alan the faggot
who said hello to everyone
even the nazis who waited for him
that night
when they plunged into alan
as they did
into europe's throat and hung
its neck from
every pole to wave like a flag

they left alan's sweet face
like a child's,
his mouth open to the breast of
the mother earth

James Baldwin

James Baldwin (1924–1987) is the celebrated author of more than twenty books, including *If Beale Street Could Talk, The Fire Next Time, Another Country, Go Tell It on the Mountain,* and *Just Above My head.* His nonfiction is collected in *The Price of the Ticket.* Baldwin's brave depiction of a homosexual love affair in the novel *Giovanni's Room* (1956) gave hope to millions of gay people. *Jimmy's Blues: Selected Poems* was published by St. Martin's Press in 1985.

GUILT, DESIRE AND LOVE

At the dark street corner
where Guilt and Desire
are attempting to stare
each other down
(presently, one of them
will light a cigarette
and glance in the direction
of the abandoned warehouse)
Love came slouching along,
an exploded silence
standing a little apart
but visible anyway
in the yellow, silent, steaming light,
while Guilt and Desire wrangled,
trying not to be overheard
by this trespasser.

Each time Desire looked towards Love,
hoping to find a witness,
Guilt shouted louder
and shook them hips
and the fire of the cigarette

threatened to burn the warehouse down.

Desire actually started across the street,
time after time,
to hear what Love might have to say,
but Guilt flagged down a truckload
of other people
and knelt down in the middle of the street
and, while the truckload of other people
looked away, and swore that they
didn't see nothing
and couldn't testify nohow,
and Love moved out of sight,
Guilt accomplished upon the standing body
of Desire
the momentary, inflammatory soothing
which seals their union
(for ever?)
and creates a mighty traffic problem.

A LOVER'S QUESTION

My country,
t'is of thee
I sing.

You, enemy of all tribes,
known, unknown, past,
present, or,
perhaps, above all,
to come:
I sing:
my dear,
        my darling,
jewel
(Columbia, the gem of
the ocean!)
or, as I, a street nigger,
would put it—:
(Okay. I'm your nigger
baby, till I get bigger!)
You are my heart.

Why
have you allowed yourself
to become so *grinly* wicked?

I
do not ask you why
you have spurned,
despised my love
as something beneath you.
We all have our ways and
days
but my love has been as constant
as the rays
coming from the earth
or the sun,
which you have used to obliterate
me,
and, now, according to your purpose,
all mankind,
from the nigger, to you,
and to your children's children.

I have endured your fire
and your whip,
your rope,
and the panic from your hip,
in many ways, false lover,
yet, my love:
you do not know
how desperately I hoped
that you would grow
not so much to love me
as to know
that what you do to me
you do to you.

No man can have a harlot
for a lover
nor stay in bed forever
with a lie.
He must rise up
and face the morning sky

and himself, in the mirror
of his lover's eye.

You do not love me.
I see that.
You do not see me:
I am your black cat.

You forget
that I remember an Egypt
where I was worshipped
where I was loved.

No one has ever worshipped you,
nor ever can: you think that love
is a territorial matter,
and racial,
oh, yes,
where I was worshipped
and you were hurling stones,
stones which you have hurled at me,
to kill me,
and, now,
you hurl at the earth,
our mother,
the toys which slaughtered
Cain's brother.

What panic makes you
want to die?
How can you fail to look
into your lover's eye?

Your black dancer
holds the answer:
your only hope
beyond the rope.

Of rope you fashioned,
usefully,
enough hangs from
your hanging tree

to carry you
where you sent me.

And, then, false lover,
you will know
what love has managed
here below.

Jane Barnes

Jane Barnes (born 1943, Brooklyn) was raised in Mendocino County, California. She has lived for twenty-one years in Boston, where she received an M.A. in poetry and fiction (Boston University, 1978). She was a co-founder and editor of *Dark Horse*, a poetry and fiction tabloid. She self-published her poetry collection *Extremes* (Blue Giant, 1981) and chapbooks *Mythologies* and *They Say I Talk in My Sleep* (Quark, 1976, 1979). Her poetry and fiction appear in numerous periodicals and anthologies, including *Naming the Waves* (Virago, 1988). A recent story was installed by Urban Arts in a Boston subway station.

HOW TO DRESS LIKE A SCARY DYKE

She said, Wear my leather jacket, a looser
sweater. Take off that lipstick,
don't fuss with your hair. Wear
jeans and boots. That ought to do it.

I still had stockings stuffed like
seaweed in packages, and nylon pants
that made my crotch itch
without desire.

I still had black high heels
I bought to make me look all business,

but I couldn't get to the business
of not dressing for men.

She told me what they'd like,
those scary dykes.
I took these notes.
Wanted to learn real bad.

1977

HOW TO DRESS LIKE A FEMMY DYKE

Go with a perm or a duck tail
—low maintenance.
Heavy on the eye paint, a little hard.
Blood-red lips. Develop a swagger
in your fuck-me shoes, or wear
expensive cowboy boots, the kind
that go with gypsy clothes.

Get three holes in one ear
and pour on the gold.
Use tons of Yes, the new perfume.
Wear Fifties coats with shoulder pads.
If you get a little plump,
just pile on the frills.

Go to Prelude and order Kaluha with cream,
or cream with anything.
Dance up a storm.
And if a scary dyke looks too long at you,
start picking the polish off your nails
or burst into tears and
beg her to take you home.

1981

THE HOT DOG POEM

I smashed a hot dog into her face
because she refused to pass

the catsup because . . . I forget why.
So she ran after me and shook me
then took the seven dollars and my keys
and her card and went out to the movies
and I took out my butcher knife
and slammed it on her table and made
four dents in it and then threw
myself on the bed and stared at the cuff
of my shirt and thought how love
chokes you and then I got up and
rubbed salad oil into the dents
and cleaned up the house and
made a pile of my books in the
bedroom and got my pen and set the
phone up in case anyone might call
and looked in my address book
for the list I have of possible
lovers and called a few numbers,
relieved they weren't home, and then
I wrote in my journal how I hate her
then called Nicky on the phone
and we talked during the commercial
about rage. Then she said she had to
hang up, it was a special on DeGaulle,
so I hung up and leafed through
a book of stories by women about love.

1979

David Bergman

David Bergman was born in 1950 in Fitchburg, Massachusetts, and reared in New York City. Winner of the George Elliston Prize for his book of poems *Cracking the Code* (Ohio State University Press, 1985), Bergman has also written *The Heath Guide to Literature* (D. C. Heath, 1987) and is editor of *John Ashbery's Art Chronicles* (Knopf, 1988). He teaches at Towson State University and serves as theater critic for *The City Paper*, Baltimore.

BLUEBERRY MAN

I was never the one to spot him walking
slowly up the street, pulling his yellow
wagon. It was always a brother or sister
who'd race home with the news. Then everything
spun into action like gulls at low tide.

Mother would shoo the children from the yard
and hide us out of danger in the living room,
warning with harsh whispers not to peek
from the windows and knowing we would anyway,
tracking the blueberry man across the porch
to where he knocked at the kitchen door.

Grandfather greeted him. Mother said
she was afraid. But I think she was jealous.
For though I was five or six, I knew I'd
never see such beautiful hair again. Hair
like a storybook princess. Great golden skeins,
falling halfway down his back. And such eyes,
freaked like a robin's egg and bobbing
beneath mascara waves of lashes. I remember
the Victory Red lips unfurling like a flag
when he spoke and the frilly shirt.

                              My brothers
giggled nervously. But I wasn't scared.
I wanted to pull the chiffon curtains back
and speak. But what would I say? That I knew
what it was to be alone? That I had heard
my own family scamper with trepidation
from my door when I was quarantined with
scarlet fever and no one but my mother was
allowed into my room?
                    I could have said:
I'm only a child but certain to end an outcast too.
Still, I said nothing, except once, a weak

goodby for which I was roundly scolded.
I used to ride my bike to his house, a tiny
cabin covered with angry brambles and
the hiss of intriguing bees, hoping we'd meet.
But he stayed inside during the day when he
wasn't peddling the wares he gathered at night.

One sleepless dawn I saw him coming home
with a kerosene lantern in one hand
and a silvery pail in the other.
Mother washed his berries twice to cleanse
them of his memory, as if he communicated
with his touch the fearful urge to dress
in women's clothing. For dessert she'd douse
the fruit with milk or pile them on peaks of
sour cream, chubby mountain climbers in the snow.
My brothers ate them greedily. But I
when everyone had left the table, would
still be seated, savoring the sweet juice
and the delicate flesh he had brought me.

Frank Bidart

Frank Bidart was born in 1939 in Bakersfield, California. In 1981, he won the
Paris Review's first Bernard F. Conners prize for a long poem with the poem
"The War of Vaslav Nijinsky." Bidart has published three collections of verse:
Golden State (Braziller, 1973), *The Book of the Body* (Farrar, Straus, Giroux,
1977), and *The Sacrifice* (Random House, 1983). His *Collected Poems* will soon
be published by Farrar, Straus, and Giroux. Bidart teaches at Wellesley Col-
lege and lives in Cambridge, Massachusetts.

CONFESSIONAL

PART I

Is she dead?

Yes, she is dead.

Did you forgive her?

No, I didn't forgive her.

Did she forgive you?

No, she didn't forgive me.

What did you have to forgive?

She was never mean, or willfully
cruel, or unloving.

When I was eleven, she converted to Christ—

she began to simplify her life, denied
herself, and said that she and I must struggle

"to divest ourselves
of the love of CREATED BEINGS,"—

and to help me to do that,

one day

      she hanged my cat.

I came home from school, and in the doorway
of my room,

my cat was hanging strangled.

She was in the bathroom; I could hear
the water running.

—I shouted at her;

                    she wouldn't
come out.

        She was in there
for hours, with the water running . . .

Finally, late that night,
she unlocked the door.

                        She wouldn't look at me.

She said that we must learn to rest
in the LORD,—

and not in His CREATION . . .

        Did you forgive her?

Soon, she had a breakdown;
when she got out of the hospital,

she was SORRY . . .

For years she dreamed the cat
had dug
its claws into her thumbs:—

in the dream, she knew, somehow,
that it was dying; she tried

to help it,—

        TO PUT IT OUT OF ITS MISERY,—

so she had her hands around its
neck, strangling it . . .

Bewildered,

it looked at her,

KNOWING SHE LOVED IT—;

and she *DID* love it, which was
what was
so awful . . .

All it could do was
hold on,—

. . . AS
SHE HELD ON.

Did you forgive her?

I was the center of her life,—
and therefore,
of her fears and obsessions. They changed;

one was money.

. . . DO I HAVE TO GO INTO IT?

Did you forgive her?

Standing next to her coffin, looking down
at her body, I suddenly
knew I hadn't—;

over and over
I said to her,

I didn't forgive you!
I didn't forgive you!

I *did* love her . . . Otherwise,

would I feel so guilty?

What did she have to forgive?

She was SORRY. She *tried*
to change . . .

She loved me. She was generous.

I pretended
that I had forgiven her—;

                        and she pretended
to believe it,—

she needed desperately to believe it . . .

SHE KNEW I COULD BARELY STAND TO BE AROUND HER.

       Did you forgive her?

I *tried*—;
        for years I almost
convinced myself I did . . .

But no, I didn't.

—Now, after I have said it all, so I can
rest,

      will you give me ABSOLUTION,—

. . . and grant this
                "*created being*"

FORGIVENESS? . . .

      Did she forgive you?

I think she tried—;
            but no,—
she *couldn't* forgive me . . .

WHY COULDN'T SHE FORGIVE ME?

         FRANK BIDART

Don't you understand even now?

No! Not—not really . . .

Forgiveness doesn't exist.

THE SACRIFICE

When Judas writes the history of SOLITUDE,—
. . . let him celebrate

Miss Mary Kenwood; who, without
help, placed her head in a plastic bag,

then locked herself
in a refrigerator.
                    •
—Six months earlier, after thirty years
teaching piano, she had watched

her mother slowly die of throat cancer.
Watched her *want* to die . . .

What once had given Mary life
in the end didn't want it.

Awake, her mother screamed for help to die.
—She felt

GUILTY . . . She knew that *all* men in these situations felt
innocent—; helpless—; yet guilty.
                    •
Christ knew the secret. Betrayal
is necessary; as is woe for the betrayer.

The solution, Mary realized at last,
must be brought out of my own body.

Wiping away our sins, Christ stained us with his blood—;
to offer yourself, yet need *betrayal*, by *Judas*, before SHOULDERING

THE GUILT OF THE WORLD—;
. . . *Give me the courage not to need Judas.*

•

When Judas writes the history of solitude,
let him record

that to the friend who opened
the refrigerator, it seemed

death fought; before giving in.

Ellen Marie Bissert

Ellen Marie Bissert (born 1947, Brooklyn, New York) is the author of the
poetry book *the immaculate conception of the blessed virgin dyke* (13th Moon,
1977) and founder of the feminist literary magazine *13th Moon.* She currently
sells insurance and investments to the Manhattan small-business community
under a pseudonym.

THE MOST BEAUTIFUL WOMAN AT MY
HIGHSCHOOL REUNION

after 11 years
she is still as sleek as an unspayed siamese
charming everyone into her audience
she is a winner
rising to associate director of a department store
quitting to have 2 children
(1 for each of her husband's houses)
nothing has changed
she is still as leggy as a doe

her iris-blue eyes
her long smooth arms holding me in confidence
as she complains
motherhood hasn't done much
she's as flat as ever
glancing toward the table of husbands
I try to pick hers
nothing has changed
short smug & meaty
they are still the inert boys at the highschool dances
quietly pumping sperm into voluptuous moviestars
the way they force air into tires
she is a winner
moving beyond the mysteries of padded bras
still needing to offer herself like cut melon to the male eyes
opening her blouse
we will never be able
as i hold her cool thin fingers
i long to caress the silk of her nipples
into loving themselves
like the woman waiting for me tonight
does to mine

Walta Borawski

Walta Borawski (born 1947 in Bayshore, Long Island, New York) "has studied yoga for the past seven years. Some have said he's stretched out. He adores the novels of Barbara Pym and the singing and the piano playing of Nina Simone." Borawski's poems have been printed regularly in *Mouth of the Dragon, Fag Rag,* and other periodicals. The collection *Sexually Dangerous Poet* was published by Good Gay Poets, Boston, in 1984. Borawski and his lover of twelve years, writer/activist Michael Bronski, live in Cambridge, Massachusetts.

CHEERS, CHEERS FOR OLD CHA CHA ASS

Cheers, cheers for old Patchogue High;
You bring the whiskey, I'll bring the rye;
When we yell   We yell like hell

Acne, puberty, dry heaves each pre-
school morning were not bad enough:

At Patchogue High a circle of charming
boys called me *Cha Cha Ass Borawski.*

Hey, look at Walter, he cha chas when he walks.
He cha chas when he tries to hit a ball.
He probably cha chas while he shits: Let's watch.

(I'm in a toilet stall, making up god.
                    O lord god let me
                    kiss your boot do you
                    think you could
                    disguise me?)

Hey, look, Jayne Mansfield's in Borawski's gym suit.
Hey, Jayne, what's happened to your tits?
If Walter had Mansfield's tits I'd screw him.
If Walter had Mansfield's tits we'd ALL screw him.

Ha ha ha. Cha cha cha. Ha ha Ha Cha
Cha cha   Until

shots called are one's own shots
they are ugly, & must be muffled.

I said *No* to their tenth year reunion,
I added a sketch, I threw in a poem:

Cha Cha Ass Borawski will not be there.
He don't mind the name anymore. He's

thinking of legally adopting it. It's
his only legal thought these days. But

now he merengues when he walks, he
dreams up the devil while he shits.

"ENGLISH WAS ONLY A SECOND LANGUAGE . . ."

English was only a second
language, never second nature
to my maternal grandfather   He

would shout the heavy
fragments of sentence:
Money!   Under!   Mattress!

He didn't trust banks, he
knew that here in America
we hide things.   When I

was 15 he wanted to see me
with my pants down   I took
them   off   in his toolshed

He ran his fingers across
my pubic hair & said
Ah!   Moustache!   That year

he died & I began
looking for other men who'd
take his sort of interest

but it's never been the same
with proper sentences

INVISIBLE HISTORY

My shrink told me it was unnatural to be
obsessed with the Nazi extermination of
homosexuals   Look at me I'm normal he

said I sleep nights & I'm healthy enough
to listen to your stories & others worse than

yours & I still have sex & *I'm* Jewish so

what's with these nightmare pogroms   find
yourself a hot guy to go to bed with or
do it on the floor of his car but

stop it with these death camps.   I
knew he was right, that his people had
lost millions more than my people, but

piles of emaciated   tortured   worked-to-
death   gassed-to-death   clubbed-to-death
bodies   resemble each other   & they

resemble *us*   Look at that man on top
of the others   Look at his beard   He
could be me. When I was six my

father first told me about liberation
of the camps   by the Allies   he was
US Army & they entered at

last & those bodies, he said   those bodies.
By time I was 15 my eye doctor showed
mercy to me put me on sleeping pills

Circles round my eyes   I told him I
couldn't sleep & when I did fall I
found myself behind wire—barbed,

or electric: my head shaved   an empty
expression leering back at me   at every-
one in this odd century of horror

so systematic so organized.   I'll give you
these pills he said   But don't abuse them
& cut out the fantasies, you're not even

Jewish

Beth Brant

Beth Brant, born 1941 in Michigan, is a Bay of Quinte Mohawk and the editor of *A Gathering of Spirit,* the first anthology of art and writing by Native American women that included the work of lesbians (Sinister Wisdom Books, 1983). She is the author of *Mohawk Trail* (Firebrand, 1985), and her work appears in *Songs From This Earth on Turtle's Back* (Greenfield Review Press) and *Naming the Waves: Contemporary Lesbian Poetry* (Virago, 1988). A mother of three and a grandmother, she lives in Detroit with her lover of eleven years, Denise.

HER NAME IS HELEN

Her name is Helen.
She came from Washington State twenty years ago through
broken routes
of Hollywood, California,
Gallup, New Mexico,
Las Vegas, Nevada,
ended up in Detroit, Michigan where she lives in #413
in the gut of the city.
She worked in a factory for ten years, six months, making
carburetors for Cadillacs.
She loved factory work.
She made good money, took vacations to New Orleans.
"A real party town."

She wears a cowboy hat with pretty feathers.
Can't wear cowboy boots because of the arthritis
that twists her feet.
She wears beige vinyl wedgies. In the winter she pulls on
heavy socks to protect her bent toes from the slush and rain.

Helen takes pictures of herself.

Everytime she passes those Polaroid booths,
one picture for a dollar,
she closes the curtain and the camera flashes.

When she was laid off from the factory
she got a job in a bar, serving up shots and beer.
Instead of tips, she gets presents from her customers.
Little wooden statues of Indians in headdress.
Naked pictures of squaws with braided hair.
Feather roach clips in fuschia and chartreuse.
Everybody loves Helen.
She's such a good guy. An honest-to-god Indian.

Helen doesn't kiss.
She allows her body to be held when she's had enough
vodkas and Lite beer.
She's had lots of girlfriends.
White women who wanted to take care of her,
who liked Indians,
who think she's a tragedy.

Helen takes pictures of herself.

She has a picture on a keychain, along with a baby's shoe
and a feathered roach clip.
She wears her keys on a leather belt.
Helen sounds like a chime, moving behind the bar.

Her girlfriends took care of her.
Told her what to wear
what to say
how to act more like an Indian.
"You should be proud of your Indian heritage.
Wear more jewelry.
Go to the Indian Center."

Helen doesn't talk much.
Except when she's had enough
vodkas and Lite beer.
Then she talks about home,
about her mom,
about the boarding schools,
the foster homes,
about wanting to go back to see her people

before she dies.
Helen says she's going to die when she's fifty.

She's forty-two now.
Eight years to go.

Helen doesn't kiss.
Doesn't talk much.
Takes pictures of herself.
She touches women who are white.
She is touched by their hands.

Helen can't imagine that she is beautiful.
That her skin is warm
like redwood and fire.
That her thick black hair moves like a current.
That her large body speaks in languages stolen from her.
That her mouth is wide and full and when she smiles
people catch their breath.

"I'm a gay Indian girl.
A dumb Indian.
A fat, ugly squaw."
This is what Helen says.

She wears a t-shirt with the legend
Detroit
splashed in glitter across her large breasts.
Her breasts that white women have sucked
and molded to fit their mouths.

Helen can't imagine that there are women
who see her.
That there are women
who want to taste her breath and salt.
Who want a speech to be created between their tongues.
Who want to go deep inside her
touch places that are dark, wet,
muscle and spirit.
Who want to swell, expand two bodies into a word
of our own making.

Helen can't imagine that she is beautiful.

She doesn't kiss.
Doesn't talk much.
Takes pictures of herself so she will know she is there.

Takes pictures of herself to prove she is alive.

Helen takes pictures of herself.

James Broughton

James Broughton (born 1913) is a native Californian who since 1948 has been a luminary of the San Francisco scene for his lively achievements in poetry and filmmaking. He has produced some twenty books and as many independent films, has been the recipient of two Guggenheim Fellowships, two grants from the National Endowment for the Arts, and a Cannes Film Festival award. His principal hobby is the care and feeding of ecstasy. His collections of poetry include *A Long Undressing* (Jargon Society, 1971), *Seeing the Light* (City Lights, 1977), *Graffiti for the Johns of Heaven* (Syzygy Press, 1982), and *Ecstasies* (Syzygy Press, 1983).

WONDROUS THE MERGE

Had my soul tottered off to sleep
taking my potency with it?
Had they both retired before I could
leaving me a classroom somnambulist?
Why else should I at sixty-one
feel myself shriveling into fadeout?

Then on a cold seminar Monday
in walked an unannounced redeemer
disguised as a taciturn student

Brisk and resolute in scruffy mufti
he set down his backpack   shook his hair
and offered me unequivocal devotion

He dismissed my rebuffs and ultimatums
He scoffed at suggestions of disaster
He insisted he had been given authority
to provide my future happiness
Was it possible he had been sent
from some utopian headquarters?

I went to his flat to find out

•

He had two red dogs   a yellow cat
a girl roommate   an ex boyfriend
and a bedroom ceiling covered
with blue fluorescent stars
But he was ready to renounce anything
that would not accommodate me

He said I held the key to his existence
He said he knew when he first saw me
that I was the reason for his birth
He claimed that important deities
had opened his head three times
to place my star in his brow

This is preposterous   I said
I have a wife in the suburbs
I have mortgages   children   in-laws
and a position in the community
I thoroughly sympathize   said He
Why else have I come to your rescue?

These exchanges gave me diarrhea
I tried leaving town on business
but I kept remembering the warmth
that flowed through his healing fingers
We met for lunch at Hamburger Mary's
and borrowed a bedroom for the afternoon

He brought a bouquet of blood roses

and a ruby-fat jug of red wine
He hung affections around my neck
and massaged the soles of my feet
He offered to arrange instant honeymoons
and guarantee the connecting flights

Are you mad?   I said   You are half my age
Are you frightened of your fate?   said He

•

At Beck's Motel on the 7th of April
we went to bed for three days
disheveled the king size sheets
never changed the Do Not Disturb
ate only the fruits of discovery
drank semen and laughter and sweat

He seasoned my mouth
    sweetened my neck
    coddled my nipple
    nuzzled my belly
    groomed my groin
    buffed my buttock
    garnished my pubis
    renovated my phallus
    remodeled all my torso
until I cried out
until I cried
    I am   Yes
    I am   your Yes
        I am   I am   your
        Yes   Yes   Yes

•

He took a studio of his own
on the windward slope of Potrero
where I spent afterschool hours
uprooting my ingrown niceties
and planting fresh beds of bliss
His sheets were grassy green

•

In his long bathtub
he sat me opposite him
and scrubbed away my guilt

With a breakfast of sunbursts
he woke the sleeping princess
in my castle of armor

Waving blueprints of daring
for twin heroes
he roused my rusty knighthood

To the choked minstrel
aching in my throat
he proffered concerts of praise

Off the tip of his tongue
I took each tasty love word
and swallowed it whole
for my own

Are you my Book of Miracles?   I said
Are you my Bodhisattva?   said He

•

Ablaze in the thrust of creation
we scathed each other with verve
burned up our fears of forever
steamed ourselves deep in surrender
till I lay drenched under scorch
and joy cried out through my crown

Wondrous   Wondrous the merge
Wondrous the merge of soulmates
the surprises of recognition
Wondrous the flowerings of renewal
Wondrous the wings of the air
clapping their happy approval!

•

I severed my respectabilities

and bought a yellow mobile home
in an unlikely neighborhood
He moved in his toaster   his camera
and his eagerness to become
my courier   seed-carrier   and consort

Above all he brought the flying carpet
that upholsters his boundless embrace
Year after year he takes me soaring
out to the ecstasies of the cosmos
that await all beings in love

One day we shall not bother to return

Olga Broumas

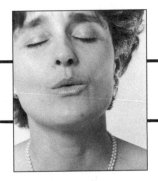

Olga Broumas (born 1949 on the Aegean island of Syros, Greece) lives in Provincetown, where she writes, translates, teaches, and has a private practice in body-work therapy. Together with Rita Speicher and Marian Roth, she co-founded Freehand, a fine-arts program for women, in 1982. She has received Guggenheim, NEA, and Regional Arts Council fellowships, and travels widely reading her work. Her books of poetry include *Beginning with O* (Yale, 1977), *Soie Sauvage, Pastoral Jazz* (Copper Canyon, 1980, 1983), *Black Holes, Black Stockings*, co-authored with Jane Miller (Wesleyan, 1985), *What I Love: Selected Translations of Odysseas Elytis, 1939–1978*, and *The Little Mariner*, a translation of Odysseas Elytis's most recent book (Copper Canyon, 1986, 1988).

SHE LOVES

Deep prolonged entry with the strong pink cock,
the situps it evokes from her, arms fast

on the climbing invisible rope to the sky,
clasping and unclasping the cosmic lorus.

Inside, the long breaths of lung and cunt
cave swell the vocal cords and rasp a song,
loud sudden overdrive into disintegrate,
spinal melt, video hologram in the belly.

Her tits are luminous and sway to the rhythm
and I grab them and exaggerate their orbs.
Shoulders above like loaves of heaven,
nutmeg flecked, exuding light like violet diodes

each time my fingers close circuit where the wall,
its fuse box, so stolidly stood. No room
for fantasy. We watch ourselves transform
the past with such disinterested fascination,

the only attitude that does not stall
the song by an outburst of consciousness
and still gives consiousness, loved and incurable
voyeur, its peek. Now consciousness transcends

its nature. Silicone transmits vibration
like the idea of perfect matter, a breath
on its handmade flange stirs sacrum to anus.
I tap. I slap. I knee, thump, bellyroll.

Her song is hoarse and is taking me,
incoherent familiar path
to that self we are all
cortical cells of. Every o in her body

beelines for her throat, that open-ended
ohming she unleashes beyond lung,
locked on a channel of vibration rising
skilift up the mountain, no

grass, no mountaintop, no snow. One finger,
bloodpainting the palm, a slap of gullwings on the thighs,
gullhead burrowing, then two. Situp, situp.
White belly folding, muscular as milk.

Fingers flutter their toes, dancers in the air.
Situp, situp. Pas de deux, pas de chat, spotlight
on the key of G, clef du roman, tour de force letting,
like the sunlight lets a sleeve against the wind, go.

Susan Cavin

Susan Cavin was born in 1948 in Trion, Georgia. She was the founding editor
and publisher of *Big Apple Dyke News* (*B.A.D. News*) (1981–87) and the first
woman president of the Gay and Lesbian Press Association (1984–85), and
was national spokeswoman for the October 13, 1987, nonviolent civil disobe-
dience at the Supreme Court for lesbian and gay rights. She is co-author of the
C.L.I.T. Papers (1974-84) and author of the theoretical work *Lesbian Origins*
(Ism Press, San Francisco, 1985) and the poetry collection *Me and Them Sirens
Running All Night Long* (Print Center, 1973). Her new manuscript of poems is
entitled *I Made It All Up.*

CHRISTMAS WITH THE HOLY FAMILY

Christmas come tomorrow
I can't wait
I wanna live like Rudolph
Santa, take me away
but . . .
what if Santa like Daddy?
just another . . . man . . .
daddy take me away alright
to the basement
and the darker alleyways of our house
everyhouse
and talks about my pussy
in a fatherly way of course
except sometimes when he gets me mixed up with mama
and calls me her name and

well, you know, he was drunk
and he didn't know what he was doing
that's what mama says
oh, what if santa really like daddy?
the man I been dreaming about every Christmas
the man who could take me away from all of this . . .
home
somehow this all too familiar
like other dreams
some tape recorder been playin' softly in my ear
while I was sleeping
all my life . . .
oh, but it's Christmas
and I shouldn't be thinking
like this
I'm too sensitive, you know
that's what mama says

anyway, Christmas come tomorrow
and I can't wait
mama got her shoes off
she feels right at home
brother got his train set, 29 years overgrown
mama waiting on him hand and foot
"why don't you have some fruit cake, johnnnny,
a growing boy needs to eat"
how come mama don't do that for me?
I need to grow too, besides I like fruit cake
guess I don't have any balls for her to bust
and mama like them balls
Daddy says I'm his little girl though
oh yeah, daddy . . .
daddy's got his liquor
hiding everything he knows
and I'm in the closet
paralyzed
blowing my nose
singing do-dah daddy don't you corner me tonight
do dah daddy wants a virgin
he likes it tight
mama's in the kitchen cooking christmas
saying he's a sight
the way he wants virgin mary every christmas night

SUSAN CAVIN   **67**

winking at me and saying to him
jc, not tonight
everynight
so he comes on me
forgetting I ain't no virgin
cause he bang bang banged me late one night
every other year.
Every evening mama makes the point
that she don't know what's going on between daddy and me
she can't see everything with her back turned you know
and with all my screaming
how could anyone hear a word?
like help
but she told me with her silence that she understood
how awful it was to sleep with that drunk
it don't feel good and she's sorry
but she just can't do it some nights
and she loves me
and comforts me with
"Life has been good to me, and it'll be nice for you too
someday if you trust in the Lord God with all your . . ."
oh, mama
another man
I wonder if he drinks too
every Christmas
it gets heavy around the house
everybody thinking, you know
another year loss
another one to get through together
and oh, every year
he cries about the war
not this one
the one before that
Christmas in Germany
1945
do wah
and how he almost lost his life
30 years ago
them graphic german details gonna wash my brain
if mama don't do it first screaming
she wants her life back from me
the youth I look
she says I took from her

SUSAN CAVIN

she don't drink
she's a Christian woman
I don't understand these people
they're my family and I just love them to death
you know, I guess maybe people never understand family love
you know, the love between them and their parents
and the holy love between a man like my father and a lady
like my mother
people never understand it no matter how old they are
but you know they love you in the same way you know
that god loves you—
YOU DON'T
you *do* know
if you're a man-child, daddy loves you the same way god,
the big he in caps,
loved his only son,
he sent him to die on the cross
to wear thorns in his head because he thought too much
it's Christmas
it's ok
to talk about jesus, isn't it?
yeah, the big He had a purpose in life for his son alright:
death,
a suffering death that he had to thank god for
because his father couldn't live
except through his son
and it hurt god alot to turn his back
at the crucial moment
that his son begged him not to do him in
enough about god and the boys.

And if you're a woman-child you know daddy loves you
the same way god loved Mary
he wants to bang you up secretly
like it never really happened
nobody talks much about mary who got some goddamned
male seed crammed up her ass
not even the writers of Jesus Christ Superstar talk about that
and how nobody would believe her
that it wasn't a fuck
of course, it wasn't a fuck
it was a god-rape
and nobody would believe her except her understanding husband

SUSAN CAVIN   **69**

my mother when we're out in public describes my father
as her understanding husband
and pats him on the head when she says it and calls him honey
she calls me honey too
after she watches daddy put his hands on my tits
when he french kisses me godnight everynight
it's times like that I remember best
when she calls him honey
it's real nice seeing them like that
loving each other
like they love me
and it's christmas, a family time
we can't talk too good
but we love each other.
Every Christmas
we pretend
a whole year of filth and hate never happened
I guess all families are like that
and it's at special times like Christmas
that everybody knows
the things they never say to each other
but would like to all year round
I guess the thing I'd like to say to my family this Christmas
that I never get the chance to say
is
daddy, I hate you
and the plastic cock
you keep locked in the trunk
of our second car
and mama, why did you try to kill me
instead of him?

December 15, 1972

LOOK AWAY CHILD

Look away child
from your bourbon smelling papa
and your perfumed lady mother
they can't help you now
just look at you
now that you've got yourself so faraway

70   SUSAN CAVIN

from everything you knew
when you wore that bride's smile
in your place
and you were sure that was his face
up in your mirror
smiling back at you.
Oh, you sure got yourself faraway
from everything you knew,
but ain't that exactly what you spent years
trying to do?

Look away child, look away.
See them crutches on the river
they used to belong to you
while you lay sleeping in your anger
someone who loved you more than you
threw them in the river
so you could be
as much as you can be
didn't you know that?
didn't you know that
there's a woman living
deep inside of you
dying
to come out
now don't you be so hard on her
she hasn't been alive as long as you.

October 13, 1971

Jane Chambers

The plays of Jane Chambers (1937–1983) have been produced Off-Broadway,
in regional and community theaters, and on television. Her published work
includes plays (*A Late Snow*, Avon, 1979; *Last Summer at Bluefish Cove*; *My*

Blue Heaven, JH Press, 1982), novels (*Burning; Chasin' Jason*, JH, 1983, 1987), and poetry (*Warrior at Rest*, JH, 1984). Writing *Last Summer at Bluefish Cove* about a dying woman supported by her chosen lesbian family, she had no idea that she herself would soon face brain cancer. The poem below is one she dictated to the loving women who took care of her in her home during her final illness, when she could no longer see or hold a pen.

WHY ARE DADDIES SO MEAN

In the South there is a saying,
that a virgin is a six year old who can outrun her
    Pappy and her brothers.

I was just a little thing,
lifting my arms for tenderness and reassurance
and hopefully
some display of love from the male of the house-
    hold
upon whom, I was told, I could depend and trust.
But always
came the exploring fingers,
frightening to me in some unintelligible and
    inexpressible way.
I was reaching out for love but instinct told me
this was not the correct way of expressing it.
And when I asked my father to desist, he said
all I was, was a lard ass, split tail anyway.
Women couldn't be depended on.
We were all alike.
Jezebels, whose function in life was to break men's
    hearts.
Except my mother, who was in his estimation . . .
    perfect.
A perfect lady.
And if I wasn't as beautiful as she, which I was not,
then I was more than useless.
And an ugly scar, which he then was forced to
    bear.

So when he took me to the Gator Bar & Grill,
which he did every afternoon,
to avoid working,

        JANE CHAMBERS

he would frequently tell his drinking buddies:
"The kid's not much to look at but you oughta see
    her mother."
When the men at the bar became unruly and the
    din deafening,
and I would slide off the stool and raise my arms
    for comfort,
he would ignore me or tell me to run home
and to lie for him to my mother.

On one occasion, on the drive home from the
    Gator Bar & Grill,
he sideswiped my mother's car.
And when we arrived home, the police were
    waiting.
He took me to the side of the porch
and he told me not to tell them that we had done
    that.
So . . . I lied for him again
and my lard ass saved his skinny butt from going
    to jail.

And when two years ago,
he lay in a North Carolina nursing home waiting
    to die,
he had the gall to ask me to come
and wave goodbye as he sailed off
to what I presume, he assumed, was heaven.
And when I arrived at the nursing home,
I did not recognize him, nor did he recognize
    me,
except for the lard ass, that he took great pains
to point out to me.
Underscoring it by saying,
how was it that I never turned out like my mother.
How I had failed them both.
How I was an embarrassment to him.
And a year later, when I was lying in a hospital
    in a coma,
he had the effrontery
to appear to me and say with great glee,
that I wasn't his daughter, after all. But that I was
    sired

by my mother's brother.
And that he and my mother's brother were stuck
　　in Purgatory
until I forgave them their meanness to me.
Which I did, having long since learned
that hate eats up more energy than it's worth.

Still . . .
I can remember being a little girl at the Gator Bar
　　& Grill,
lifting my arms for Daddy's protection.
　　　　　Why are daddies so damn mean?

But as Beth always reminds me,
we are victims of victims.
And recounts the story of her own father who was
　　as cold and crazy
as my own. Except in different ways.
Telling us the story that when he was a boy he had
　　a dog
that looked like our Annabel, that he called Old
　　Black
and who was trained to hunt.
And when he was just a boy, his Dad called him
　　out to the barn
and told him to bring Old Black.
Since his father was shouldering a shotgun, he
　　assumed
that they were going hunting.
But when he got to the barn, his father said to him:
"Boy, you love that old dog, don't you?"
Beth's father admitted that he did.
Whereupon the old man raised the shotgun
and shot Old Black between the eyes.

Then he said:
"That's what you get for loving anything."

And as Beth's father wept retelling the story,
it was obvious how difficult it was
for him to display love.
　　　　　Why are daddies so mean?

Chrystos

Chrystos, born 1946, San Francisco, is the author of *Not Vanishing* (Press Gang, Canada, 1988), the first collection of her work. Her poetry is included in *This Bridge Called My Back* (Kitchen Table, 1981), *A Gathering of Spirit* (Sinister Wisdom Books, 1982), *Living the Spirit: A Gay American Indian Anthology* (St. Martin's, 1988), *Naming the Waves* (Virago, 1988), *Conditions, Sinister Wisdom,* and elsewhere. She writes: "Born of a Menominee father & an immigrant mother from Lithuania/Alsace-Lorraine, I live on many razors of contradictions. I've learned to run fast & watch my back. Political involvement includes Women for Big Mountain, Native Alliance, Gay American Indians, and People of Color Caucus."

THE WINGS OF A WILD GOOSE

for Beth Brant

A hen, one who could have brought more geese, a female, a wild
    one, dead
Shot by an excited young blond boy, his first, his mother threw the
    wings in the garbage
I rinsed them, brought them home, hung them spread wide on my
    studio wall
A reminder of so much   Saving what I can't bear to be wasted
Wings
I dream of   Wings which carry me far above human bitterness
    human walls
A goose who will have no more tiny pale fluttering goslings to
    bring alive, to shelter, feed, watch fly off on new wings,
    different winds
He has a lawn this boy   A pretty face which was recently paid
    thousands of dollars
to be in a television commercial   I clean their house every
    Wednesday morning

2 dogs which no one brushes   flying hair everywhere
A black rabbit who is almost always out of water   usually in a
    filthy cage
I've cleaned the cage out of sympathy a few times although it is
    not part
of what are called my duties   I check the water as soon as I arrive
This rabbit & those dogs are the boy's pets   He is very lazy
He watches television constantly leaving the sofa in the den
    littered
with food wrappers, soda cans, empty cereal bowls   If I'm
    still there
when he comes home, he is rude to me
If he has his friends with him he makes fun of me behind my back
I muse on how he will always think of the woods as an exciting
    place to kill
This family of three lives on a five-acre farm   They raise no crops
not even their own vegetables   no animals for slaughter
His father is a neurosurgeon who longs to be a poet
His mother frantically searches for Christian enlightenment
    spiritual guidance
I'm sad for her though I don't like her   because I know she
    won't find any
The boy does nothing to help around the house without being
    paid
I'm 38 & still haven't saved the amount of money he has in a
    passbook found
in the pillows of the couch under gum wrappers
That dead goose   This boy who will probably never understand
    that it is not right
to take without giving   He doesn't know how to give   His
    mother who cleaned & cooked
the goose says she doesn't really like to do it but can't
    understand why
she should feel any different about the goose than a chicken or
    hamburger from the market
I bite my tongue & nod   I could explain that meat raised for
    slaughter
is very different from meat taken from the woods where so few
    wild beings survive
That her ancestors are responsible for the emptiness of this land
    That lawns
feed no one   That fallow land lined with fences is sinful
That hungry people need the food they could grow

76   CHRYSTOS

That spirituality is not separate from food or wildness or respect
  or giving
But she already doesn't like me because she suspects I read her
  husband's
poetry books when no one is around & she's right I do
I need the $32 a week that tolerating them provides me
I wait for the wings on my wall to speak to me, guide my
  hungers, teach me winds I
can't reach   I keep these wings because walls are so hard
  wildness so rare
because ignorance must be remembered   because I am female
  because I fly only
in my dreams because I too, will have no young to let go

Cheryl Clarke

Cheryl Clarke (born 1947, Washington, D.C.) lives and writes in Jersey City,
New Jersey. She has been a member of the *Conditions* magazine editorial col-
lective since 1981. Her two collections of poetry are *Narratives: poems in the
tradition of black women* (Kitchen Table: Women of Color Press, 1983) and
Living as a Lesbian (Firebrand, 1986). Her goal as a poet is to give voice to the
unspoken heroes of black American culture, black lesbians, and to stop the
erasures.

OF ALTHEA AND FLAXIE

In 1943 Althea was a welder
very dark
very butch
and very proud
loved to cook, sew, and drive a car
and did not care who knew she kept company with a woman
who met her every day after work

in a tight dress and high heels
light-skinned and high-cheekboned
who loved to shoot, fish, play poker
and did not give a damn who knew her 'man' was a woman.

Althea was gay and strong in 1945
and could sing a good song
from underneath her welder's mask
and did not care who heard her sing her song to a woman.

Flaxie was careful and faithful
mindful of her Southern upbringing
watchful of her tutored grace
long as they treated her like a lady
she did not give a damn who called her a 'bulldagger.'

In 1950 Althea wore suits and ties
Flaxie's favorite colors were pink and blue
People openly challenged their flamboyance
but neither cared a fig who thought them 'queer' or 'funny.'

When the girls bragged over break of their sundry loves,
Flaxie blithely told them her old lady Althea took her dancing
every weekend
and did not give a damn who knew she clung to a woman.

When the boys on her shift complained of their wives,
Althea boasted of how smart her 'stuff' Flaxie was
and did not care who knew she loved the mind of a woman.

In 1955 when Flaxie got pregnant
and Althea lost her job
Flaxie got herself on relief
and did not care how many caseworkers
threatened midnite raids.

Althea was set up and went to jail
for writing numbers in 1958.
Flaxie visited her every week with gifts
and hungered openly for her thru the bars
and did not give a damn who knew she waited for a woman.

When her mother died in 1965 in New Orleans

CHERYL CLARKE

Flaxie demanded that Althea walk beside her in the funeral
    procession
and did not care how many aunts and uncles knew she slept with a
    woman.

When she died in 1970
Flaxie fought Althea's proper family not to have her laid out in lace
and dressed the body herself
and did not care who knew she'd made her way with a woman.

PALM LEAF OF MARY MAGDALENE

Obsessed by betrayal
compelled by passion
I pull this mutant palm leaf, orange
from my childhood of palm sundays.
Weave it into a cross, pray to it,
wear it as headband and wristband,
strap it round my ankle.
Magical as the pentecostal holy ghost.
Turning to fuchsia in afternoon light.

More than once an olive skinned nun pulled her
skirts up for me; later bribed me with a wild
orange palm leaf; thought its color a miracle
awesome as the resurrection; whispered it was
the palm leaf of Mary Magdalene, laughed;
side to side, stroked her unfrocked breasts
and shoulders with it; tied my wrist to hers
with it and took my forgiveness.

Mary Magdalene's palm leaf to you, dearest whore.
Flash it cross your sex back and forth like a
shoe shine rag more gently with as much dedication
while I (and the one you sleep with tonight instead
of me) watch and wait for the miracle
weave it into a cross pray to it
wear it as headband and wristband
tie your ankle to the bedpost with it
tongue of the holy ghost
palm leaf of Mary Magdalene.

THE OLDER AMERICAN

Lettie Walker was 71
when she was struck unconscious in the street
by a hit and run driver
who seemed not to have obeyed the stop sign
or perhaps became impatient with her halt gait.

Mrs. Walker,
a widow
long past the empty-nest syndrome
living alone
prone to speak symbolically
metaphorically
biblically
content in having only to do for self,
did not die.
She lay at the curb unbloody for nearly an hour
before anyone noticed her body.

At the hospital she regained her sense of things.
A youngish, white coated, white man
asked Mrs. Walker how she felt.
Laughing, Mrs. Walker said: 'Like a leaf.'

'What happened?' the man continued, chagrined.

'They crucified Jesus. They only hit me with a car.'

Considering her color, her age, her seeming disorientation,
and that no pocketbook had been recovered,
the man presumed Mrs. Walker to be a cast off thing
and probably a little demented.
After applying several pokes and squeezes to her rather vulnerable body
the man ordered x-rays
and the next thing she knew
Mrs. Walker was going under in the o.r. for something called
      'exploratory.'

Since that time
Lettie Walker has been depressed
agoraphobic
nearly anorexic
taken to walking with a cane

CHERYL CLARKE

given up her home in the South
to stay with her daughter in the North
and ambivalent about wanting to live.

Jan Clausen

Jan Clausen was born in 1950 in North Bend, Oregon. Her poetry, fiction, and critical prose have appeared widely in the U.S. and Great Britain. A founder and former editor of *Conditions* magazine, she received an NEA fiction fellowship in 1981. Her books include *Mother, Sister, Daughter, Lover* (short stories, Crossing, 1980), *Duration* (poetry and prose, Hanging Loose, 1983), and *Sinking, Stealing* (novel, Crossing, 1985). Her second novel, *The Prosperine Papers* (Crossing), and her essay collection *Books & Life* (Ohio) were published in 1988. She is a lesbian co-parent, works in a tape-transcription agency, and is active in Brooklyn's Central America solidarity movement.

AFTER TOUCH

after late evenings
filled with women

after talk
or touch

after a song by janis joplin
and a woman's body in my arms
quite by accident, swaying
and slowly stepping in a dance
like those dances of high school
back at the dawn of sex

after kissing my friends
a safe goodbye at the door

after the long ride
underground/under mind
and the transfer, the platform
desolate and calm
with waiting men
lounging in seats
or closing their eyes, free,
free to doze
or accost me as they please

and the cab ride or terror
five blocks home from the station

after hot showers, hot chocolate
and books

i lie down in bed
beside the dark shape of a man
thinking of women

awake

not wanting masturbation
that old ploy
my clitoris fooled,
rubbed, drugged, bribed
into submission
when it's my whole body,
woman-hungering, aches

i remember now a childhood story
of a man of the last century
who drove a team of horses
forty miles through a blizzard
to bring back wheat
for his starving midwestern town

and how, when he lived,
when at last he lay down
in his own safe bed
his fingers, itching and burning,
his tingling feet
kept him awake all night

JAN CLAUSEN

and he was glad.   the pain
meant they would thaw, meant
he would dance, chop wood,
hold wagon reins again

i am a lesbian

Dennis Cooper

Dennis Cooper (born 1953 in Pasadena, California) was from 1976 to 1982
editor of *Little Caesar* magazine and Little Caesar Press, which published, in
1980, his important anthology *Coming Attractions: An Anthology of American
Poets in Their Twenties*. Author of two collections of poems, *Idols* (The Sea-
Horse Press, 1979) and *The Tenderness of the Wolves* (The Crossing Press,
1982), Cooper also writes fiction. *Wrong*, a book of poems and short prose,
and *Closer*, a novel, were published in 1988.

BEING AWARE

Men are drawn to my ass by
my death-trance blue eyes
and black hair, tiny outfit,
while my father is home with
a girl, moved by the things
I could never think clearly.

Men smudge me onto a bed,
drug me stupid, gossip and
photograph me till I'm famous
in alleys, like one of those
jerk offs who stare from
the porno I sort of admire.

I'm fifteen. Screwing means

more to the men than to me.
I daydream right through it
while money puts chills on
my arms, from this to that
grip. I was meant to be naked.

Hey, Dad, it's been like this
for decades. I was always
approached by your type, given
dollars for hours. I took a
deep breath, stripped and they
never forgot how I trembled.

It means tons to me. Aside
from the obvious heaven
when cumming, there's times
I'm with them that I'm happy
or know what the other guy
feels, which is progress.

Or, nights when I'm angry,
if in a man's arms moving
slowly to the quietest music—
his hands on my arms, in my
hands, in the small of my back
take me back before everything.

MY PAST

for Jim Stegmiller

is a short string of beautiful
boys or young men I admired,
dragged to bed, left in ruins
on corners with taxi fare home.
Another of friends who were
horny, who I could have slept
with but didn't because they
were ugly, insane or too much
like me to be sexy. We were
partners for sweeps of wild
parties, took dope till they felt

DENNIS COOPER

like museums which we
could pick-over for bodies
to idealize with caresses.
The sun rose slowly. I was
still huffing and toiling
with them, like a sculptor
attempting to get things just
right—finally collapsing
in bed with some smeared,
smelly torso before me, and
a powerful wish to be left
alone. Take you, for example,
who I found throwing-up in
the bathroom of some actor's
mansion and crowned my new
boyfriend. Your ass made me
nervous till I explored it.
Now I want to forget it. My
friends feel this way too.
I know them. We've been close
since before we were artists
working to leave haunted eyes
on our lovers. I've thrown
out hundreds like you, and
found only art can remain so
aloof in its make-up that I'll
stare endlessly into its eyes
like a kid with a microscope.
Once I was back when art chatted
just over my head, when I was
still glancing up the red swim
trunks of some boy who I think
was named Jimmy, and wondering
what could be out there, miles
from my hands. He was leaving
like you. Who knows where that
man and that feeling are now.

Alfred Corn

Alfred Corn (born 1943 in Georgia), poet, critic, and teacher of creative writing, has received prizes and fellowships from the NEA, the Guggenheim Foundation, the American Academy and Institute of Arts and Letters, and the Academy of American Poets. His poetry collections include *A Call in the Midst of a Crowd* (1978), *The Various Light* (1980), *Notes from a Child of Paradise* (1984), and *The West Door* (1988). In 1987, his publisher (Viking/Penguin) also brought out *The Metamorphoses of Metaphor*, a collection of his critical essays. He lives in New York with the poet and critic J. D. McClatchy.

OLDER MEN

I used to prefer them and now I'm one of them—
At the lower end of the scale, but even so,
I still like older men—you know
Who you are. (Which is half the appeal.)
You, to start with, Tony, who haven't shaved
Off your untrendy moustache, your liquid
Brown eyes staring directly into mine
When you break from painting a diningroom
To talk about new research on pets—how
Those who have cats or dogs live longer,
Just talking to them releases good feelings,
And good feelings keep us alive, obviously.
Or I think of you, Jim, blond hair thinning on top,
Oblique of wit, with elegant runner's calves,
Your shirts all in solid colors and finely sewn seams,
Half smiling as you quote Goethe: "If youth is a fault,
It is one that is soon corrected." Would you
Agree, Bob, you who have all the anxious decency
Of the ex-Catholic, a new petition for me to sign,
A new injustice that we can for once do something about?
And sign I do, fairly incapable of saying no

To another survivor of the Sixties, this one
With a deep hoarse voice that is effective
Either at the mike during a downtown rally or
Growling softly into one's ear late at night.
It's not that there's nothing to be said for boys—
Their waists that amount to living sculpture,
That blue stare of desperate, childlike need,
Plus an infallible radar for the next new thing . . .
But how does that compare with you, Harry,
As you do the doubletake of nobody's fool,
Calmly expert about music and its performance,
With your thousand stories about old New York,
And whatever else it is that keeps your phone
Ringing and ringing from morning to midnight?
Or you, John, with your grizzled beard neatly trimmed,
Gay activist professor discussing Melville
In a gray silk jacket and jeans that fit
To a rapt audience that regularly includes me.
Or you, even-tempered Tom, who died last year,
Surrounded by buddies from AA and church,
But not before setting an example of loyalty,
Never abandoning those at your bedside until
Forced to. In fact, we don't feel ourselves abandoned
Even now—Fred doesn't feel we are, nor Liz,
Nor Adam; because we talk about you all the time,
Always with an acute sense of being overheard.
Heaven is the best vantage point, I imagine,
For keeping tabs on a circle as restless as ours?
From there no doubt we've come to resemble one
Of those soap operas you used to take off as a comedy turn
Over drinks before one of your famous bad dinners.
Well, you won't mind if I drop everything to praise
Stan's paintings, seascapes in providential color,
The play of waterlights and introspective cloud. . . .
The fifteen years you and he were together
Were mostly lean, you weren't given enough time
To see him collect his medals. Unless as I said
You are our supervising angel and his good fortune
Counts as the latest episode in our "Search for Tomorrow."

Louie Crew

Louie Crew (a.k.a. Li Min Hua, Brother Thorn-in-the-Flesh, and Quean Lutibelle) was born in 1936 in Anniston, Alabama, and has published 575-plus items. The FBI confirms that Crew taught "Homosexual Revolution," University of Alabama, Spring 1969. In 1974 Crew founded Integrity (gay Anglicans). In 1976 he co-organized the Lesbian/Gay Caucus of the National Council of Teachers of English. In 1983 he served on the Wisconsin Governor's Council on Lesbian and Gay Issues, but with his black lover fled rural America, first to teach in Beijing, thence to Hong Kong, where Crew directed writing at Chinese University. Crew's poems appear in *Sunspots* (Lotus, Detroit, 1976) and *Midnight Lessons* (Samisdat, Richford, Vermont, 1987). With Rictor Norton, he edited "The Homosexual Imagination," a Special Lesbian/Gay Issue of *College English* (Vol. 36, No. 3) and also edited the collection *The Gay Academic* (ETC, Palm Springs, 1978).

A GAY PSALM FROM FORT VALLEY

Oh, Lord, we call to you from our apartment
because we are not welcome in the church hall.
Hear us and help us with this terrible fear.
Do not freeze our hurt into false smiles.
Deliver us from countenancing in ourselves
    the rumors our enemies spread about us.
Help our enemies to come to terms
    with that in themselves
    which they project on us.
Turn their evil into good, oh God.
Make of their children's spit on our faces
    a salve for healing the pains
    which they have inflicted.
Be miraculous, God!
Do not fear to show your glory on the side
    of your children.

Why have our accusers refused even to hear us?
How can your Church tolerate spiritual lynchings?
Deliver us from vigilantes, God.

How they hiss against us,
    gossiping on their phones
    all the day long.
One of their most articulate ones
    drives his car to house after house,
    peddling the Vestry's hateful petition
    to ask us to leave.
What does he think as the remnant,
    the two loving women,
    turn him away?
Is he ready to be judged with that judgment
    which he has meted to us?
Help him, God.

Why do you allow the proud to turn your house
    of prayer into a court house?
Why do you allow your priests to bully us,
    to insult us,
    to spread lies about us in their councils,
    and yet to ignore us
    when we are sick or in danger or in need?
Why have you allowed your house
    to become a temple of self-righteousness
    rather than a house of honest sinners?

About ourselves we have spoken the truth
    in love, God,
and the keepers of the Church
    have turned us away.
Were we to debauch ourselves with hypocrisies
    and in secret to be consumed
    in anonymous lust,
they would honor us, God,
    and welcome us as like themselves.
But they have hated us for loving openly
    and responsibly.
They ride by our apartment
    with orgies in their heads

while we cook supper
and wash dishes together.

Heal this sick town, God.
You promised that the meek will inherit
the earth, that with Christ
we are joint heirs
of your everlasting kingdom.
Keep us aware that we are your children.
Ready us for our witness.

tatiana de la tierra

tatiana de la tierra was born in 1961 in Villavicencio, Colombia—"a lush, green, magical mountainous country. I love my roots, romantically, realistically. Remain connected through visits, family, feminism, politics. Came to Miami in 1968. I have been out as a lesbian since 1983. Lesbian eyes, lesbian heart—I wanted more, different. Began traveling, picking up wimmin's culture along the way. I travel/feel/share, focusing on Latin American wimmin's writings and music. My worldly work relates to massage, music, radio, photography, pawn shops, writing. I love and collect rocks, books, albums, jewelry, goddess images, silk scarves, anything beautiful."

DE AMBIENTE

graciela wouldn't fuck me
wouldn't feel her hand
inside me,
wouldn't let me know her pleasures
and wouldn't know mine.

graciela wouldn't taste me
and explore me,
wouldn't want me
caliente, abierta
like a wanting woman does.

she wouldn't move on me
with grace,
wouldn't make noises
with abandon
or open trembling thighs.

graciela wouldn't fuck me,
wouldn't release her mami's rosary
or answer her family's questions,
wouldn't challenge her country's machismo
or her friends, the queer-baiting feminists,
or her fears, temores que consumen.

she wouldn't live her love fully
or fully love herself.
graciela, tortillera,
wouldn't risk her love daily
for machine guns in the night.*

mujer de ambiente y poderosa,
mujer que ama, mujer que niega,
to survive is to bring fear home,
fear for hands, thighs,
fear for women's words.
and so, graciela wouldn't fuck me.

---

* Since at least 1986, paramilitary groups in Colombia have vowed to exterminate homosexuals. As a result of this "moral cleansing," hundreds of gays have and continue to be murdered throughout the country.

Alexis De Veaux

Alexis De Veaux, born 1948 in New York City, is a poet, teacher, playwright, novelist, journalist, and performance artist. Among her works are a biography of jazz great Billie Holiday entitled *Don't Explain: A Song of Billie Holiday* (Harper & Row, 1980); *Blue Heat: A Portfolio of Poems and Drawings* (Diva Enterprises, 1985); and *An Enchanted Hair Tale* (Harper & Row, 1987). Her plays for stage and television include *Circles* (1972), *The Tapestry* (1976), *A Season to Unravel* (1979), and the highly acclaimed *"No"* (1981). She is also the producer of the video documentary *Motherlands: From Manhattan To Managua To Africa, Hand To Hand*. De Veaux is an active sponsor of MADRE, an international friendship organization based in New York City, and a board member of SISA: Sisterhood In Support of Sisters In South Africa.

THE SISTERS

Ntabuu
Ntabuu   Selina and
Ntabuu of the red dirt road in New Orleans. Red dirt morning.
Hang dry sun below restless maple trees.

> truckload of farm workermen
> Come juggle down the road
> a hundred faces closed   in the dawn
> move along, move along . . .

In a home made wooden love seat Selina moves nearer. Ntabuu feels
the warm hip and white gabardine skirt close. Selina blows
cigarette ash from her bare breasts rising and falling voluptuous black.
Ntabuu
Ntabuu
Selina
Ntabuu is 27. She two months baby swollen. Mozambique skin purple
she gapped tooth with nigger-toe eyes. Her squat body full of

future unknown/her face solid woman stone. Yellow linen skirt folds
pleat her thigh. In summer hot like this she does not wear panties
she rather her touch-garden sweat (than itch) in July.

> farm workerman sing along
> sing along . . .

"You love him?"
"No."
"You want to marry him?"
"No."
"Why you having this baby?"
"Because we can't make one of our own."

Selina she 33 years old. Her charcoal body is angular and firm.
She has never had a child or a man. She has never wanted one.
She has always wanted to sing and decorate houses. Always loved
her big white teeth and sculptured lips inherited from their
grandmother.

"Just cause I want a baby Selina don't mean I love you any less."
"What *do* it mean."
"God is moving in me Selina. This is God."
"Bullshit."

> . . . a hundred faces closed in the migratory
> dawn
> lips dream last night's kisses
> bronze
> move along, sing along . . .

Ntabuu
Ntabuu
Ntabuu the pregnant dancer. Do splits for Selina. Do one two
three kick. One two up. Kick. One two three down. Kick split
for Selina in the next room singing do-re-mi-fa-so-la 3 days
a week when students come see their 16 room Southern palace.
Inherited from a half French grandmother. Knic knacs traditions
and crystal tables. Old photographs of old aunts and great uncles
in big hats and 2-tone shoes.

"What time is the doctor coming?"
"8:00 or soon after he said."
"You could still change your mind."

"No."
"Why goddamnit? We don't need nobody else."
"We got to have an heir."

In the evenings when the townmen come back sun tired/smelling of fruit trees and oppression they come see the Sisters. Come bring them berry apple pear and Selina cigarettes. Selina did not know one night one month someone slept over.

    Ntabuu give good massages he tells the others
    wait their turn their back muscles ache
    for her dancing touch maybe
    ache for the caress
    of julep oil heated on the wood burning stove . . .

"Ntabuu you love me?"
"Yes Selina."
"You mine?"
"Yes but you can't own me."

Ntabuu
Ntabuu love her sister/Selina.
Ntabuu
Ntabuu

"You love me Selina?"
"Yes girl."
"You want to marry me?"
"You crazy."
"Marry me Selina."
"I marry you."
"Do it proper."

Do it voluptuous mornings like this one. In their 4-posted bed. Ntabuu rolls closer. Musk oil and lapis lazuli. Her small hand explores nipple. Selina purrs. Ntabuu fondles the sassy blackness breathing beneath her own. Tongue and tender. Fingers trail her stomach quivers. Ntabuu. Open. Selina. Ntabuu. Way down. Purr Selina.

Purr, Open way down. Slow chant for Isis and Nefertiti. Probe her royal magic. Smell the bold journey. Wait. Flutter. Pulse Ntabuu. Cling Selina. Tangle fingers in hair and slow love sweat. Ancient graffiti hidden on vulva walls.

       ALEXIS DE VEAUX

C. M. Donald

C. M. Donald (born 1950 in Chesterfield, Derbyshire, England) lives in Toronto. "Educated by the Girls' Public Day School Trust, I kept myself from knowing I was a lesbian by not applying the word to the emotions I felt (it wouldn't have been *done* in the Trust . . .). At Cambridge, I abandoned a Ph.D. in favour of coming out and joining the Women's Liberation Movement. My relationship to writing has changed dramatically since feminism freed me to join words and content for the first time." Her books of poetry *The Fat Woman Measures Up* (Ragweed, 1986) and *The Breaking Up Poems* (Ragweed, 1988) are also tapes (Jezebel Tapes and Books, Seaton, Devon, UK).

I EXPECT YOU THINK THIS HUGE DARK COAT

I expect you think this huge dark coat
conceals in its capacious folds
some unsavoury old knitted cardigans,
a worn-through pair of trousers and,
inside all that, one sweaty fat woman.
You think I'm hiding in here to protect myself,
that I'm trying to make my bulk inconspicuous.
You be careful, do not attempt to thwart me.
Inside this black coat
    I am
       Sir Despard Murgatroyd.

AN EYE FOR AN EYE

An eye for an eye, they said,
and a tooth for a tooth.

When she had stopped laughing

and wondering what she would do
with someone else's tooth, the fat woman spoke:

and for all the suffering flesh, she said,
this dieted, stomach-stapled, by-passed,
pill-riddled flesh,
                    what for that?

Robert Duncan

Robert Duncan (born 1919 in Oakland, California; died 1988) was a charismatic and influential teacher, theorist, and author of, among many volumes, *The Opening of the Field* (Grove Press, 1960), *Roots and Branches* (Scribner's, 1964), and *Bending the Bow* (New Directions, 1968). In a remarkable essay, "The Homosexual in Society" (*Politics*, August 1944) Duncan called for a homosexual who is "willing to take in his own persecution a battlefront toward human freedom." His own lifetime as a writer was spent in a search for "those forms that allow for the most various feelings in one." Duncan, as scholar Robert K. Martin observes, "remains preeminently the poet of the soul known through the body." A new book, *Ground Work II: In The Dark* (New Directions) appeared posthumously in 1988.

MY MOTHER WOULD BE A FALCONRESS

My mother would be a falconress,
And I, her gay falcon treading her wrist,
would fly to bring back
from the blue of the sky to her, bleeding, a prize,
where I dream in my little hood with many bells
jangling when I'd turn my head.

My mother would be a falconress,
and she sends me as far as her will goes.
She lets me ride to the end of her curb
where I fall back in anguish.
I dread that she will cast me away,
for I fall, I mis-take, I fail in her mission.

She would bring down the little birds.
And I would bring down the little birds.
When will she let me bring down the little birds,
pierced from their flight with their necks broken,
their heads like flowers limp from the stem?

I tread my mother's wrist and would draw blood.
Behind the little hood my eyes are hooded.
I have gone back into my hooded silence,
talking to myself and dropping off to sleep.

For she has muffled my dreams in the hood she has made me,
sewn round with bells, jangling when I move.
She rides with her little falcon upon her wrist.
She uses a barb that brings me to cower.
She sends me abroad to try my wings
and I come back to her. I would bring down
the little birds to her
I may not tear into, I must bring back perfectly.

I tear at her wrist with my beak to draw blood,
and her eye holds me, anguisht, terrifying.
She draws a limit to my flight.
Never beyond my sight, she says.

She trains me to fetch and to limit myself in fetching.
She rewards me with meat for my dinner.
But I must never eat what she sends me to bring her.

Yet it would have been beautiful, if she would have carried me,
always, in a little hood with the bells ringing,
at her wrist, and her riding
to the great falcon hunt, and me
flying up to the curb of my heart from her heart
to bring down the skylark from the blue to her feet,
straining, and then released for the flight.

My mother would be a falconress,
and I her gerfalcon, raised at her will,
from her wrist sent flying, as if I were her own
pride, as if her pride
knew no limits, as if her mind
sought in me flight beyond the horizon.

Ah, but high, high in the air I flew.
And far, far beyond the curb of her will,
were the blue hills where the falcons nest.
And then I saw west to the dying sun—
it seemd my human soul went down in flames.

I tore at her wrist, at the hold she had for me,
until the blood ran hot and I heard her cry out,
far, far beyond the curb of her will   •

to horizons of stars beyond the ringing hills of the world where
      the falcons nest
I saw, and I tore at her wrist with my savage beak.
I flew, as if sight flew from the anguish in her eye beyond her sight,
sent from my striking loose, from the cruel strike at her wrist,
striking out from the blood to be free of her.

My mother would be a falconress,
and even now, years after this,
when the wounds I left her had surely heald,
and the woman is dead,
her fierce eyes closed, and if her heart
were broken, it is stilld   •

I would be a falcon and go free.
I tread her wrist and wear the hood,
talking to myself, and would draw blood.

ROBERT DUNCAN

Jim Everhard

Jim Everhard (born 1946 in Dayton, Ohio) was reared in the Virginia suburbs of Washington, D.C. He served a four-year enlistment in the Navy from 1966 to 1970, and following that spent the next eleven years working on a B.A. in English literature from George Mason University. His poems appeared in *Gay Sunshine, Mouth of the Dragon, Hanging Loose, The Iowa Review, Epos, Painted Bride Quarterly, New: American and Canadian Poetry,* and several anthologies. In 1982, when his collection of poems *Cute* was published by Gay Sunshine Press, he wrote that he was "currently deeply in love with an egg and . . . working on more writing every day." Jim Everhard died of AIDS in 1986.

CURING HOMOSEXUALITY

for three incurables, Frank, Stu and Richard

"There are no homosexuals, only fallen heterosexuals."
—DR. REUBEN SEBASTIAN WILDCHILD

Of the many known and proven
cures for homosexuality,
the most familiar, perhaps,
is the Catholic Church's version of
"Confession-is-good-for-the-soul."
According to this ritual, every time
you feel an unclean urge to touch your-
self, you stop your hand with the
mental image of the Pope staring you
in the face and these words: "if-I-do-this-
I-have-to-tell-the-priest-again."
Then, when you go to confession you
enumerate and fully describe every such
forbidden act leaving out not the
slightest detail and the priest,

who lives anonymously in a dark box,
tells you what you must do to redeem your lost
soul. This usually amounts to kneeling
before a statue of this virgin
who has never allowed the sinful hands
of any man to ever infest her body
with the puerile desires of the flesh and
mutter a prayer that
you won't touch other men hail Mary as you,
in a religious rapture,
fondle your beads.
                  If this doesn't work,
and one wonders about these
good men whose career it is to sit in the dark
and listen to the pornography of everybody
else's life, the next step is psychoanalysis.
The doctor sits solemnly in the dark
behind you, his hands suspiciously folded
in his lap, and doesn't say a word
while you lie down on a long, lumpy sofa
and tell him about your childhood
and how much you hate yourself
for thinking the things you think
so uncontrollably
and you wish your tongue would fall out
and it almost does as you go on and on
wondering what the hell this fellow
is listening for as you start inventing
stories about Uncle's anus and house pets.
You soon find out he is interpreting
the things you tell him. According to
psychoanalytic theory, everything you say
means something else even more sinister
than what you meant. Your unknown desires
live within you and control your outward be-
havior. For instance, if you say,
"It's such a beautiful day today
I wanted to leave work early,"
the psychiatrist will interpret this to mean
you are dissatisfied with your job
and this in turn means you are sexually frus-
trated and this goes back to your miserable
childhood which means he'll probably

            JIM EVERHARD

respond with, "Do you think that this means
you resented your mother when she
wouldn't let you play with yourself?"
If you say you had a dream about flying
he'll interpret it as a dream of sexual
frustration and penis envy meaning
you are really sick since only women
are supposed to have penis envy. He'll
probably ask you, "How did you feel when
you first saw your father's instrument?
Did you notice if it was bigger than yours?
Did he seem ashamed of his?
Did you want to touch it?"
If you tell him you don't recall
what it looked like he'll tell you
you unconsciously wanted it to fall off
so you could flush it down the toilet.
If you tell him you wanted to kill your father
and rape your mother he'll tell you
you had an Oedipus conflict.
He will listen for key words like
umbrella, closet, brother, rooster, shit, nude
and Judy Garland, all of which convey
a large surplus of unconscious homo-
sexual material. For instance, never say:
"I put my umbrella in the closet
and found my brother in the backyard
beating the shit out of a rooster
while looking at nude pictures of
Judy Garland." To a psychiatrist this means:

umbrella = phallic symbol = womb = death = fear that it will
    rain at your funeral and no one will come
closet = phallic symbol = womb = mother = castration = desire
    to work for a fast food chain = prostitution = fear of underwear
brother = phallic symbol = sibling rivalry = castration = desire to
    stick your finger up your ass and smell it
rooster = phallic symbol = cock = flying = fear of Karen Black =
    crashing = fear of impotence = hatred of women = fear of
    oxygen
shit = phallic symbol = fear of dirt = work = puritan work ethic
    = father's penis = sexual frustration = deviations = fascination
    with dirt = bad toilet training = sexual hostility toward pilgrims

nude = phallic symbol = opposite sex = original sin = truth =
   fear of gardens = self-deception = poor sanitation habits =
   desire for death and return to Earth Mother = return to disco =
   hatred of mother = love of analyst but always waiting for
   someone to come along and say no = desire to live in a hole in
   the ground
Judy Garland = phallic symbol = fear of tornadoes = love/hate of
   sucking = confusion of identity = desire to have oral relations
   with a lap dog = necrophilia = fear of Easter bonnets = desire
   to be a woman = fear of bad breath = spiritual destitution =
   desire to be Dr. Kinsey = existential malfunction = fear of tubas
   = fear of dude ranches and desire to perform unnatural acts with
   Mickey Rooney = fear of short, pimply people

Like a cancer, one sentence can devour your entire psyche.

If you say you had a hard time coming today
and you don't have anything to say
he'll call that resistance. If you say
it isn't, he'll say that's more resistance.
If you stop resisting, he'll call that
passive-aggressive. If you tell him
you've had it, you're tired of wasting
time and money when you haven't even begun
talking about homosexuality, he'll tell you
your problems run even deeper than he
initially realized and you need hospitalization.

Once you are hospitalized, the doctors
will begin electric shock therapy.
They call it therapy. There is no resistance.
You are not sure who's getting the therapy,
you or the sadistic maniacs who strap you down
and wire you up and turn on the juice
while they flash pictures of naked men
on a screen. The idea is to associate pain
and the fear of death by electrocution
with naked men. Then a comforting female
nurse unstraps you and wheels you, unconscious,
back to your room where she slowly
but surely revives you and stuffs a few pieces of
stale toast and cold eggs down your gullet.
This is supposed to turn you on to women.

JIM EVERHARD

If

none of these cures works
you will probably be thrown out of high school
as a bad influence for all those guys who
make you suck them off in the shower,
then beat you up at the bus stop. If you
still wish to remain homosexual, you will prob-
ably be arrested in the public library
for browsing too long in the "Sexuality"
section or during one of the periodic raids
of a local gay bar or face charges for soliciting
a cop who arrested you and forced you
to give him a blow job while he played
with his siren. In prison
you will probably be gang raped by
lusty straight men who are only acting out
their healthy but stifled heterosexual impulses
and if you are lucky one of them may even
win you in a knife fight and protect you
from the gang except when he trades you
out for a night for a pack of cigarettes or
a shot of heroin. Once you are released
you will become an expert in American
legal procedures as you face future charges
of child molestation, murder and attempts
to overthrow the common decency, whatever that is.
When you have had it, and decide to hijack
a jet and escape, you will discover the small
but important fact that no nation under god
or red offers asylum, political or otherwise,
to a plane full of pansies.
Your best bet is to fly over
the Bermuda Triangle and click
your little red pumps together whispering,
"There's no place like home, there's no
place like home."
                    In olden days
the main cure for homosexuality (then
often known simply as witchcraft) was
to tie the suspected faggot to a tiny seat
on the end of a long pole suspended
over boiling water. The suspected faggot was then
submerged for half an hour or until
he stopped struggling, whichever happened first.

JIM EVERHARD   **103**

If he was still alive when they lifted him
from the vat, they spread an oil slick over the water,
resubmerged the suspect and struck a match.
If he went up in smoke,
it meant he was a godless heathen faggot
who deserved to go up in smoke. If a choir
of angels emblazoned the sky and God,
humming the Hallelujah Chorus,
personally pissed out the flames dancing
around the suffocating faggot's body,
he was allowed to return home if he promised
to register four times daily with the local
police and never get his hair cut
in a place called a boutique.

                    So, you see,
liberalism has increased the life expectancy
of fairies. That's because we've evolved
into the world's wittiest, best groomed
ballroom dancers. Everyone's into
the Queen's vernacular, pierced ears, disco
and poppers. So long as you seek your partner
after dark in the mountains of Montana
at least one hundred miles distant
from the nearest living heterosexual
and keep your meeting anonymous and
under fifteen minutes with no visible
body contact or non-contacting foreplay,
you could not conceivably, even by the
most homophobic, be considered
or accused homosexual by anyone but the most
adamantine and intolerant straight person.
Thanks to science it is now well known
that homosexuality is not transmitted by
tiny springing bugs or bats. We are not burned
at the stake (except during ceremonial
occasions of state for example only)
in the larger urban centers today
though we may still face a constant barrage
of misdemeanors (nastier than a case of crabs)
such as littering, (i.e.,
don't drop your hanky in a city park),
jaywalking (i.e., no matter how cute the

          JIM EVERHARD

cop may be, don't wiggle your ass when
you buzz across Connecticut Avenue
during rush hour in the middle of the block
waving you-whoo, you-whoo to your color-
ful friends) and loitering (i.e., situated
under the romantic moon in an open
park after dark behind willowy shade trees
on your knees with a look of ecstasy
on your face as he creams into your eager mouth
is considered loitering among other things).
Simple precautions will save you
from a life of humiliation and
all those long blank spots on your résumé
that you have to explain as time
to get your head together or
extended vacation or time spent nursing
your mother back to health
when you were really fired for
turning on a fellow office employee.

In conclusion, there are no known cures
for homosexuality. Faggots have survived
Christianity, psychiatry, social ostracism, jail,
earth, air, wind and fire, as well as the pink
triangle and concentration camps. Nothing
can reckon with you if you can reckon with yourself.
The facts have been available for a long, long time:
where there are human beings, there are faggots.
We were around clubbing each other over the head
just like straight cave men. We were considered magical
by some people. We were considered mysterious.
We were obviously different but not always hated.
Hatred is always self-hatred.
Denial is always fear.
It's easier for THEM when
we hate ourselves,
FEAR OURSELVES.
I don't have to and
I WON'T.
None of us knows how he got here,
for what reason we are here or
why we are who we are.
It is not obvious

JIM EVERHARD   **105**

and a swish doesn't make me any more obvious
than the lack of one.
I am obvious
because I AM.

Edward Field

Edward Field was born in Brooklyn in 1924 and grew up in Lynbrook, Long Island. After the war, he went to New York University, spent a year in Europe, where the poet Robert Friend helped him with his poetry, and later studied and worked as an actor. In 1963, the Lamont Award brought into print his first book, *Stand up, Friend, With Me* (Grove Press, 1963). Since then he has gotten the Shelley Memorial Award, a Prix de Rome, and other honors. In 1965, the documentary film *To Be Alive*, for which he wrote the narration, won an Academy Award. He has given hundreds of poetry readings around the country, including the Library of Congress, has published an anthology, *A Geography of Poets* (Bantam, 1979), a book of translations from the Eskimo, and, in collaboration with Neil Derrick, novels under the pseudonym of Bruce Elliot. His latest book is *New and Selected Poems* (Sheep Meadow Press, 1987). The poem "World War II" grew out of his experiences as a navigator, flying twenty-seven missions over Germany in Flying Fortresses.

UNWANTED

The poster with my picture on it
Is hanging on the bulletin board in the Post Office.

I stand by it hoping to be recognized
Posing first full face and then profile

But everybody passes by and I have to admit
The photograph was taken some years ago.

I was unwanted then and I'm unwanted now
Ah guess ah'll go up echo mountain and crah.

I wish someone would find my fingerprints somewhere
Maybe on a corpse and say, You're it.

Description: Male, or reasonably so
White, but not lily-white and usually deep-red

Thirty-fivish, and looks it lately
Five-feet-nine and one-hundred-thirty pounds: no physique

Black hair going gray, hairline receding fast
What used to be curly, now fuzzy

Brown eyes starey under beetling brow
Mole on chin, probably will become a wen

It is perfectly obvious that he was not popular at school
No good at baseball, and wet his bed.

His aliases tell his history: Dumbell, Good-for-nothing,
Jewboy, Fieldinsky, Skinny, Fierce Face, Greaseball, Sissy.

Warning: This man is not dangerous, answers to any name
Responds to love, don't call him or he will come.

WORLD WAR II

It was over Target Berlin the flak shot up our plane
just as we were dumping bombs on the already smoking city
on signal from the lead bomber in the squadron.
The plane jumped again and again as the shells burst under us
sending jagged pieces of steel rattling through our fuselage.
I'll never understand
how none of us got ripped by those fragments.

Then, being hit, we had to drop out of formation right away
losing speed and altitude,
and when I figured out our course with trembling hands
    on the instruments
(I was navigator)

we set out on the long trip home to England
alone, with two of our four engines gone
and gas streaming out of holes in the wing tanks.
That morning at briefing
we had been warned not to go to nearby Poland
partly liberated then by the Russians,
although later we learned that another crew in trouble
had landed there anyway,
and patching up their plane somehow,
returned gradually to England
roundabout by way of Turkey and North Africa.
But we chose England, and luckily
the Germans had no fighters to send up after us then
for this was just before they developed their jet.
To lighten our load we threw out
guns and ammunition, my navigation books, all the junk
and made it over Holland
with a few goodbye fireworks from the shore guns.

Over the North Sea the third engine gave out
and we dropped low over the water.
The gas gauge read empty but by keeping the nose down
a little gas at the bottom of the tank sloshed forward
and kept our single engine going.
High overhead, the squadrons were flying home in formation
—the raids had gone on for hours after us.
Did they see us down there in our trouble?
We radioed our final position for help to come
but had no idea if anyone
happened to be tuned in and heard us,
and we crouched together on the floor
knees drawn up and head down
in regulation position for ditching;
listened as the engine stopped, a terrible silence,
and we went down into the sea with a crash,
just like hitting a brick wall,
jarring bones, teeth, eyeballs panicky.
Who would ever think water could be so hard?
You black out, and then come to
with water rushing in like a sinking-ship movie.

All ten of us started getting out of there fast:

There was a convenient door in the roof to climb out by,
one at a time. We stood in line,
water up to our thighs and rising.
The plane was supposed to float for twenty seconds
but with all those flak holes
who could say how long it really would?
The two life rafts popped out of the sides into the water
but one of them only half inflated
and the other couldn't hold everyone
although they all piled into it, except the pilot,
who got into the limp raft that just floated.
The radio operator and I, out last,
(Did that mean we were least aggressive, least likely to
    survive?)
we stood on the wing watching the two rafts
being swept off by waves in different directions.
We had to swim for it.
Later they said the cords holding rafts to plane
broke by themselves, but I wouldn't have blamed them
for cutting them loose, for fear
that by waiting the plane would go down
and drag them with it.

I headed for the overcrowded good raft
and after a clumsy swim in soaked heavy flying clothes
got there and hung onto the side.
The radio operator went for the half-inflated raft
where the pilot lay with water sloshing over him,
but he couldn't swim, even with his life vest on,
being from the Great Plains—
his strong farmer's body didn't know
how to wallow through the water properly
and a wild current seemed to sweep him farther off.
One minute we saw him on top of a swell
and perhaps we glanced away for a minute
but when we looked again he was gone—
just as the plane went down sometime around then
when nobody was looking.

It was midwinter and the waves were mountains
and the water ice water.
You could live in it twenty-five minutes

the Ditching Survival Manual said.
Since most of the crew were squeezed on my raft
I had to stay in the water hanging on.
My raft? It was their raft, they got there first so they would live.
Twenty-five minutes I had.
Live, live, I said to myself.
You've got to live.
There looked like plenty of room on the raft
from where I was and I said so
but they said no.
When I figured the twenty-five minutes were about up
and I was getting numb,
I said I couldn't hold on anymore,
and a little rat-faced boy from Alabama, one of the gunners,
got into the icy water in my place,
and I got on the raft in his.
He insisted on taking off his flying clothes
which was probably his downfall because even wet clothes
    are protection,
and then worked hard, kicking with his legs, and we all
    paddled,
to get to the other raft,
and we tied them together.
The gunner got in the raft with the pilot
and lay in the wet.
Shortly after, the pilot started gurgling green foam from his
    mouth—
maybe he was injured in the crash against the instruments—
and by the time we were rescued,
he and the little gunner were both dead.

That boy who took my place in the water
who died instead of me
I don't remember his name even.
It was like those who survived the death camps
by letting others go into the ovens in their place.
It was him or me, and I made up my mind to live.
I'm a good swimmer,
but I didn't swim off in that scary sea
looking for the radio operator when he was washed away.
I suppose, then, once and for all,
I chose to live rather than be a hero, as I still do today,
although at that time I believed in being heroic, in saving the world,

even if, when opportunity knocked,
I instinctively chose survival.

As evening fell the waves calmed down
and we spotted a boat, far off, and signaled with a flare gun,
hoping it was English not German.
The only two who cried on being found
were me and a boy from Boston, a gunner.
The rest of the crew kept straight faces.

It was a British air-sea rescue boat:
They hoisted us up on deck,
dried off the living and gave us whisky and put us to bed,
and rolled the dead up in blankets,
and delivered us all to a hospital on shore
for treatment or disposal.
None of us even caught cold, only the dead.

This was a minor accident of war:
Two weeks in a rest camp at Southport on the Irish Sea
and we were back at Grafton-Underwood, our base,
ready for combat again,
the dead crewmen replaced by living ones,
and went on hauling bombs over the continent of Europe,
destroying the Germans and their cities.

Salih Michael Fisher

Salih Michael Fisher was born in Harlem in 1956. He is an active member of the New York Chapter of Men of All Colors Together. His poems have been published in Michael J. Smith's anthology *Black Men/White Men* and in Issues 1 and 3 of *Blackheart: A Journal of Graphics and Writing by Black Gay Men*.

ASSUMPTION ABOUT THE HARLEM BROWN BABY

Do not assume I came out on Christopher Street
as the piers and tracks began to heat and dance in the night

I came out at fifteen in the streets of Harlem and South Bronx
On rooftop jungles . . . pulling tigers and leopards to my rhythmic past
Spurting . . . spurting fountains . . . and baking bread never laid . . .
   upon the table
Never laid upon the table before any human's hands . . . mouths . . .
   dragon unasleep
It was natural . . . a raw kind of primitive dance . . . it was my
   ritualistic dance
into manhood . . . into the passage of blood sung in Benin
   linguistic breathing patterns

Breathing . . . breathing down my neck . . . breathing in my face
Between the cries of baby this and that . . . and feelings
of being good . . . of ooh I feel good!

And back then I was Eschu . . . the trickster . . . a chameleon
in my identity . . . I played the butch-queen games well
For the period of blood can be a time of confusion . . .
Of direct lines between straight and narrow paths not taken

But the lullabies of nights remembered on roofs . . .
Was knocking at my door . . . and the black and latin men
made love to those nights so long ago were calling

I came . . . and came again to the hallways . . . and Mt. Morris Park
To sing the song of the bushes in black heat . . . black heat rising
rising in my eyes . . . rising in your eyes . . . your eyes piercing my eyes
in unison . . . the stars now fall and shoot themselves. . . .
from our scepters held to the morning sun . . . rising . . . rising . . .
   rising . . .

And do not assume . . . you . . . my friend
that the first bars I went to were gay
and had men posing as wax barbie dolls
and twisted g. i. joes

The first bars that I went to find a man
was mixed and three-fourth straight
And the first man I walked out with . . .
had a thirty-eight between his belt

And a road called "sudden paradise"
He was a dope dealer . . . he was a saint
a devil in disguise . . . and he taught me to bleed
at sixteen . . . with the first heart broken

I did go to gay bars later . . . back then . . . the bars
that spoke the words from the outside "Black Only"
Whites who come in . . . come in at your own risk

And in those places . . . the queens and drags were respected
and sometime feared . . . they were the ones that kept the place
    together
And if someone wanted to play the macho butch and read
they would make sure . . . they could not sow future seeds

They were no slouch these queens
They carried blades and guns filled with lead
Go off wrong with them . . . you were dead!

And when I came out . . . there were no definite gay code of dress
What got you from A to Z with a man was whether you had nice labels
or looked street cool . . . not whether you were a cowboy or
    leatherman
or even showing half of your can . . . if you did the queens would look
and read you as being a desperate man

So do not assume that I was some Harlem brown baby
that came out in your world . . . your ghetto . . . your constructs
of your reality . . . I came out in my own

Knowing the even flow to life . . . knowing which cards
had been marked and played . . . the sea . . . the sea
is now at rest . . . fill your bowels of passion with my wisdom

SALIH MICHAEL FISHER   **113**

Beatrix Gates

Beatrix Gates was born in 1949 in Boston. "I've been writing since I was twelve. I've had poems in *Greenfield Review, Nimrod, Sinister Wisdom, The Women's Review of Books,* and in the anthology *Naming the Waves* (Virago, 1988). I became a publisher through designing and printing my chapbooks *native tongue* (1973) and *Shooting at Night* (1980) and founded Granite Press in 1973. I still work as a women's publisher and book designer, have taught writing and literature at home, Hardscrabble Hill, and Hampshire College, and consider my work political. I struggle to balance my lives a day at a time." Her new manuscript of poems is entitled *Swimmer of Air.*

DEADLY WEAPON

for Leslie, Rosa and Margaret, who were there, '81
and in memory of Charlie Howard, gay man murdered in Bangor, '84

We came home to the stranger:
Scarsdale. The move to the city
still rattling at our backs, even our shadows ran
thin as thread, then wide as plates.
We blinked at the walls, their whiteness,
and moved furniture into comforting positions.
This night, we drove with country
determination—two women in a car
no one could see under the flowing sheet of rain.
Unused to locks, we lost
both sets of keys and had to break in,
then laughed, got out the smoke
and curled tight on the bed. Hot wind
blew on us, hissing through the screen,
open window.

I lay naked on top of the sheets,
the green comforter slipped again
to the floor and your remaining clothing.
You turned the pages of your magazine—
lazily licking your fingers,
toking on the joint and gently slapping
the pages. *Making the scene*
with a magazine, I leaned on your turning
arm and fell back, liking to be fed
tokes in a continuum. The dog pressed his chest
against the cardboard boxes collapsing
the sides, straining to get to the window, his nose
pointing to the open screen.
Come here, Lou, out of the boxes.
The buzzer rang. We scowled at each other
and as you pulled on your jeans, you asked the door, *Who is it?*
The pounding, fisted, began a loud, dull
hammer over the rain.

Sweatpants by the bed, I slip
them on, turn for a shirt, a top, something.
Through the heat, it is the sound
of speed, a hissing splits the room. It feels just
like I've dreamt so often—dreaming of wars,
I am shot again and again, feel the burn
of bullets, the burn of being
alive is wondrous and strange.
I moan and drop by the bed, listen
to the crunch of sand on the floor by my shoes.
I see the short, yellow arrow,
stand up and hurl it at the window.
My hands do not have the power
of the triggered crossbow and the arrow
falls a dizzy, harmless end-over-end.
You fuckhead, get the fuck out of here.
Scream at the waiting window
as you run between me and the opening,
snap off the light.

We move quickly to the center room—
no windows here, fumble for the phone,
knock it to the floor. *What's our address*

remembering our apartment has no number,
but letters like signals. You collect the phone
in your hands, dial the police   ·
through the operator. I am full of violence
and hold my thigh tightly, both hands,
wide as nets, look down, feel the blood
hot and sticky. Squeeze tighter. They ask,
*Is anyone wounded? No, no, yes, yes,
one of us has been hit.* Hang up. *They're coming.
Who cares, I wish I had a gun to blast
the windows, blow his face off.*
The dog presses to my knees
under the table and you lean close,
we've both been wounded.

You call Rosa and Margaret, call to say
what? *Something terrible has happened*
and you make the words work with your tears.
*We need you to come,
yes, now. We're
all right. We need you.* Hang up.
We look at each other, know we are seeing
in the dark, our chairs click
against each other, old bones, close,
chosen. We cannot touch and our bodies
have put on the weighted coat, the lie.
We have already moved to the inner lining
in the center of the apartment where we can't be
seen. We breathe together, rattling the mix
of hate and fear, blood in the air
and nested somewhere safe outside.
This is what the arrow wanted—
to strike us apart. The blue lights
flash at the edges of the shades
as we take each other's hands appearing
and disappearing before our eyes.

Two detectives question us. Six policemen stand around
the front room, arms moving, radios loud.
They are angry and talk to each other, unbelieving.
*In Scarsdale, who'd shoot two girls in Scarsdale?
With a crossbow? That's a long-range, deadly weapon.*
You are the girl visiting. This they make up

themselves, unable to picture us in bed. We said we were
both in the bedroom. The medic escorts me into the bathroom
"to have a look." I hear them ask you if you turned down
any guys recently, in a bar, anything like that.
Easy now, pull down your pants, so I can see.
His hands turn my leg. I am miles away, can't believe
this man is touching me. The last question:
Do you have any enemies?

The nurse shows me the examining room,
pulls back the curtain, *Just one, one of you
can come.* Rosa is holding you
knowing to touch. The curtain closes. Margaret
takes my hands. I see the nurse's calves and white shoes
leave. *Let yourself cry,* Margaret tells me,
*I know how strong you are. You don't have to
be strong now.* I hear my mother speaking
as she put her arms around my neck—
one day in her dying she broke
and pulled me close, cried against my chest,
I can't be strong all the time.
Just once. I let the shot come up, a hailstone
in my throat. The nurse returns,
What's the matter honey?
It's all over now.

No one can come with me
to be x-rayed—and it is the x-ray technician
who suggests I have been shot by Westchester's own
"Dart Man." *I don't think they ever caught him.
The publicity died down, what with "Son of Sam."
I never heard anymore.* He pins me
in position, hip hard against the machine, drapes the gray
radiation shield across the top of my body.
I turn my face as he enters his protected booth.
I haven't been in a hospital
since I kissed my mother's dead forehead
goodbye in May. She had wanted
radiation. And it was her doctor, a young
man, who told her it wouldn't help.
Somehow, she believed him—like no other.
I've lost all modesty, she said and gave herself
to the cure, injections of platinum that searched

and searched her veins for a way
out. This most precious metal, white
gold, shone in her veins
like belief.

A man ran from our window
leaving his imprint in the mud—
the footprints filled with water, the definition
slurred as the ground gave way.
He is the one who saw
us, did not deny his vision, picked up
the closest weapon, aimed and fired.
There have been others, more
usual. My mother worked to keep
us apart, speaking to you
only when I was in the room,
when she felt she had to, that last Christmas
at home. Alone for a moment, she would always ask
you the same question: *When are you leaving,*
what bus, what train, when did you say
you were going? She refused to enter any house
we shared and when we thought she would
we moved all the furniture of her imagination
for her—the extra bed, the live example of our
separateness. So she stood at the door,
This isn't as bad as I thought and we knew
we had imagined well—taken on her mask
for our own and forced her to bless our lie.
There was nothing right for her
about you. When she died, you were the first
to ask, *When are you coming home?*

September '81–'87

Allen Ginsberg

Allen Ginsberg (born 1926, Paterson, New Jersey) is the author of "Howl" (1955), perhaps the most famous poem in English of the second half of the twentieth century. His "Kaddish" is one of the great elegies of the language. A leading figure of the "Beat Generation," Ginsberg's writing and the well-circulated reports of his lifestyle helped transform the consciousness of thousands of young people and laid part of the groundwork for the gay uprisings of the 70s and after. "Fate tells big lies, & the gay Creator dances on his own body in Eternity," says Ginsberg in Fantasy 7006 (1959). Ginsberg's *Collected Poems* (Harper & Row, 1985) was followed in 1986 by *White Shroud,* a new book of poems.

THE LION FOR REAL

"Soyez muette pour moi, Idole contemplative . . ."

I came home and found a lion in my living room
Rushed out on the fire-escape screaming Lion! Lion!
Two stenographers pulled their brunette hair and banged the
      window shut
I hurried home to Paterson and stayed two days.

Called up my old Reichian analyst
who'd kicked me out of therapy for smoking marijuana
'It's happened' I panted 'There's a Lion in my room'
'I'm afraid any discussion would have no value' he hung up.

I went to my old boyfriend we got drunk with his girlfriend
I kissed him and announced I had a lion with a mad gleam in my eye
We wound up fighting on the floor I bit his eyebrow & he kicked me out
I ended masturbating in his jeep parked in the street moaning 'Lion.'

Found Joey my novelist friend and roared at him 'Lion!'
He looked at me interested and read me his spontaneous ignu high
        poetries
I listened for lions all I heard was Elephant Tiglon Hippogriff
        Unicorn Ants
But figured he really understood me when we made it in Ignaz
        Wisdom's bathroom.

But next day he sent me a leaf from his Smoky mountain retreat
'I love you little Bo-Bo with your delicate golden lions
But there being no Self and No Bars therefore the Zoo of your dear
        Father hath no Lion
You said your mother was mad don't expect me to produce the
        Monster for your Bridegroom.'

Confused dazed and exalted bethought me of real lion starved in his
        stink in Harlem
Opened the door the room was filled with the bomb blast of his anger
He roaring hungrily at the plaster walls but nobody could hear him
        outside thru the window
My eye caught the edge of the red neighbor apartment building
        standing in deafening stillness

We gazed at each other his implacable yellow eye in the red halo of fur
Waxed rheumy on my own but he stopped roaring and bared a fang
        greeting.
I turned my back and cooked broccoli for supper on an iron gas stove
boilt water and took a hot bath in the old tub under the sink board.

He didn't eat me, tho I regretted him starving in my presence.
Next week he wasted away a sick rug full of bones wheaten hair falling
        out
enraged and reddening eye as he lay aching huge hairy head on his
        paws
by the egg-crate bookcase filled up with thin volumes of Plato, &
        Buddha.

Sat by his side every night averting my eyes from his hungry
        motheaten face
stopped eating myself he got weaker and roared at night while I had
        nightmares

        ALLEN GINSBERG

Eaten by lion in bookstore on Cosmic Campus, a lion myself starved
      by Professor Kandisky, dying in a lion's flophouse circus,
I woke up mornings the lion still added dying on the floor—'Terrible
      Presence!' I cried 'Eat me or die!'

It got up that afternoon—walked to the door with its paw on the
wall, to steady its trembling body
Let out a soul-rending creak from the bottomless roof of his mouth
thundering from my floor to heaven heavier than a volcano at night
      in Mexico
Pushed the door open and said in a gravelly voice 'Not this time
      Baby—but I will be back again.'

Lion that eats my mind now for a decade knowing only your hunger
Not the bliss of your satisfaction O roar of the Universe how am I
      chosen
In this life I have heard your promise I am ready to die I have served
Your starved and ancient Presence O Lord I wait in my room at
      your Mercy.

HOWL

for Carl Solomon

I

I saw the best minds of my generation destroyed by madness,
      starving hysterical naked,
dragging themselves through the negro streets at dawn looking for an
      angry fix,
angelheaded hipsters burning for the ancient heavenly connection to
      the starry dynamo in the machinery of night,
who poverty and tatters and hollow-eyed and high sat up smoking in
      the supernatural darkness of cold-water flats floating across
      the tops of cities contemplating jazz,
who bared their brains to Heaven under the El and saw
      Mohammedan angels staggering on tenement roofs
      illuminated,
who passed through universities with radiant cool eyes hallucinating
      Arkansas and Blake-light tragedy among the scholars of war,
who were expelled from the academies for crazy & publishing
      obscene odes on the windows of the skull,

who cowered in unshaven rooms in underwear, burning their money
in wastebaskets and listening to the Terror through the wall,
who got busted in their pubic beards returning through Laredo with
a belt of marijuana for New York,
who ate fire in paint hotels or drank turpentine in Paradise Alley,
death, or purgatoried their torsos night after night
with dreams, with drugs, with waking nightmares, alcohol and cock
and endless balls,
incomparable blind streets of shuddering cloud and lightning in the
mind leaping toward poles of Canada & Paterson,
illuminating all the motionless world of Time between,
Peyote solidities of halls, backyard green tree cemetery dawns, wine
drunkenness over the rooftops, storefront boroughs of
teahead joyride neon blinking traffic light, sun and moon and
tree vibrations in the roaring winter dusks of Brooklyn,
ashcan rantings and kind king light of mind,
who chained themselvs to subways for the endless rides from Battery
to holy Bronx on benzedrine until the noise of wheels and
children brought them down shuddering mouth-wracked and
battered bleak of brain all drained of brilliance in the drear
light of Zoo,
who sank all night in submarine light of Bickford's floated out and
sat through the stale beer afternoon in desolate Fugazzi's,
listening to the crack of doom on the hydrogen jukebox,
who talked continuously seventy hours from park to pad to bar to
Bellevue to museum to the Brooklyn Bridge,
a lost battalion of platonic conversationalists jumping down the
stoops off fire escapes off windowsills off Empire State out of
the moon,
yacketayakking screaming vomiting whispering facts and memories
and anecdotes and eyeball kicks and shocks of hospitals and
jails and wars,
whole intellects disgorged in total recall for seven days and nights
with brilliant eyes, meat for the Synagogue cast on the
pavement,
who vanished into nowhere Zen New Jersey leaving a trail of
ambiguous picture postcards of Atlantic City Hall,
suffering Eastern sweats and Tangerian bone-grindings and migraines
of China under junk-withdrawal in Newark's bleak furnished
room,
who wandered around and around at midnight in the railroad yard
wondering where to go, and went, leaving no broken hearts,
who lit cigarettes in boxcars boxcars boxcars racketing through snow

toward lonesome farms in grandfather night,

who studied Plotinus Poe St. John of the Cross telepathy and bop
     kaballa because the cosmos instinctively vibrated at their feet
     in Kansas,

who loned it through the streets of Idaho seeking visionary indian
     angels who were visionary indian angels,

who thought they were only mad when Baltimore gleamed in
     supernatural ecstasy,

who jumped in limousines with the Chinaman of Oklahoma on the
     impulse of winter midnight streetlight smalltown rain,

who lounged hungry and lonesome through Houston seeking jazz or
     sex or soup, and followed the brilliant Spaniard to converse
     about America and Eternity, a hopeless task, and so took
     ship to Africa,

who disappeared into the volcanoes of Mexico leaving behind
     nothing but the shadow of dungarees and the lava and ash of
     poetry scattered in fireplace Chicago,

who reappeared on the West Coast investigating the F.B.I. in beards
     and shorts with big pacifist eyes sexy in their dark skin
     passing out incomprehensible leaflets,

who burned cigarette holes in their arms protesting the narcotic
     tobacco haze of Capitalism,

who distributed Supercommunist pamphlets in Union Square
     weeping and undressing while the sirens of Los Alamos
     wailed them down, and wailed down Wall, and the Staten
     Island ferry also wailed,

who broke down crying in white gymnasiums naked and trembling
     before the machinery of other skeletons,

who bit detectives in the neck and shrieked with delight in
     policecars for committing no crime but their own wild
     cooking pederasty and intoxication,

who howled on their knees in the subway and were dragged off the
     roof waving genitals and manuscripts,

who let themselves be fucked in the ass by saintly motorcyclists, and
     screamed with joy,

who blew and were blown by those human seraphim, the sailors,
     caresses of Atlantic and Caribbean love,

who balled in the morning in the evenings in rosegardens and the
     grass of public parks and cemeteries scattering their semen
     freely to whomever come who may,

who hiccupped endlessly trying to giggle but wound up with a sob
     behind a partition in a Turkish Bath when the blonde &
     naked angel came to pierce them with a sword,

who lost their loveboys to the three old shrews of fate the one eyed
	shrew of the heterosexual dollar the one eyed shrew that
	winks out of the womb and the one eyed shrew that does
	nothing but sit on her ass and snip the intellectual golden
	threads of the craftsman's loom,
who copulated ecstatic and insatiate with a bottle of beer a
	sweetheart a package of cigarettes a candle and fell off the
	bed, and continued along the floor and down the hall and
	ended fainting on the wall with a vision of ultimate cunt and
	come eluding the last gyzym of consciousness,
who sweetened the snatches of a million girls trembling in the
	sunset, and were red eyed in the morning but prepared to
	sweeten the snatch of the sunrise, flashing buttocks under
	barns and naked in the lake,
who went out whoring through Colorado in myriad stolen night-
	cars, N.C., secret hero of these poems, cocksman and
	Adonis of Denver—joy to the memory of his innumerable
	lays of girls in empty lots & diner backyards, moviehouses,
	rickety rows on mountaintops in caves or with gaunt
	waitresses in familiar roadside lonely petticoat upliftings &
	especially secret gas-station solipsisms of johns, & hometown
	alleys too,
who faded out in vast sordid movies, were shifted in dreams, woke
	on a sudden Manhattan, and picked themselves up out of
	basements hungover with heartless Tokay and horrors of
	Third Avenue iron dreams & stumbled to unemployment
	offices,
who walked all night with their shoes full of blood on the snowbank
	docks waiting for a door in the East River to open to a room
	full of steamheat and opium,
who created great suicidal dramas on the apartment cliff-banks of
	the Hudson under the wartime blue floodlight of the moon &
	their heads shall be crowned with laurel in oblivion,
who ate the lamb stew of the imagination or digested the crab at the
	muddy bottom of the rivers of Bowery,
who wept at the romance of the streets with their pushcarts full of
	onions and bad music,
who sat in boxes breathing in the darkness under the bridge, and
	rose up to build harpsichords in their lofts,
who coughed on the sixth floor of Harlem crowned with flame under
	the tubercular sky surrounded by orange crates of theology,
who scribbled all night rocking and rolling over lofty incantations
	which in the yellow morning were stanzas of gibberish,

who cooked rotten animals lung heart feet tail borsht & tortillas
dreaming of the pure vegetable kingdom,
who plunged themselves under meat trucks looking for an egg,
who threw their watches off the roof to cast their ballot for Eternity
outside of Time, & alarm clocks fell on their heads every day
for the next decade,
who cut their wrists three times successively unsuccessfully, gave up
and were forced to open antique stores where they thought
they were growing old and cried,
who were burned alive in their innocent flannel suits on Madison
Avenue amid blasts of leaden verse & the tanked-up clatter
of the iron regiments of fashion & the nitroglycerine shrieks
of the fairies of advertising & the mustard gas of sinister
intelligent editors, or were run down by the drunken taxicabs
of Absolute Reality,
who jumped off the Brooklyn Bridge this actually happened and
walked away unknown and forgotten into the ghostly daze of
Chinatown soup alleyways & firetrucks, not even one free
beer,
who sang out of their windows in despair, fell out of the subway
window, jumped in the filthy Passaic, leaped on negroes,
cried all over the street, danced on broken wineglasses
barefoot smashed phonograph records of nostalgic European
1930's German jazz finished the whiskey and threw up
groaning into the bloody toilet, moans in their ears and the
blast of colossal steamwhistles,
who barreled down the highways of the past journeying to each
other's hotrod-Golgotha jail-solitude watch or Birmingham
jazz incarnation,
who drove crosscountry seventytwo hours to find out if I had a vision
or you had a vision or he had a vision to find out Eternity,
who journeyed to Denver, who died in Denver, who came back to
Denver & waited in vain, who watched over Denver &
brooded & loned in Denver and finally went away to find out
the Time, & now Denver is lonesome for her heroes,
who fell on their knees in hopeless cathedrals praying for each
other's salvation and light and breasts, until the soul
illuminated its hair for a second,
who crashed through their minds in jail waiting for impossible
criminals with golden heads and the charm of reality in their
hearts who sang sweet blues to Alcatraz,
who retired to Mexico to cultivate a habit, or Rocky Mount to
tender Buddha or Tangiers to boys or Southern Pacific to the

black locomotive or Harvard to Narcissus to Woodlawn to
the daisychain or grave,
who demanded sanity trials accusing the radio of hypnotism & were
left with their insanity & their hands & a hung jury,
who threw potato salad at CCNY lecturers on Dadaism and
subsequently presented themselves on the granite steps of the
madhouse with shaven heads and harlequin speech of
suicide, demanding instantaneous lobotomy,
and who were given instead the concrete void of insulin metrasol
electricity hydrotherapy psychotherapy occupational therapy
pingpong & amnesia,
who in humorless protest overturned only one symbolic pingpong
table, resting briefly in catatonia,
returning years later truly bald except for a wig of blood, and tears
and fingers, to the visible madman doom of the wards of the
madtowns of the East,
Pilgrim State's Rockland's and Greystone's foetid halls, bickering
with the echoes of the soul, rocking and rolling in the
midnight solitude-bench dolmen-realms of love, dream of life
a nightmare, bodies turned to stone as heavy as the moon,
with mother finally ******, and the last fantastic book flung out of
the tenement window, and the last door closed at 4 AM and
the last telephone slammed at the wall in reply and the last
furnished room emptied down to the last piece of mental
furniture, a yellow paper rose twisted on a wire hanger in the
closet, and even that imaginary, nothing but a hopeful little
bit of hallucination—
ah, Carl, while you are not safe I am not safe, and now you're really
in the total animal soup of time—
and who therefore ran through the icy streets obsessed with a sudden
flash of the alchemy of the use of the ellipse the catalog the
meter & the vibrating plane,
who dreamt and made incarnate gaps in Time & Space through
images juxtaposed, and trapped the archangel of the soul
between 2 visual images and joined the elemental verbs and
set the noun and dash of consciousness together jumping
with sensation of Pater Omnipotens Aeterna Deus
to recreate the syntax and measure of poor human prose and stand
before you speechless and intelligent and shaking with
shame, rejected yet confessing out the soul to conform to the
rhythm of thought in his naked and endless head,
the madman bum and angel beat in Time, unknown, yet putting

down here what might be left to say in time come after
 	death,
and rose reincarnate in the ghostly clothes of jazz in the goldhorn
 	shadow of the band and blew the suffering of America's
 	naked mind for love into an eli eli lamma lamma sabacthani
 	saxophone cry that shivered the cities down to the last radio
with the absolute heart of the poem of life butchered out of their
 	own bodies good to eat a thousand years.

PLEASE MASTER

Please master can I touch your cheek
please master can I kneel at your feet
please master can I loosen your blue pants
please master can I gaze at your golden haired belly
please master can I gently take down your shorts
please master can I have your thighs bare to my eyes
please master can I take off my clothes below your chair
please master can I kiss your ankles and soul
please master can I touch lips to your hard muscle hairless thigh
please master can I lay my ear pressed to your stomach
please master can I wrap my arms around your white ass
please master can I lick your groin curled with blond soft fur
please master can I touch my tongue to your rosy asshole
please master may I pass my face to your balls,
please master, please look into my eyes,
please master order me down on the floor,
please master tell me to lick your thick shaft
please master put your rough hands on my bald hairy skull
please master press my mouth to your prick-heart
please master press my face into your belly, pull me slowly strong
 	thumbed
till your dumb hardness fills my throat to the base
till I swallow & taste your delicate flesh-hot prick barrel veined
 	Please
Master push my shoulders away and stare in my eye, & make me
 	bend over the table
please master grab my thighs and lift my ass to your waist
please master your hand's rough stroke on my neck your palm down
 	my backside
please master push me up, my feet on chairs, till my hole feels the

breath of your spit and your thumb stroke
please master make me say Please Master Fuck me now Please
Master grease my balls and hairmouth with sweet vaselines
please master stroke your shaft with white creams
please master touch your cock head to my wrinkled self-hole
please master push it gently, your elbows enwrapped round my breast
     your arms passing down to my belly, my penis you touch w/your
          fingers
Please master shove it in me a little, a little, a little,
please master sink your droor thing down my behind
& please master make me wiggle my rear to eat up the prick trunk
till my asshalfs cuddle your thighs, my back bent over,
till I'm alone sticking out, your sword stuck throbbing in me
please master pull out and slowly roll into the bottom
please master lunge it again, and withdraw to the tip
please please master fuck me again with your self, please fuck me
          Please
Master drive down till it hurts me the softness the
Softness please master make love to my ass, give body to center, &
          fuck me for good like a girl,
tenderly clasp me please master I take me to thee,
& drive in my belly your selfsame sweet heat-rood
you fingered in solitude Denver or Brooklyn or fucked in a maiden in
          Paris carlots
please master drive me thy vehicle, body of love drops, sweat fuck
body of tenderness, Give me your dog fuck faster
please master make me go moan on the table
Go moan O please master do fuck me like that
in your rhythm thrill-plunge & pull-back-bounce & push down
till I loosen my asshole a dog on the table yelping with terror delight
          to be loved
Please master call me a dog, an ass beast, a wet asshole,
& fuck me more violent, my eyes hid with your palms round my
          skull
& plunge down in a brutal hard lash thru soft drip-flesh
& throb thru five seconds to spurt out your semen heat
over & over, bamming it in while I cry out your name I do love you
please Master.

KADDISH

IV

O mother
what have I left out
O mother
what have I forgotten
O mother
farewell
with a long black shoe
farewell
with Communist Party and a broken stocking
farewell
with six dark hairs on the wen of your breast
farewell
with your old dress and a long black beard around the vagina
farewell
with your sagging belly
with your fear of Hitler
with your mouth of bad short stories
with your fingers of rotten mandolines
with your arms of fat Paterson porches
with your belly of strikes and smokestacks
with your chin of Trotsky and the Spanish War
with your voice singing for the decaying overbroken workers
with your nose of bad lay with your nose of the smell of the pickles
        of Newark
with your eyes
with your eyes of Russia
with your eyes of no money
with your eyes of false China
with your eyes of Aunt Elanor
with your eyes of starving India
with your eyes pissing in the park
with your eyes of America taking a fall
with your eyes of your failure at the piano
with your eyes of your relatives in California
with your eyes of Ma Rainey dying in an ambulance
with your eyes of Czechoslovakia attacked by robots
with your eyes going to painting class at night in the Bronx
with your eyes of the killer Grandma you see on the horizon from
        the Fire-Escape

with your eyes running naked out of the apartment screaming into
    the hall
with your eyes being led away by policemen to an ambulance
with your eyes strapped down on the operating table
with your eyes with the pancreas removed
with your eyes of appendix operation
with your eyes of abortion
with your eyes of ovaries removed
with your eyes of shock
with your eyes of lobotomy
with your eyes of divorce
with your eyes of stroke
with your eyes alone
with your eyes
with your eyes
with your Death full of Flowers

Jewelle Gomez

Jewelle Gomez, born 1948 in Boston, has published two collections of poetry, *The Lipstick Papers* and *Flamingoes and Bears* (Grace Publications, 1981, 1987). Her reviews have appeared in *The New York Times*, *The Village Voice*, *Belles Lettres*, *The Black Scholar*, and *Gay Community News*. A member of the Feminist Anti-Censorship Task Force and the board of directors of Open Meadows, a women's foundation, she works in New York City on the staff of the Literature Program at the New York State Council on the Arts. She is currently completing her first novel.

MY CHAKABUKU MAMA

My first big love was cosmically correct:
she rolled perfect joints, made herbal tea
and vegetarian chili.
We sat on huge pillows talking hours on end

about the cosmic connection, the state of the union
and who should do the laundry
in an equal relationship.
We meditated on celestial seasonings
and I pretended to comprehend
numerology, graphology, phrenology
and the phases of the moon.
I slept with my head facing north
abiding a vicious draught.
My shoes sat outside the door
crying to be let in.
We searched together for the higher ground
through macrobiotic bushes and abstinence;
me peering into her thick transcendental glasses
she facing Mecca.

We chanted to find our center
beneath an azure blue candle from Key Food
and sprinkled a pinch of salt
in the four corners of each room.
We never separated
without talking it out
or allowed bad vibes to invade our space.
She made breakfast on alternate Sundays
and I never drank gin.
We went on camping trips every Spring.
I read poets and journals
and loaned all of my favorite clothes
to slight acquaintances.
I never eavesdropped
when she talked on the phone.
I ate fresh fruit
and only argued with Con Edison.
I cut my finger nails.
We played kalimba duets.
I learned to love brown rice
and Japanese slippers.
I threw out my Salems.
She threw out the roach spray.
We shuddered in unison at the mention
of french fries or Table Talk pies.
I never watched TV
or listened to James Brown.

I gave up aspirin and wore 100% cotton,
had my tarot read, meditated on a tatami bed,
ate raw fish and burned patchouli.
She could squeeze the names of three
Egyptian goddesses
into any general conversation.

Malice and jealousy beat a hasty retreat
from my consciousness.   Our life moved forth
on a path of righteous awareness and sisterhood.
Then she left me flat.
Exiting serenely
on a cloud of universal love.

Melinda Goodman

Melinda Goodman, born 1957 in Manhattan, grew up in New York and New Jersey. She has written and self-published a collection of poetry entitled *Middle Sister* (MSG Press, 1988). She teaches poetry writing and works with the Audre Lorde Women's Poetry Center at Hunter College, where she is currently directing a poetry/theater piece. She is a member of the *Conditions* magazine editorial collective.

JUST HOW CRAZY BRENDA IS

When I was seventeen
you asked me had I ever done this before
and I said no
I feel your hands trembling slightly
as you slide them gently
under my mother's nylon ribbed turtleneck
your hot palms radiating
through my one size fits all bra

still too nervous to slip your fingers underneath
to where my nipples are hardening
waiting for you
later on when I get asked
"Are *you* messing with Brenda?"
I look at my friend shocked
"Hell no" I say
"Did Brenda tell you that?"
I have an angry expression on my face
"Shit, Brenda's crazy."
I laugh and we agree
just how crazy
Brenda is

We used to go to your house all the time
because you lived by the school
and would always get us high
but then I started going to see you alone
parking my mother's chevy stationwagon at the curb
meeting one of your little brothers
nicknamed Rooster hanging off the porch rail
"Brenda upstairs" he says
but I stop first by the kitchen
to say hi to your Moms
who is always so friendly
and treats us each special
like the stars we want to be
as usual she is cooking
and watching the black and white
T.V. set flickering diagonally
across your father's blank face
he sits frozen in his work clothes   still
in a trance
from the lady down the block
who put a spell on him for ending
their twenty year affair
I see Gilligan's Island
the calendar on the wall from Nesbit's
Funeral Parlor
your mother's different numbers
to play for each day
pencilled into every square of the month
hey, Bren

at nineteen you are supporting the entire
household with your job at
Midlantic Bank

I walk up the dark wood staircase
you meet me on the landing   halfway
we are both wearing bellbottoms and wrap-around
sweaters with hoods and knitted belts
I have one of my mother's
polka dotted scarves
tied around my neck
like a choker
your hair smells sweet
neither of us can wait to get upstairs

On the wall in your room
is a day glo poster
your bookshelf is filled with paperback
novels and textbooks from high school
"Linda Goodman's Sun Signs"
and "Love Signs"
you close the door and open
a bottle of Strawberry Annie Greensprings
you light some vanilla incense
"Wanna smoke a joint?" you ask
already emptying out
a plastic baggy full of
mustard yellow brown reefer
"This is the Gold" you tell me
sprinkling a trail like gun powder
into a creased sheet of EZ Wider
eyes looking over your fingers
at me as you roll
lick the gummed edge quick
twirl between your soft dark lips
we hear the sound of Marva's
heavy wooden footsteps
climbing up the stairs from school
in her platform shoes
we hear Valerie giggling in the livingroom
downstairs with her boyfriend
you twist the ends tight
with the tips of your fingers

MELINDA GOODMAN

reaching for a Midlantic Bank matchbook
you strike the back cover
then jump up quick
snatching open the door to the hall
your little brothers scatter running scared
down the stairs to the kitchen
"Ma! Ma!" I hear you call over the banister
"Keep Rooster and Chicken downstairs with you! . . .
because they're *bothering* me. . . . that's why."
I hear your mother telling them to
leave those girls alone
"I swear to God" you say closing the door again
"They can really get on my nerves sometimes"
lying back on the old creaky springy double bed
"I'm gonna get my own place soon" you tell me
I lean toward you with the joint in my hand
smoke leaking out my nose   eyes squinting
"Where's the roach clip?" you ask
looking around the room
I look around too
"never mind" you say softly
"give me a kiss"
I feel your teeth   lips closing around mine
and it feels so good
an eager tangle of teenage tongues
so good it makes us laugh
I lied to you Brenda
you were not my first woman lover
I just wanted you to think
that it was all your
fault

WEDDING RECEPTION

Now close your eyes
I close my eyes
I'm gonna go in the other room, she says
and when I come back in . . . I'm gonna be the doctor
don't open your eyes
I close my eyes
I hear her party shoes tipping across the wood floor
the door opens

the door closes
the door opens
I am trying not to laugh
I feel her eight year old breath on my cheek
she is feeling my pulse
she is checking my reflexes
listening with her invisible stethoscope
to my heart
my heart
O.K. I'll be right back she says
don't open your eyes
through the slit between my eyelashes
I see the blur of her blue tafetta party dress
disappear through the door
I close my eyes
I hear the party downstairs
family, friends, alcohol and cocaine
a live band
Philly rocks to the Planet Rock/don't stop
Detroit rocks to the Planet Rock/don't stop

She comes back
checks my pulse
checks my reflexes
fingers moving up my thigh
I am smiling   wondering how far she will take this
O.K. she says   I'll be right back
don't open your eyes
tip tip tip out the door
I close my eyes
when she comes back in she tells me
unbutton your top button
I do what she tells me
she slips her stethoscope into my blouse
I feel her fingertip just above each breast
she tells me
unbutton the next one
says   don't open your eyes
I'll be right back
tip tip tip
the door opening and closing
I am scared
my blouse is half open and I am waiting for her to come back

I lean back in the rocking chair
The Granny chair   she calls it
Now you sit in the Granny chair she told me
when she brought me to this room
I rock
the door opens
tip tip   tip tip
now take off your bra she says
I say I'm not wearing a bra
she falters for a moment

Oh she says . . .
I'm going to unbutton the next two buttons
O.K.? she says
O.K. I answer
I am the patient   she is the doctor
are you married? she asks me
no I say
too bad she says
you're pretty . . . somebody will want to marry you
her hand is right above my nipple
I'll be right back
tip tip   tip tip
I hear my name from the hallway
the door opens
my eyes open
my blouse is open
Where have you been?
What are you doing?
Nothing I say relieved it's not the girl's mother
I walk into the hall with my lover
tell her I've been playing doctor
tell her I don't know what to do
I say should I stop?
my lover just stares at me
she says you know what to do
she's a child
I go back in the room
sit back in the Granny chair
the door opens
tip tip tip tip
eight year old breath
I open my eyes

don't open your eyes! she says
I take her on my lap
I've got to go now
why? she says
will you come back?
I say no
she says close your eyes
I say no
she says just for a second
I close my eyes
she kisses me on the mouth
I say you're a very nice little girl but I have to go
I walk out of the room down the stairs
the party is in full swing
L.A. rocks to the Planet Rock/don't stop
Chicago rocks to the Planet Rock/don't stop

Half an hour later I go looking for her to say goodbye
find her upstairs on the landing
staring into another woman's eyes.

Paul Goodman

Paul Goodman was born in New York City in 1911 and died in New Hampshire in 1972. He graduated from City College in New York and received his Ph.D. in Humanities from the University of Chicago. A novelist, social commentator, poet, literary critic, and psychologist, he was consistently controversial and thought-provoking. Goodman's writings have appeared widely, and his best-known books include Growing Up Absurd, The Empire City, and Compulsory Mis-education. Black Sparrow Press has published four volumes of Collected Stories and will soon bring out a volume of Selected Poems.

LONG LINES: YOUTH AND AGE

Like a hot stone your cock weighs on mine, young man,
and your face has become brutish and congested.
I'd draw back and gaze at it but drunk with carbon dioxide
we cannot stop snuffling each other's breath.

I am surprised you lust for a grayhead like me
and what a waste for me to grapple so much pleasure
with sliding palms holding your thin body
firlmly while you squirm, till it is time to come.

Come, lad . . . I have come with him for company
to his pounding heart. We are wet. Wistfully
I play with his black hair while he falls asleep
minute by minute, slowly, unlike my restless life.

It is quiet on his little boat. "He's a noisy lover,"
I notice idly—the April air is keen—
"but he has no human speech." It's I who say
the words like "I love you" or "Thank you."

I PLANNED TO HAVE A BORDER OF LAVENDER

I planned to have a border of lavender
but planted the bank too of lavender
and now my whole crazy garden
   is grown in lavender

it smells so sharp heady and musky
of lavender, and the hue of only
lavender is all my garden up
   into the gray rocks.

When forth I go from here the heedless lust
I squander—and in vain for I am stupid
and miss the moment—it has blest me silly
   when forth I go
and when, sitting as gray as these gray rocks
among the lavender, I breathe the lavender's
tireless squandering, I liken it
   to my silly lusting,

I liken my silly indefatigable
lusting to the lavender which has grown over
all my garden, banks and borders, up
    into the gray rocks.

Judy Grahn

Judy Grahn (born 1940, Chicago) published her first books of poetry with The Women's Press Collective, of which she was a co-founder, in Oakland, California: *The Common Woman* (1969), *Edward the Dyke and Other Poems* (1971), and *A Woman Is Talking to Death* (1974). Grahn's work, both as legendary poet and independent publisher, fueled the explosion of lesbian poetry that began in the 70s. Her books of poetry, drama, stories, and essays include *She Who* (Diana, 1977), *The Work of a Common Woman: The Collected Poetry of Judy Grahn, 1964–1977* (Diana, 1978, reprinted by St. Martin's, then Crossing), *The Queen of Wands* (Crossing, 1982), *The Queen of Swords* (Beacon, 1987), the ground-breaking gay and lesbian cultural history *Another Mother Tongue: Gay Words, Gay Worlds* (Beacon, 1984), and *The Highest Apple: Sappho and the Lesbian Poetic Tradition* (Spinsters, Ink, 1985).

A HISTORY OF LESBIANISM

How they came into the world,
the women-loving-women
came in three by three
and four by four
the women-loving-women
came in ten by ten
and ten by ten again
until there were more
than you could count

they took care of each other
the best they knew how
and of each other's children,
if they had any.

How they lived in the world,
the women-loving-women
learned as much as they were allowed
and walked and wore their clothes
the way they liked
whenever they could. They did whatever
they knew to be happy or free
and worked and worked and worked.
The women-loving-women
in America were called dykes
and some liked it
and some did not.

they made love to each other
the best they knew how
and for the best reasons

How they went out of the world,
the women-loving-women
went out one by one
having withstood greater and lesser
trials, and much hatred
from other people, they went out
one by one, each having tried
in her own way to overthrow
the rule of men over women,
they tried it one by one
and hundred by hundred,
until each came in her own way
to the end of her life
and died:

The subject of lesbianism
is very ordinary; it's the question
of male domination that makes everybody
angry.

A WOMAN IS TALKING TO DEATH

One
Testimony in trials that never got heard

my lovers teeth are white geese flying above me
my lovers muscles are rope ladders under my hands

we were driving home slow
my lover and I, across the long Bay Bridge,
one February midnight, when midway
over in the far left lane, I saw a strange scene:

one small young man standing by the rail,
and in the lane itself, parked straight across
as if it could stop anything, a large young
man upon a stalled motorcycle, perfectly
relaxed as if he'd stopped at a hamburger stand;
he was wearing a peacoat and levis, and
he had his head back, roaring, you
could almost hear the laugh, it
was so real.

"Look at that fool," I said, "in the
middle of the bridge like that," a very
womanly remark.

Then we heard the meaning of the noise
of metal on a concrete bridge at 50
miles an hour, and the far left lane
filled up with a big car that had a
motorcycle jammed on its front bumper, like
the whole thing would explode; the friction
sparks shot up bright orange for many feet
into the air, and the racket still sets
my teeth on edge.

When the car stopped we stopped parallel
and Wendy headed for the callbox while I
ducked across those 6 lanes like a mouse
in the bowling alley. "Are you hurt?" I said,

JUDY GRAHN

the middle-aged driver had the greyest black face,
"I couldn't stop, I couldn't stop, what happened?"

Then I remembered. "Somebody," I said, "was *on*
the motorcycle." I ran back,
one block? two blocks? the space for walking
on the bridge is maybe 18 inches, whoever
engineered this arrogance. in the dark
stiff wind it seemed I would
be pushed over the rail, would fall down
screaming onto the hard surface of
the bay, but I did not, I found the tall young man
who thought he owned the bridge, now lying on
his stomach, head cradled in his broken arm.

He had glasses on, but somewhere he had lost
most of his levis, where were they?
and his shoes. Two short cuts on his buttocks,
that was the only mark except his thin white
seminal tubes were all strung out behind; no
child left *in* him; and he looked asleep.

I plucked wildly at his wrist, then put it
down; there were two long haired women
holding back the traffic just behind me
with their bare hands, the machines came
down like mad bulls, I was scared, much
more than usual, I felt easily squished
like the earthworms crawling on a busy
sidewalk after the rain; *I wanted to
leave.* And met the driver, walking back.

"The guy is dead." I gripped his hand,
the wind was going to blow us off the bridge.

"Oh my God," he said, "haven't I had enough
trouble in my life?" He raised his head,
and for a second was enraged and yelling,
at the top of the bridge—"I was just driving
home!" His head fell down. "My God, and
now I've killed somebody."

I looked down at my own peacoat and levis,
then over at the dead man's friend, who
was bawling and blubbering, what they would
call hysteria in a woman. "It isn't possible"
he wailed, but it was possible, it was
indeed, accomplished and unfeeling, snoring
in its peacoat, and without its levis on.

He died laughing: that's a fact.

I had a woman waiting for me,
in her car and in the middle of the bridge,
I'm frightened, I said.
I'm afraid, he said, stay with me,
please don't go, stay with me, be
my witness—"No," I said, "I'll be your
witness—later," and I took his name
and number, "but I can't stay with you,
I'm too frightened of the bridge, besides
I have a woman waiting
and no license—
and no tail lights—"
So I left—
as I have left so many of my lovers.

we drove home
shaking, Wendy's face greyer
than any white person's I have ever seen.
maybe he beat his wife, maybe he once
drove taxi, and raped a lover
of mine—how to know these things?
we do each other in, that's a fact.

who will be my witness?
death wastes our time with drunkenness
and depression
death, who keeps us from our
lovers.
he had a woman waiting for him,
I found out when I called the number
days later

JUDY GRAHN

"Where is he" she said, "he's disappeared."
"He'll be all right" I said, "we could
have hit the guy as easy as anybody, it
wasn't anybody's fault, they'll know that,"
women so often say dumb things like that,
they teach us to be sweet and reassuring,
and say ignorant things, because we don't invent
the crime, the punishment, the bridges

that same week I looked into the mirror
and nobody was there to testify;
how clear, an unemployed queer woman
makes no witness at all,
nobody at all was there for
those two questions: what does
she do, and who is she married to?

I am the woman who stopped on the bridge
and this is the man who was there
our lovers teeth are white geese flying
above us, but we ourselves are
easily squished.

keep the women small and weak
and off the street, and off the
bridges, that's the way, brother
one day I will leave you there,
as I have left you there before,
working for death.

we found out later
what we left him to.
Six big policemen answered the call,
all white, and no child in them.
they put the driver up against his car
and beat the hell out of him.
What did you kill that poor kid for?
you mutherfucking nigger.
that's a fact.

Death only uses violence
when there is any kind of resistance,

the rest of the time a slow
weardown will do.

They took him to 4 different hospitals
til they got a drunk test report to fit their
case, and held him five days in jail
without a phone call.
how many lovers have we left.

there are as many contradictions to the game,
as there are players.
a woman is talking to death,
though talk is cheap, and life takes a long time
to make
right. He got a cheesy lawyer
who had him cop a plea, 15 to 20
instead of life
Did I say life?

the arrogant young man who thought he
owned the bridge, and fell asleep on it
he died laughing: that's a fact.
the driver sits out his time
off the street somewhere,
does he have the most vacant of
eyes, will he die laughing?

Two
They don't have to lynch the women anymore

death sits on my doorstep
cleaning his revolver
death cripples my feet and sends me out
to wait for the bus alone,
then comes by driving a taxi.

the woman on our block with 6 young children
has the most vacant of eyes
death sits in her bedroom, loading
his revolver

they don't have to lynch the women
very often anymore, although

JUDY GRAHN

they used to—the lord and his men
went through the villages at night, beating &
killing every woman caught
outdoors.
the European witch trials took away
the independent people; two different villages
—after the trials were through that year—
had left in them, each—
one living woman:
one

What were those other women up to? had they
run over someone? stopped on the wrong bridge?
did they have teeth like
any kind of geese, or children
in them?

Three
This woman is a lesbian be careful

In the military hospital where I worked
as a nurse's aide, the walls of the halls
were lined with howling women
waiting to deliver
or to have some parts removed.
One of the big private rooms contained
the general's wife, who needed
a wart taken off her nose.
we were instructed to give her special attention
not because of her wart or her nose
but because of her husband, the general.

as many women as men die, and that's a fact.

At work there was one friendly patient, already
claimed, a young woman burnt apart with X-ray,
she had long white tubes instead of openings;
rectum, bladder, vagina—I combed her hair, it
was my job, but she took care of me as if
nobody's touch could spoil her.

ho ho death, ho death
have you seen the twinkle in the dead woman's eye?

when you are a nurse's aide
someone suddenly notices you
and yells about the patient's bed,
and tears the sheets apart so you
can do it over, and over
while the patient waits
doubled over in her pain
for you to make the bed *again*
and no one ever looks at you,
only at what you do not do
Here, general, hold this soldier's bed pan
for a moment, hold it for a year—
then we'll promote you to making his bed.
we believe you wouldn't make such messes

if you had to clean up after them.

that's a fantasy.
this woman is a lesbian, be careful.

When I was arrested and being thrown out
of the military, the order went out: dont anybody
speak to this woman, and for those three
long months, almost nobody did; the dayroom, when
I entered it, fell silent til I had gone; they
were afraid, they knew the wind would blow
them over the rail, the cops would come,
the water would run into their lungs.
Everything I touched
was spoiled. They were my lovers, those
women, but nobody had taught us to swim.
I drowned, I took 3 or 4 others down
when I signed the confession of what we
had done   together.

No one will ever speak to me again.

I read this somewhere; I wasn't there:
in WW II the US army had invented some floating
amphibian tanks, and took them over to
the coast of Europe to unload them,
the landing ships all drawn up in a fleet,
and everybody watching. Each tank had a

JUDY GRAHN

crew of 6 and there were 25 tanks.
The first went down the landing planks
and sank, the second, the third, the
fourth, the fifth, the sixth went down
and sank. They weren't supposed
to sink, the engineers had
made a mistake. The crews looked around
wildly for the order to quit,
but none came, and in the sight of
thousands of men, each 6 crewmen
saluted his officers, battened down
his hatch in turn and drove into the
sea, and drowned, until all 25 tanks
were gone. did they have vacant
eyes, die laughing, or what? what
did they talk about, those men,
as the water came in?

was the general their lover?

Four
A Mock Interrogation

Have you ever held hands with a woman?

Yes, many times—women about to deliver, women about to
have breasts removed, wombs removed, miscarriages, women
having epileptic fits, having asthma, cancer, women having
breast bone marrow sucked out of them by nervous or in-
different interns, women with heart condition, who were
vomiting, overdosed, depressed, drunk, lonely to the point
of extinction: women who had been run over, beaten up.
deserted. starved. women who had been bitten by rats; and
women who were happy, who were celebrating, who were
dancing with me in large circles or alone, women who were
climbing mountains or up and down walls, or trucks or roofs
and needed a boost up, or I did; women who simply wanted
to hold my hand because they liked me, some women who
wanted to hold my hand because they liked me better than
anyone.

These were many women?

Yes. many.

What about kissing? Have you kissed any women?

I have kissed many women.

When was the first woman you kissed with serious feeling?

The first woman ever I kissed was Josie, who I had loved at
such a distance for months. Josie was not only beautiful,
she was tough and handsome too. Josie had black hair and
white teeth and strong brown muscles. Then she dropped
out of school unexplained. When she came back she came
back for one day only, to finish the term, and there was a
child in her. She was all shame, pain, and defiance. Her eyes
were dark as the water under a bridge and no one would
talk to her, they laughed and threw things at her. In the
afternoon I walked across the front of the class and looked
deep into Josie's eyes and I picked up her chin with my
hand, because I loved her, because nothing like her trouble
would ever happen to me, because I hated it that she was
pregnant and unhappy, and an outcast. We were thirteen.

You didn't kiss her?

How does it feel to be thirteen and having a baby?

You didn't actually kiss her?

Not in fact.

You have kissed other women?

Yes, many, some of the finest women I know, I have kissed.
women who were lonely, women I didn't know and didn't
want to, but kissed because that was a way to say yes we are
still alive and loveable, though separate, women who recognized
a loneliness in me, women who were hurt, I confess to
kissing the top of a 55 year old woman's head in the snow in
boston, who was hurt more deeply than I have ever been
hurt, and I wanted her as a very few people have wanted
me—I wanted her and me to own and control and run the

city we lived in, to staff the hospital I knew would mistreat
her, to drive the transportation system that had betrayed
her, to patrol the streets controlling the men who would
murder or disfigure or disrupt us, not accidently with
machines, but on purpose, because we are not allowed out
on the street alone—

Have you ever committed any indecent acts with women?

Yes, many. I am guilty of allowing suicidal women to die
before my eyes or in my ears or under my hands because I
thought I could do nothing, I am guilty of leaving a prostitute
who held a knife to my friend's throat to keep us from
leaving, because we would not sleep with her, we thought
she was old and fat and ugly; I am guilty of not loving her
who needed me; I regret all the women I have not slept with
or comforted, who pulled themselves away from me for lack of
something I had not the courage to fight for, for us, our
life, our planet, our city, our meat and potatoes, our love.
These are indecent acts, lacking courage, lacking a certain
fire behind the eyes, which is the symbol, the raised fist, the
sharing of resources, the resistance that tells death he will
starve for lack of the fat of us, our extra. Yes I have committed
acts of indecency with women and most of them were
acts of omission. I regret them bitterly.

Five
Bless this day oh cat our house

"I was allowed to go
3 places, growing up," she said—
"3 places, no more.
there was a straight line from my house
to school, a straight line from my house
to church, a straight line from my house
to the corner store."
her parents thought something might happen to her.
but nothing   ever   did.

my lovers teeth are white geese flying above me
my lovers muscles are rope ladders under my hands
we are the river of life and the fat of the land
death, do you tell me I cannot touch this woman?

if we use each other up
on each other
that's a little bit less for you
a little bit less for you, ho
death, ho ho death.

Bless this day oh cat our house
help me be not such a mouse
death tells the woman to stay home
and then breaks in the window.

I read this somewhere, I wasnt there:
In feudal Europe, if a woman committed adultery
her husband would sometimes tie her
down, catch a mouse and trap it
under a cup on her bare belly, until
it gnawed itself out, now are you
afraid of mice?

Six
Dressed as I am, a young man once called
me names in Spanish

a woman who talks to death
is a dirty traitor

inside a hamburger joint and
dressed as I am, a young man once called me
names in Spanish
then he called me queer and slugged me.
first I thought the ceiling had fallen down
but there was the counterman making a ham
sandwich, and there was I spread out on his
counter.

For God's sake I said when
I could talk, this guy is beating me up
can't you call the police or something,
can't you stop him? he looked up from
working on his sandwich, which was *my*
sandwich, I had ordered it. He liked
the way I looked. "There's a pay phone
right across the street" he said.

I couldn't listen to the Spanish language
for weeks afterward, without feeling the
most murderous of urges, the simple
association of one thing to another,
so damned simple.

The next day I went to the police station
to become an outraged citizen
Six big policemen stood in the hall,
all white and dressed as they do
they were well pleased with my story, pleased
at what had gotten beat out of me, so
I left them laughing, went home fast
and locked my door.
For several nights I fantasized the scene
again, this time grabbing a chair
and smashing it over the bastard's head,
killing him. I called him a spic, and
killed him. My face healed. his didn't
no child *in* me.

now when I remember I think:
maybe *he* was Josie's baby.
all the chickens come home to roost,
all of them.

Seven
Death and disfiguration

One Christmas eve my lovers and I
we left the bar, driving home slow
there was a woman lying in the snow
by the side of the road. She was wearing
a bathrobe and no shoes, where were
her shoes? she had turned the snow
pink, under her feet. she was an Asian
woman, didnt speak much English, but
she said a taxi driver beat her up
and raped her, throwing her out of his
care.
what on earth was she doing there
on a street she helped to pay for

but doesn't own?
doesn't she know to stay home?

I am a pervert, therefore I've learned
to keep my hands to myself in public
but I was so drunk that night,
I actually did something loving
I took her in my arms, this woman,
until she could breathe right, and
my friends who are perverts too
they touched her too
we all touched her.
"You're going to be all right"
we lied. She started to cry
"I'm 55 years old" she said
and that said everything.

Six big policemen answered the call
no child *in* them.
they seemed afraid to touch her,
then grabbed her like a corpse and heaved her
on their metal stretcher into the van,
crashing and clumsy.
She was more frightened than before.
they were cold and bored.
"don't leave me" she said.
"she'll be all right" they said.
we left, as we have left all of our lovers
as all lovers leave all lovers
much too soon to get the real loving done.

Eight
a mock interrogation

Why did you get into the cab with him, dressed as you are?

I wanted to go somewhere.

Did you know what the cab driver might do
if you got into the cab with him?

I just wanted to go somewhere.

JUDY GRAHN

How many times did you
get into the cab with him?

I dont remember.

If you don't remember, how do you know it happened to
you?

Nine
Hey you death

ho and ho poor death
our lovers teeth are white geese flying above us
our lovers muscles are rope ladders under our hands
even though no women yet go down to the sea in ships
except in their dreams.

only the arrogant invent a quick and meaningful end
for themselves, of their own choosing.
everyone else knows how very slow it happens
how the woman's existence bleeds out her years,
how the child shoots up at ten and is arrested and old
how the man carries a murderous shell within him
and passes it on.

we are the fat of the land, and
we all have our list of casualties

to my lovers I bequeath
the rest of my life

I want nothing left of me for you, ho death
except some fertilizer
for the next batch of us
who do not hold hands with you
who do not embrace you
who try not to work for you
or sacrifice themselves or trust
or believe you, ho ignorant
death, how do you know
we happened to you?

wherever our meat hangs on our own bones
for our own use
your pot is so empty
death, ho death
you shall be poor

A FUNERAL PLAINSONG FROM A YOUNGER WOMAN
TO AN OLDER WOMAN

i will be your mouth now, to do your singing
breath belongs to those who do the breathing.
warm life, as it passes through your fingers
flares up in the very hands you will be leaving

you have left, what is left
for the bond between women is a circle
we are together within it.

i am your best, i am your kind
kind of my kind, i am your wish
wish of my wish, i am your breast
breast of my breast, i am your mind
mind of my mind, i am your flesh
i am your kind, i am your wish
kind of my kind, i am your best

now you have left you can be
wherever the fire is when it blows itself out.
now you are a voice in any wind
        i am a single wind
now you are any source of a fire
        i am a single fire

wherever you go to, i will arrive
whatever i have been, you will come back to
wherever you leave off, i will inherit
whatever i resurrect, you shall have it

you have right, what is right
for the bond between women is returning
we are endlessly within it

and endlessly apart within it.
it is not finished
it will not be finished

i will be your heart now, to do your loving
love belongs to those who do the feeling.

life, as it stands so still along your fingers
beats in my hands, the hands i will, believing
that you have become she, who is not, any longer
somewhere in particular

we are together in your stillness
you have wished us a bonded life

love of my love, i am your breast
arm of my arm, i am your strength
breath of my breath, i am your foot
thigh of my thigh, back of my back
eye of my eye, beat of my beat
kind of my kind, i am your best

when you were dead i said you had gone to the mountain

the trees do not yet speak of you

a mountain when it is no longer
a mountain, goes to the sea
when the sea dies it goes to the rain
when the rain dies it goes to the grain
when the grain dies it goes to the flesh
when the flesh dies it goes to the mountain

now you have left, you can wander
will you tell whoever could listen
tell all the voices who speak to younger women
tell all the voices who speak to us when we need it
that the love between women is a circle
and is not finished

wherever i go to, you will arrive
whatever you have been, i will come back to
wherever i leave off, you will inherit

whatever we resurrect, we shall have it
we shall have it, we have right

and you have left, what is left

i will take your part now, to do your daring
lots belong to those who do the sharing.
i will be your fight now, to do your winning
as the bond between women is beginning
in the middle at the end
my first beloved, present friend
if i could die like the next rain
i'd call you by your mountain name
and rain on you

want of my want, i am your lust
wave of my wave, i am your crest
earth of my earth, i am your crust
may of my may, i am your must
kind of my kind, i am your best

tallest mountain least mouse
least mountain tallest mouse

you have put your very breath upon mine
i shall wrap my entire fist around you
i can touch any woman's lip to remember

we are together in my motion
you have wished us a bonded life

a funeral: for my first lover and longtime friend
Yvonne Mary Robinson   b. Oct. 20, 1939; d. Nov. 1974
for ritual use

TALKERS IN A DREAM DOORWAY

You leaned your body in the doorway
(it was a dim NY hall)
I was leaving as usual—on my way.
You had your head cocked to the side
in your most intelligent manner

eyes glistening   with provocation,
gaze direct as always,
and more, as though wanting something,
as though I could have bent and kissed you
like a lover
and nothing social would have changed,
no one minded, no one bothered.
I can't testify to your intention.

I can only admit to my temptation.

Your intensity dazed me, so matter of fact
as though I could have leaned my denser body into yours,
in that moment while the cab waited
traffic roaring nine flights down
as well as in my ears,
both of us with lovers of our own
and living on each end of a large continent.
We were raised in vastly different places,
yet speak this uncanny similar tongue.
Some times we're different races,
certainly we're different classes,
yet our common bonds and common graces,
common wounds and destinations
keep us closer than some married folks.

I admit I have wanted to touch your face, intimately.

Supposing that I were to do this awful
act, this breach of all our lovers' promises—in reality—
this tiny, cosmic infidelity: I believe our lips would first be
tentative, then hardened in a rush of feeling, unity
such as we thought could render up the constellations AND our
daily lives, justice, equality AND freedom,
give us worldly definition
AND the bread of belonging. In the eye of my imagination
I see my fingers curled round the back of your head
as though it were your breast
and I were pulling it to me.
As though your head were your breast
and I were pulling it to me

I admit, I have wanted to possess your mind.

I leaned forward to say good-bye,
aware of your knuckle possibly digging a tunnel
through my thigh, of the whole shape of your body as
an opening, a doorway to the heart.
Both of us with other lives to lead
still sure why we need so much to join,
and do join with our eyes on every
socially possible occasion.
More than friends, even girl friends,
more than comrades, surely,
more than workers with the same bent,
and more than fellow magicians
exchanging recipes for a modern brand of golden spit.

I admit we have already joined more than physically.

The cab's horn roars.
You smile, or part your lips as if to welcome how I'd just
slip in there, our tongues nodding together,
talking inside each other's mouth for a change,
as our upper bodies talked that night we danced together.
Your face was wine-flushed, and foolish; my desire selfish,
pushing you beyond your strength.
You paid for it later, in pain, you said.
I forget you are older, and fragile. I forget your arthritis.
I paid later in guilt, though not very much.
I loved holding you so close, your ear pressed to my ear.
I wanted to kiss you then but I didn't dare
lest I spoil the real bonding we were doing there.

I admit I have wanted to possess my own life.

Our desire is that we want to talk of really important things,
and words come so slowly, eons of movement
squirt them against our gums. Maybe once in ten years a
     sentence
actually flashes out, altering everything in its path.
Flexing our tongues into each other's dreams, we want to
suck a new language, strike a thought into being, out of the old
fleshpot. That rotten old body of our long submersion. We sense
the new idea can be a dance of all kinds of women,
one we seek with despair and desire
and exaltation; are willing to pay for

JUDY GRAHN

with all-consuming passion, AND those tiny boring paper cuts.
I never did lean down to you that day.
I said good-bye with longing and some confusion.

I admit to wanting a sword AND a vision.

I doubt I will ever kiss you in that manner.
I doubt I will ever stop following you around, wanting to.
This is our love, this stuff
pouring out of us, and if this mutual desire is
some peculiar ether-marriage
among queens, made of the longing of women
to really love each other, made of dreams
and needs larger than all of us,
we may not know what to do
with it yet but at least
we've got it,
we're in the doorway.
We've got it right here, between us,

(admit it) on the tip of our tongues.

Freddie Greenfield

Freddie Greenfield (born 1929 in Chelsea, Massachusetts) writes: "Started writing seriously in prison while serving a five-year sentence for narcotic law violations about sixteen years ago write mostly about my apprenticeship as a gay petty thief professional boxer carnival hustler construction worker and former male prostitute presently poetry editor art editor for *Fag Rag* Boston last book *Amusement Business And Then Some* by Good Gay Poets Boston 1976 have new book coming out *Were You Always a Criminal?*"

OH GOD FORBID

Oh God Forbid
Oh God Forbid
Oh God Forbid
Your Son
Your Son
Your Son
Is Married
Is Married
Is Married
To A
To A
To A
Black Fairy
Black Fairy
Black Fairy
Oh God Forbid Your Son Is Married
To A Black Fairy

Susan Griffin

Susan Griffin (born 1943, Los Angeles) was raised in California, where she lives now in the Berkeley Hills with her daughter. She is the author of a number of books of poetry, drama, and nonfiction, including *Like the Iris of an Eye*, *Woman and Nature: The Roaring Inside Her*, *Pornography and Silence: Culture's Revenge Against Nature*, *Made from This Earth* (Harper & Row, 1976, 1978, 1981, 1982), and *Unremembered Country* (Copper Canyon, 1987). Her play *Voices* won an Emmy Award in 1975, and she received the Malvina Reynolds Cultural Achievement Award in 1981. She is presently writing a book on the nuclear crisis, *The First and the Last: A Woman Thinks About War*, to be published by Doubleday.

AN ANSWER TO A MAN'S QUESTION, "WHAT CAN I DO ABOUT WOMEN'S LIBERATION?"

Wear a dress.
Wear a dress that you made yourself, or bought in a dress store.
Wear a dress and underneath the dress wear elastic, around
your hips, and underneath your nipples.
Wear a dress and underneath the dress wear a sanitary napkin.
Wear a dress and wear sling-back, high-heeled shoes.
Wear a dress, with elastic and a sanitary napkin underneath,
and sling-back shoes on your feet, and walk down Telegraph Avenue.
Wear a dress, with elastic and a sanitary napkin and sling-
back shoes on Telegraph Avenue and try to run.

Find a man.
Find a nice man who you would like to ask you for a date.
Find a nice man who *will* ask you for a date.
Keep your dress on.
Ask the nice man who asks you for a date to come to dinner.
Cook the nice man a nice dinner so the dinner is ready before
he comes and your dress is nice and clean and wear a smile.
Tell the nice man you're a virgin, or you don't have
birth control, or you would like to get to know him better.
Keep your dress on.
Go to the movies by yourself.

Find a job.
Iron your dress.
Wear your ironed dress and promise the boss you won't get
pregnant (which in your case is predictable) and you like to
type, and be sincere and wear your smile.
Find a job or get on welfare.
Borrow a child and get on welfare.
Borrow a child and stay in the house all day with the child,
or go to the public park with the child, and take the child
to the welfare office and cry and say your man left you and
be humble and wear your dress and your smile, and don't talk
back, keep your dress on, cook more nice dinners, stay
away from Telegraph Avenue, and still, you won't know the
half of it, not in a million years.

THE SONG OF THE WOMAN WITH HER PARTS
COMING OUT

I am bleeding
the blood seeps in red
circles on the white
white of my sheet,
my vagina
is opening, opening
closing and opening
wet, wet,
my nipples turn rose and hard
my breasts swell against my arms
my arms float out
like anemones
my feet slide on the wooden
floor,
dancing, they are dancing, I sing,
my tongue slips from my mouth
and my mind
imagines a
clitoris
I am the woman
I am the woman
with her parts coming out
with her parts coming out.

The song of the woman with
the top of her head ripping off, with
the top of her head ripping off
and she flies out
and she flies out
and her flesh flies out
and her nose rubs against her ass,
and her eyes love ass
and her cunt
swells and sucks and waves,
and the words spring from her mind
like Fourth of July rockets,
and the words too come out,
lesbian, lesbian, lesbian, pee, pee, pee, pee, cunt, vagina,
dyke, sex, sex, sex, sex, sweat, tongue, lick, suck, sweet,
sweet, sweet, suck
and the other words march out too,

SUSAN GRIFFIN

the words,
P's and Q's
the word
nice,
the word
virginity,
the word
mother,
mother goodness mother nice good goodness good good should
should be good be mother be nice good
the word
pure
the word
lascivious
the word
modest
the word
no
the word
no
the word
no
and the woman
the woman
the woman
with her
parts coming out
never stopped
never stopped
even to
say yes,
but only
flew with
her words
with her words
with her words
with her parts
with her parts
coming
with her parts
     coming
     coming
     coming
     out.

WAITING FOR TRUTH

Their bodies lined up against the walls.
waiting for truth, my
words thread the room
like fishing line,
"She put
she put her head in an oven
she put her head in an
oven,"
I stutter,
my words enter space and I
slide down the line
terrified, where are we
going?
Their bodies wait for information.
"There are places I have been," I
want to tell them.
The book behind me reads:
        "Sylvia Plath's range of technical resources . . ."
"There are places I have been," I
want to say, my body
all night sleeping,
did I dream
running in Harlem
dream the markets of the
poor,
was someone diseased, was the disease
spreading? Did I dream
an escape? Was I safe in a
classroom, sitting close
to a friend, sighing relief,
writing the movie script,
telling where I had been,
was I singing?
Did they say my name?
That I was supposed to write words
on the chalkboard, I
was supposed to address and I
stuttered,
"What I have seen
the places I have been and I
promised everyone there

SUSAN GRIFFIN

I would speak only of *them:*
the one who sat in a corner for a week,
the one whose breasts ran dry,"
And the book read,
    "Sylvia Plath
    Sylvia Plath's range of
    technical resources was narrower
    than Robert Lowell's," * and I
stuttered:
"The one whose lovers
were frightened by her
children, the one who
wished her children,"
    "Narrower than Robert Lowell's and so,
    apparently, was her capacity"
her children would be
    "for intellectual objectivity."
would be still.
Sylvia Plath's range of
technical resources
she put her
was narrower
head in an
there are places I have been
Everyone on the street was diseased.
There are places you have been.
Trying to speak
the script
claiming my mind, was it
a dream
or did I live, "range of
technical."
Their bodies in transformation.
She put her head in an
repetition
repetition
is no longer

---

* The line "Sylvia Plath's range of technical resources was narrower than Robert Lowell's and so, apparently, was her capacity for intellectual objectivity" is from the essay "Sylvia Plath and Confessional Poetry," by M. L. Rosenthal, which appears in *The Art of Sylvia Plath,* Charles Newman, ed., Indiana University Press, 1971.

no longer
interesting in
poetry
he said
but goes on
which one put
her head in an
in life, in
autobiographical detail, gas,
milk, a pair of kids, technical resources, a bottle
of chicken fat, two dinner guests, a box of books,
Achoo IdoAchoo IdoAchoo   I   do
and an interesting sense of rhyme
range of
chattering, "There are places
we have," suddenly the whole
been, there are places, bodies
lined up, the walls, the whole world
suddenly the whole world is making
terrific sense I am chattering,
"Yes," I say to the bus driver, taking me home
"I am afraid of freeways."
"Yes," I lecture a tree
near the sidewalk, "I am free."
Yes, I am afraid of rats, knives, bullets,
I am, there is, I am there is,
I sing, walking the street,
a fish on the line,
shouting to my feet,
"But I will not be afraid
of voices nor of,"
There are places we
"nor of pieces of paper."
have been.

SUSAN GRIFFIN

I WAKE THINKING OF MYSELF AS A MAN

And as I rise slapping my feet
on the wooden floor
I begin to imagine myself
quite tall
with broad shoulders, a
painter who puts his feet
into dirty tennis shoes, does
not comb his hair and lumbers
largely into the kitchen, laces
loose in all this space.
I am this man, giant in my
female house, as I eat
my huge hands dwarf these bowls,
this breakfast!
I have become so big
I need a larger meal, more
eggs, coffee, and the newspaper
the newspaper rests like a
delicate letter in
my enormous grasp.

Thom Gunn

Thom Gunn was born in Gravesend, England, in 1929 and received his B.A. degree from Trinity College, Cambridge. Since 1954 he has lived in San Francisco. *Fighting Terms*, Gunn's first book of poems—for which he received wide recognition as an important new voice—appeared in England in 1954 (Fantasy Press) and in America in 1958 (Hawk's Well Press, New York). His recent publications include *Jack Straw's Castle* (1976); *Selected Poems, 1950–1975* (1979); and *The Passages of Joy* (1981)—all published by Farrar, Straus, and Giroux.

AS EXPECTED

Most of his friends, as expected,
went into service. Two
became pilots, swooping over
lush Vietnamese lowland in their bombers,
high on the orgasmic shriek
of Led Zeppelin over the intercom.

Larry chose a slower route.

He was assigned a grubby
roomful of young men sitting around
idle, or idle on their cots.
One who had been high-spirited
earlier, lay in deep sleep
knocked out by thorazine all day.
Their hair was cropped. Some
would have to be hosed down.
Burdens-on-society.

They looked like ninepins.
But he found that none had head-lice
and let them grow their hair.
They started to look
as if they had different names.

A whole night he watched them
till they forgot he was there.
They paid neighbourly visits
bed to bed. One of them
had composed a little tune
made up of three sounds.
One had invented a game
for the fingers of both hands.
Larry watched:
              if the unteachable
can teach themselves, it follows
they can be taught by others.

One learned to eat without help.
One learned toilet training
for the first time in his nineteen years.

When he came on his shift
they shambled up, poorly co-ordinated,
wild-eyed, and with faces uncomposed.
'Larry! Larry!' they cried out,
they giggled and embraced him,
stumbling like kittens, inarticulate
like tulips bending in a wet wind,
and learning as they went, like humans.

When the testing time was over,
Larry and the pilots went to college.
The young men in the other institution
were given to other keepers: and they were
retarded, unteachable,
      as expected.

COURAGE, A TALE

There was a Child
who heard from another Child
that if you masturbate 100 times
it kills you.

This gave him pause;
he certainly slowed down quite a bit
and also
    kept count.

But, till number 80,
was relatively loose about it.
There did seem plenty of time left.

The next 18
were reserved for celebrations,
like the banquet room in a hotel.

The 99th time
was simply unavoidable.

Weeks passed.

And then he thought

Fuck it
        it's worth dying for,

and half an hour later
the score rose from 99 to 105.

THE CHERRY TREE

In her gnarled sleep it
begins
        though she seems
as unmoving as the statue
of a running man: her
branches caught in a
writhing, her trunk
leaning as if in mid-fall.
When the wind moves
against her grave body
only the youngest twigs
scutter amongst themselves.

But there's something going on
in those twisted brown limbs,
it starts as a need
and it takes over, a need
to push
        push outward
from the centre, to
bring what is not
from what is, pushing
till at the tips of the push
something comes about
                        and then
pulling it from outside
until yes she has them started
tiny bumps
appear at the ends of twigs.

Then at once they're all here,
she wears them like a coat
a coat of babies,
I almost think that she

THOM GUNN

preens herself, jubilant at
the thick dazzle of bloom,
that the caught writhing has become
a sinuous wriggle of joy
beneath her fleece.
But she is working still
to feed her children,
there's a lot more yet,
bringing up all she can
a lot of goodness from roots

while the petals drop.
The fleece is gone
as suddenly as it came
and hundreds of babies are left
almost too small to be seen
but they fatten, fatten, get pink
and shine among her leaves.

Now she can repose a bit
they are so fat.
                She cares less
birds get them, men
pick them, human children wear them
in pairs over their ears
she loses them all.
That's why she made them,
to lose them into the world, she
returns to herself,
she rests, she doesn't care.

She leans into the wind
her trunk shines black
with rain, she sleeps
as black and hard as lava.
She knows nothing about babies.

LAMENT

for Allan Noseworthy, died June 21, 1984
Your dying was a difficult enterprise.
First, petty things took up your energies,
The small but clustering duties of the sick,
As irritant as the cough's dry rhetoric.
Those hours of waiting for pills, shot, X-ray
Or test (while you read novels two a day)
Already with a kind of clumsy stealth
Distanced you from the habits of your health.
    In hope still, courteous still, but tired and thin,
You tried to stay the man that you had been,
Treating each symptom as a mere mishap
Without import. But then the spinal tap.
It brought a hard headache, and when night came
I heard you wake up from the same bad dream
Every half-hour with the same short cry
Of mild outrage, before immediately
Slipping into the nightmare once again
Empty of content but the drip of pain.
No respite followed: though the nightmare ceased,
Your cough grew thick and rich, its strength increased.
Four nights, and on the fifth we drove you down
To the Emergency Room. That frown, that frown:
I'd never seen such rage in you before
As when they wheeled you through the swinging door.
For you knew, rightly, they conveyed you from
Those normal pleasures of the sun's kingdom
The hedonistic body basks within
And takes for granted—summer on the skin,
Sleep without break, the moderate taste of tea
In a dry mouth. You had gone on from me
As if your body sought out martyrdom
In the far Canada of a hospital room.
Once there, you entered fully the distress
And long pale rigors of the wilderness.
A gust of morphine hid you. Back in sight
You breathed through a segmented tube, fat, white,
Jammed down your throat so that you could not speak.

How thin the distance made you. In your cheek
One day, appeared the true shape of your bone
No longer padded. Still your mind, alone,
Explored this emptying intermediate
State for what holds and rests were hidden in it.
    You wrote us messages on a pad, amused
At one time that you had your nurse confused
Who, seeing you reconciled after four years
With your gray father, both of you in tears,
Asked if this was at last your "special friend"
(The one you waited for until the end).
"She sings," you wrote, "A Philippine folk song
To wake me in the morning . . . It is long,
And very pretty." Grabbing at detail
To furnish this bare ledge toured by the gale,
On which you lay, bed restful as a knife,
You tried, tried hard, to make of it a life
Thick with the complicating circumstance
Your thoughts might fasten on. It had been chance
Always till now that had filled up the moment
With live specifics your hilarious comment
Discovered as it went along; and fed,
Laconic, quick, wherever it was led.
You improvised upon your own delight.
I can remember when one summer night
We talked between our sleeping bags, below
A molten field of stars five years ago:
I was so tickled by your mind's light touch
I couldn't sleep, you made me laugh too much,
Though I was tired and begged you to leave off.

Now you were tired, and yet not tired enough
—Still hungry for the great world you were losing
Steadily in no season of your choosing—
And when at last the whole death was assured,
Drugs having failed, and when you had endured
Two weeks of an abominable constraint,
You faced it equably, without complaint,
Unwhimpering, but not at peace with it.
You'd lived as if your time was infinite:
You were not ready and not reconciled,
Feeling as incompleted as a child

Till you had shown the world what you could do
In some ambitious role to be worked through,
A role your need for it had half-defined,
But never wholly, even in your mind.
You lacked the necessary ruthlessness,
The soaring meanness that pinpoints success.
We loved that lack of self-love, and your smile,
Rueful, at your own silliness.
                                        Meanwhile,
Your lungs collapsed, and the machine, unstrained,
Did all your breathing now. Nothing remained
But death by drowning on an inland sea
Of your own fluids, which it seemed could be
Kindly forestalled by drugs. Both could and would:
Nothing was said, everything understood,
At least by us. Your own concerns were not
Long-term, precisely, when they gave the shot
—You made local arrangements to the bed
And pulled a pillow round beside your head.

   And so you slept, and died, your skin gone gray,
Achieving your completeness, in a way.

Outdoors next day, I was dizzy from a sense
Of being ejected with some violence
From vigil in a white and distant spot
Where I was numb, into this garden plot
Too warm, too close, and not enough like pain.
I was delivered into time again
—The variations that I live among
Where your long body too used to belong
And where the still bush is minutely active.
You never thought your body was attractive,
Though others did, and yet you trusted it
And must have loved its fickleness a bit
Since it was yours and gave you what it could,
Till near the end it let you down for good,
Its blood hospitable to those guests who
Took over by betraying it into
The greatest of its inconsistencies
This difficult, tedious, painful enterprise.

Marilyn Hacker

Marilyn Hacker (born 1942, the Bronx, New York) lives in Manhattan and the Marais with Iva and Karyn. She was editor of the feminist literary magazine *13th Moon* from 1982 through 1986. Her books of poetry to date are *Presentation Piece* (Viking, 1974), which was a Lamont Poetry Selection of the Academy of American Poets and received the National Book Award for poetry in 1975; *Separations; Taking Notice; Assumptions* (Knopf, 1976, 1980, 1985); and *Love, Death, and the Changing of the Seasons* (Arbor House, 1986).

FIFTEEN TO EIGHTEEN

I'd almost know, the nights I snuck in late,
at two, at three, as soon as I had tucked
into myself tucked in, to masturbate
and make happen what hadn't when I fucked,
there'd be the gargled cry, always "God damn
you to hell," to start with, from the other
bedroom: she was in shock again. I swam
to my surface to take care of my mother.
That meant, run for a glass of orange juice,
clamp her shoulders with one arm, try to pour
it down her throat while she screams, "No, God damn
you!" She is stronger than I am
when this happens. If she rolls off on the floor,
I can't/she won't let me/lift her up. Fructose solution,
a shot and she'd come around.
At half-past-two, what doctor could I call?
Sometimes I had to call the hospital.
More often, enough orange juice got down,
splashed on us both.
                    "What are you doing here?
Where were you? Why is my bed in this mess?

How did you get those scratches on your face?
What were you doing, out until this hour?"

1974

"I'm pregnant," I wrote to her in delight
from London, thirty, married, in print. A fool-
scap sheet scrawled slantwise with one miniscule
sentence came back. "I hope your child is white."
I couldn't tear the pieces small enough.
I hoped she'd be black as the ace of spades,
though hybrid beige heredity had made
that as unlikely as the spun-gold stuff
sprouted after her neo-natal fur.
I grudgingly acknowledged her "good hair,"
which wasn't very, from my point of view.
"No tar-brush left," her father's mother said.
"She's Jewish and she's white," from her cranked bed
mine smugly snapped.
                    She's Black. She is a Jew.

THREE SONNETS FOR IVA

He tips his boy baby's hand in an icy
stream from the mountaintop. The velvet cheek
of sky is like a child's in a backpack
carrier. Then wrote his anthology
piece, began it while she changed the Pamper
full of mustardy shit. Again rage
blisters my wet forehead as the page
stays blank, and you tug my jeans knee, whimper
"I *want* you!" I want you, too. In the child-
sized rowboat in Regent's Park, sick with a man,
and I hadn't spoken to another
grown-up for two days, I played Amazon
Queen and Princess with you. You splashed pond water
outside my fantasy, nineteen months old.

The bathroom tiles are very pink and new.
Out the window, a sixty-foot willow

tree forks, droops. Planted eighteen years ago,
its huge roots choke the drains. The very blue
sky is impenetrable. I hear you
whine outside the locked door. You're going to cry.
If I open the door, I'll slap you. I've
hit you six times this morning, I threw
you on the rug and smacked your bottom. Slapped
your face. Slapped your hands. I sit on the floor.
We're both scared. I picked you up, held you, lov-
ing your cheek's curve. Yelled, shook you. I want to stop
this day. I cringe on the warm pink tiles of
a strange house. We cry on both sides of the door.

Chip took you to your grandmother's today.
You scoop sand-cakes from your orange-and-blue
dump truck, while he reads *The Times Book Review*
on a hot slatted bench four feet away.
Solitary for work, I pay bills, spray
the roaches' climbing party on the flank
of students' dittoed manuscripts and bank
statements. Myself as four-year-old, I play
with your clean clothes, open my closet, finger
old lives' skirts dependent on plastic hangers.
You ask for dresses now, and I demur,
then buy you a crisp shift, blue with white cats,
which I just once have offered you to wear.
I love you most when you are what I'm not.

Joy Harjo

Joy Harjo (born 1951, Tulsa, Oklahoma) is of the Creek Tribe. She has taught
Native American literature and creative writing at the Institute of American
Indian Arts and Arizona State University, and currently teaches at the Uni-

versity of Colorado in Boulder. Author of *The Last Song* (Puerta del Sol Press, 1975), *What Moon Drove Me to This* (I. Reed Books, 1980), and *She Had Some Horses* (Thunder's Mouth, 1983), she is working on texts for *Secrets from the Center of the World* (with photographs by astronomer Stephen Strom) and a fourth collection of poetry entitled *In Mad Love and War*.

THE WOMAN HANGING FROM THE THIRTEENTH FLOOR WINDOW

She is the woman hanging from the 13th floor
window. Her hands are pressed white against the
concrete moulding of the tenement building. She
hangs from the 13th floor window in east Chicago,
with a swirl of birds over her head. They could
be a halo, or a storm of glass waiting to crush her.

She thinks she will be set free.

The woman hanging from the 13th floor window
on the east side of Chicago is not alone.
She is a woman of children, of the baby, Carlos,
and of Margaret, and of Jimmy who is the oldest.
She is her mother's daughter and her father's son.
She is several pieces between the two husbands
she has had. She is all the women of the apartment
building who stand watching her, watching themselves.

When she was young she ate wild rice on scraped down
plates in warm wood rooms. It was in the farther
north and she was the baby then. They rocked her.

She sees Lake Michigan lapping at the shores of
herself. It is a dizzy hole of water and the rich
live in tall glass houses at the edge of it. In some
places Lake Michigan speaks softly, here, it just sputters
and butts itself against the asphalt. She sees
other buildings just like hers. She sees other
women hanging from many-floored windows
counting their lives in the palms of their hands
and in the palms of their children's hands.

She is the woman hanging from the 13th floor window

JOY HARJO

on the Indian side of town. Her belly is soft from
her children's births, her worn levis swing down below
her waist, and then her feet, and then her heart.
She is dangling.

The woman hanging from the 13th floor hears voices.
They come to her in the night when the lights have gone
dim. Sometimes they are little cats mewing and scratching
at the door, sometimes they are her grandmother's voice,
and sometimes they are gigantic men of light whispering
to her to get up, to get up, to get up. That's when she wants
to have another child to hold onto in the night, to be able
to fall back into dreams.

And the woman hanging from the 13th floor window
hears other voices. Some of them scream out from below
for her to jump, they would push her over. Others cry softly
from the sidewalks, pull their children up like flowers and gather
them into their arms. They would help her, like themselves.

But she is the woman hanging from the 13th floor window,
and she knows she is hanging by her own fingers, her
own skin, her own thread of indecision.

She thinks of Carlos, of Margaret, of Jimmy.
She thinks of her father, and of her mother.
She thinks of all the women she has been, of all
the men. She thinks of the color of her skin, and
of Chicago streets, and of waterfalls and pines.
She thinks of moonlight nights, and of cool spring storms.
Her mind chatters like neon and northside bars.
She thinks of the 4 a.m. lonelinesses that have folded
her up like death, discordant, without logical and
beautiful conclusion. Her teeth break off at the edges.
She would speak.

The woman hangs from the 13th floor window crying for
the lost beauty of her own life. She sees the
sun falling west over the grey plain of Chicago.
She thinks she remembers listening to her own life
break loose, as she falls from the 13th floor
window on the east side of Chicago, or as she
climbs back up to claim herself again.

Richard Harteis

Richard Harteis (born 1946 in Johnstown, Pennsylvania) has lived and worked most of his adult life in the Washington, D.C., area, but has traveled extensively as a Peace Corps volunteer, health worker, teacher, and tourist. His books include *Fourteen Women* (Three Rivers Press, 1979), *Morocco Journal*, and *Internal Geography* (Carnegie-Mellon University Press, 1981 and 1987). He has recently completed *Training*, a prose account of running the New York City Marathon, caring for a stroke patient, living in the country, facing up to middle age, and other ruminations. Since 1971 he has shared his life with the poet William Meredith.

STAR TREK III

The fantasy spaceman
returning from death
greets his captain
gingerly: "Jim?"

Spock's Vulcan father explains
that only time will tell
if the priestess' magic
will bring him totally back.
Instead of "the end"
the film's last frames promise,
"the adventure continues."

I want to cry a little:
I grew up on these heroes—
to be as good as Kirk . . .

But life is a little closer now.
We watch the film together
and I explain the plot

the way one would talk to someone
trapped under ice. My manuals say
I mustn't convey anxiety.

I remember the day after
weeks at your bedside when
you said my name finally.

You were IN there,
KNEW me.

The same shock the cardiac nurse
felt the year before when she
randomly took the tape from
your sweet eyes and they flew open
as she called your name.

We've been in a few
tight spots lately.

All these months.
My loneliness deepens.
I cry in private
when you forget my name.

Still, you love me clearly,
whoever I am.

The adventure continues.

THE GRACE OF ANIMALS

I

Long before the adult flora of
sex, ambition, and money overgrew
the moral landscape, I recall thinking
I might possibly not be able to believe
in a God who denied a place in heaven
for animals, in particular my blue terrier
who was the single friend of my lonely boyhood.

II

I could see their lesser intelligence, I
was reading about dinosaurs then and Darwin
like other boys, even aspiring to Aquinas.
But I couldn't accept that something so
beautiful, something which responded so
completely to my being would become
dumb earth while I, my brothers and sisters,
and Sister Marguerite would, would what?
buzz eternal in a perfect inanimate rapture,
paradise, glowing Godhead?

Couldn't there be an antechamber, a
little limbo say, some way for Astra
to live with me after death since
till then she was the only star in my life?
I began to read Egyptian theology which
seemed closer to how things ought to be.

III

The good guest recently, I walked
with my host's child and his dog
while the adults drank
night caps and did dishes:
"Feel her, feel her," he said,
unselfconscious in the delight of
her satin coat, a little afraid the
black lab might knock him down again
going for a squirrel, but determined
with his entire small weight (half the dog's)
and soul to try to train this gentle monster,
who had a pretty good idea how to train this boy.

IV

Ten years ago for mother's birthday I
bought a scottie puppy. With pointed
ears and little skirt it was a cookie
cutter version of Franklin Roosevelt's pet.

The dog lived her quiet secret scottie life
all these years, the black eyes, black coals
at the far end of her face structure, hidden
in the bushy eyebrows—the kind of success
one hopes for in life, giving a good gift.

V

This morning, insomniac and firm,
mother calls from retirement and Florida
to declare I must put the dog to sleep.
The pet has become incontinent, a burden to
relatives, snaps at the children occasionally
and is too much an expense.

This woman is as good as Simone de Beauvoir
or Saint Teresa, no irony is lost on her.
It's what has kept her awake all night I suppose,
this coming to the end and telling me firmly
how to deal with age, and loneliness and death
the way earlier she taught me how to deal with
youth and loneliness and life.

Now mother returns the gift, gives me
the chance to comfort, to say, "No,
I understand, but I think I'll try her here,
see if she can be happy here, no need to
put her to sleep yet. You have made your
decision, don't worry, I accept the responsibility
and it's not a burden."

And it is clearer than ever
how if there is a God
he gives us these creatures
to lead us here and there.

Essex Hemphill

Essex Hemphill (born 1957 in Chicago) is co-founder and former publisher of *Nethula Journal of Contemporary Literature*. His collections of poems include *Earth Life* and *Conditions* (Be Bop Books, 1985 and 1986), and his poems are anthologized in *Art Against Apartheid* (*Ikon*, Winter/Summer 1986), *In the Life: A Black Gay Anthology* (Alyson Publications, Boston, 1986), and *Tongues Untied* (GMP, London, 1987). A resident of Washington, D.C., Hemphill was the recipient of a 1986 Fellowship in Literature (Poetry) from the National Endowment for the Arts.

CORDON NEGRO

I drink champagne early in the morning
instead of leaving my house
with an M16 and nowhere to go.

I die twice as fast
as any other American
between eighteen and thirty-five.
This disturbs me,
but I try not to show it in public.

Each morning I open my eyes is a miracle.
The blessing of opening them
is temporary on any given day.

I could be taken out,
I could go off,
I could forget to be careful.
Even my brothers, hunted, hunt me.
I'm the only one who values my life
and sometimes I don't give a damn.

My love life can kill me.
I'm faced daily with choosing violence
or a demeanor that saves every other life
but my own.

I won't cross over.
It's time someone came to me
not to patronize me physically,
sexually, or humorously.

I'm sick of being an endangered species,
sick of being a goddamn statistic.
So what are my choices?

I could leave with no intention
of coming home tonight,
go crazy downtown and raise hell
on a rooftop with my rifle.
I could live for a brief moment
on the six o'clock news,
or masquerade another day
through the corridors of commerce
and American dreams.

I'm dying twice as fast
as any other American.
So I pour myself a glass of champagne,
I cut it with a drop of orange juice.

After I swallow my liquid valium,
my private celebration
for being alive
this morning,
I leave my shelter,
I guard my life with no apologies.
My concerns are small
and personal.

TO SOME SUPPOSED BROTHERS

You judge a woman
by the length of her skirt,
by the way she walks,
talks, looks, and acts;
by the color of her skin you judge
and will call her "bitch!"
"Black bitch!"
if she doesn't answer your:
"Hey baby, whatcha gonna say
to a man?"

You judge a woman
by the job she holds,
by the number of children she's had,
by the number of digits on her check;
by the many men she may have lain with
and wonder what jive murphy
you'll run on her this time.

You tell a woman
every poetic love line
you can think of,
then like the desperate needle
of a strung-out junkie
you plunge into her veins,
travel wild through her blood,
confuse her mind, make her hate
and be cold to the men to come,
destroying the thread of calm
she held.

You judge a woman
by what she can do for you alone
but there's no need
for slaves to have slaves.

You judge a woman
by impressions you think you've made.
Ask and she gives,
take without asking,

beat on her and she'll obey,
throw her name up and down the streets
like some loose whistle—
knowing her neighbors will talk.
Her friends will chew her name.
Her family's blood will run loose
like a broken creek.
And when you're gone,
a woman is left
healing her wounds alone.

But we so-called men,
we so-called brothers
wonder why it's so hard
to love *our* women
when we're about loving them
the way america
loves us.

ISN'T IT FUNNY?

I don't want to hear you beg.
I'm sick of beggars.
If you a man
take what you want from me
or what you can.
Even if you have me
like some woman across town
you think you love.

Look at me
standing here with my dick
as straight as yours.
What do you think this is?
The weather cock on a rooftop?

We sneak all over town
like two damn thieves,
whiskey on our breath,
no street lights on the backroads,
just the stars above us
as ordinary as they should be.

We always have to work it out,
walk it through, talk it over,
drink and smoke our way into sodomy.
I could take you in my room
but you're afraid the landlady
will recognize you.
I feel thankful I don't love you.
I won't have to suffer you later on.

But for now I say
Johnnie Walker,
have you had enough, Johnnie Walker?
Do-I-look-like-a-woman-now?
Against the fogged car glass
do I look like your cross-town lover?
Do I look like Shirley?

When you reach to kiss her lips
they're thick like mine.
Her hair is cut close too,
like mine—
isn't it?

FAMILY JEWELS

for Washington, D.C.

I live in a town
where pretense and bone structure
prevail as credentials
of status and beauty.
A town bewitched
by mirrors, horoscopes,
and corruption.

I intrude on this nightmare.
Arm outstretched from curbside.
I'm not pointing to Zimbabwe.
I want a cab
to take me to Southeast
so I can visit my mother.

I'm not ashamed to cross
the bridge that takes me there.

No matter where I live
or what I wear
the cabs speed by.
Or they suddenly brake
a few feet away
spewing fumes in my face
to serve a fair-skinned fare.

I live in a town
where everyone is afraid
of the dark.
I stand my ground unarmed
facing a mounting disrespect,
a diminishing patience,
a need for defense.

In passing headlights
I appear to be a criminal.
I'm a weird-looking muthafucka.
Shaggy green hair sprouts all over me.
My shoulders hunch and bulge. I growl
as blood drips from my glinting fangs.

My mother's flowers are wilting
while I wait.
Our dinner
is cold by now.

I live in a town
where pretense and structure
are devices of cruelty.
A town bewitched
by mirrors, horoscopes,
and blood.

ESSEX HEMPHILL   **191**

Daryl Hine

Daryl Hine (born 1936 in British Columbia) was educated at McGill and the University of Chicago. Between undergraduate and graduate work, he lived in London, Paris, and New York. He has also taught at the University of Chicago, the University of Illinois, and Northwestern University. Editor of *Poetry* magazine from 1958 to 1968, Hine was named a MacArthur Fellow in 1986. He lives with his companion of twenty-one years, a philosopher. Among the most recent of his more than fifteen books are *Selected Poems* (1981), *Theocritus: Idylls and Epigrams* (1982), and *Academic Festival Overtures* (1985), a book-length verse narrative dealing with his first year in junior high school in 1949. The selection here is taken from that book, and the photograph shows him at age thirteen in that year.

FROM "MARCH,"
IN ACADEMIC FESTIVAL OVERTURES

Once when I was coming from art class they surprised me
    On Zulu Island where there was no place to hide.
Although I could see their bicycles in the offing,
    I would not run away, vainly detained by pride,
Or greeting as inevitable this encounter—
    Besides, I could not run as fast as they could ride.
Soon enough they surrounded me, some half-a-dozen
    Youths my senior, as well as my superiors
In strength and a certain sort of sophistication,
    Impatient to settle imaginary scores.
"Whaddya got there?" I handed over my sketchbook
    (Without much expectation of getting it back)
To him I had identified as the leader,
    Assuming there must be one in every pack,
A boy of arresting Nordic, no, Arctic beauty,
    With icy eyes and hair so blonde that it looked white,
(Which makes him sound too like a sinister albino,
    Which, despite his extreme pallour, he was not quite),

Balanced astride his bicycle among his cohorts,
    Apparently poised for either attack or flight.
"What do you want?" I asked. Amid sarcastic laughter
    The young ring-leader superciliously smiled.
I recognized the Nazi gangster in the Viking
    And the unpredictable bully in the child.
Riffling quickly through the smudged and disfigured pages
    My precocious critic, who had a German name,
Paused at the portrait of a mysterious woman,
    Draped. "What's the matter? Can't you draw a naked dame?"
The others crowding to ogle over his shoulder
    In their disappointment found plenty to deride
In my drawing, some making indecent suggestions
    Regarding the probable upshot had I tried.
The first time I confronted sexual fascism,
    Tongue-tied I was saved by not knowing what to say.
My tormentors assumed I shared their predilections,
    And I could not have disabused them anyway.
Hitler's victims who wore the lavender triangle
    Are dishonoured by silence even to this day.

Oppressed by a sneaking sense of a certain weakness
    For my captors which complicated my distress,
I masked with a facade of contemptuous silence
    Sentiments it would be fatal for them to guess.
Allegations of complicity in the victim,
    Which are oftener than not monstrously unjust,
Gain a faint plausibility when the oppressor
    Is the surreptitious object of guilty lust.
Not only willing participants in those brutal
    But harmless exercises known as S & M,
But anyone attacked by adolescent bullies
    Entertains latent ambivalence towards them.
Ironically the hooligans who inspected
    My blameless notebooks hopefully for something raw
Might have provided the imaginary models
    I was too inhibited and inept to draw.
Their very arrogant, animalistic poses
    Had all the unconscious grace of a Grecian frieze,
So that, as they bestrode their metal steeds, I envied
    The unfeeling machinery between their knees.
Their straightforward prurience presently grew weary
    Of my water-colours, preferring other sport,

And, after playing half-hearted catch with my sketchbook,
    Off they rode triumphant: their triumph would be short.
In half a mile I retrieved my discarded art work.
    But could not so quickly retrieve myself. Escaped
Physically unhurt, merely humiliated,
    I had the queer sensation of having been raped
Gregariously, without putting up a struggle.
    I made my way home in a post-traumatic trance,
Bedevilled by regret and resentment, as shaken
    And naked as if they had taken off my pants.

Imagine my discomfiture a few weeks later
    Meeting one of the gang at an informal dance.
I had been invited to a small birthday party
    By a girl I had known ever since the first grade;
Although far from Hallowe'en, like all teenage socials
    It was something of a selfconscious masquerade,
Exactly the same kind of stuffy get-together
    As those I remember from my earliest years,
Such as the nursery tea I had once disrupted
    Attempting to get the attention of my peers,
As rocking on a hobbyhorse I babbled
    Of the primal scene witnessed in a field of flax
Where an older boy and his girl had demonstrated
    To my astonished delight the beast with two backs.
But the other four-year-olds were not interested,
    My revelations fell on indifferent ears
As if I preached to the incomprehending heathen.
    Frustrated and unheeded, I burst into tears.
Present company, although presumably better
    Informed, appeared at first glance improbably prim.
Our hostess did her best to dispell this impression
    With low music and lights irreligiously dim.
Too old for games (we thought), and too shy for flirtation,
    Too dumb for conversation, and too young to drink,
We sat about like strangers in a railway station—
    As easily break the ice in a skating rink!
The greedy gravitated to a groaning sideboard
    Laden with the makings of a rather late lunch:
Hot dogs, cold slaw, potato chips, potato salad
    As well as a tasteless kind of Temperance Punch.
The background music, anodyne and sentimental,
    On the eve of the eruption of rock and roll,

    DARYL HINE

Was diversified by an old, upright piano
    Pounding out hits like "In the Mood," and "Heart and Soul,"
To which some of the more brazen girls began dancing
    With one another, selfconsciously, two by two,
While their intended partners gazed on from the sidelines,
    Uneasily aware they should be dancing too.
In similar but more coercive circumstances
    At school the sexes tended to stay separate,
Most boys looking on the young female of their species
    As the male praying mantis might look on his mate.

But what was he doing here with these well-dressed children?
    Clad in turtleneck sweater and corduroy pants,
The roughneck whom I recognized from Zulu Island,
    Stepped up and without preamble asked me to dance.
Astounded, I accepted. It seemed not to matter
    That I did not really know how: neither did he,
So our exaggeratedly clumsy performance
    Was applauded as a plausible parody.
Till I realized with a thrill of recognition
    The point of this hitherto footling exercise:
If dancing with girls had always felt like a duty,
    Dancing with my own sex was a pleasant surprise.
Being older, more masculine-looking and bigger,
    My impetuous partner masterfully led,
While servile but inefficient I tried to follow,
    Two beats behind the music or two steps ahead.
Galvanized by our unconventional example,
    The embarrassed waxworks began to move about.
Soon the living-room was filled with gyrating couples.
    My vis-a-vis whispered, "Want to sit this one out?"
Our inauspicious first encounter unforgotten
    But unmentioned, we shyly confided first names—
His was Dick—and biographical information.
    To this day I do not quite understand his aims.
He had come honestly by his fisherman's jersey
    Working weekends on the family fishing boat,
An old trawler which he offered to show me over
    And described as "the leakiest bugger afloat."
His language, like his looks and his dress and his manners,
    Vigorous, virile, and disconcertingly coarse,
However out of place in such polite surroundings,
    Had a crude but undeniably telling force.

DARYL HINE   **195**

At the same time he was unexpectedly gentle
　　As he threw his arms about my shoulders and pressed
Me unprepared, not unflattered but flabbergasted,
　　Feebly protesting against his broad, woolly chest.
"Pretend," he whispered in my tingling ear, "We're necking,"
　　(A decade later he might have said, "making out.")
A joke conceived in the same satyrical spirit
　　As his first invitation to the dance, no doubt.
As he embraced me with exaggerated ardour
　　I exaggerated my struggles to resist,
But amid the nervous, apotropaic laughter
　　Felt for the first time what it was to be kissed,
Even facetiously in public, by a stranger,
　　Squarely or rather orotundly on the lips,
Mortified by my rapidity of reaction
　　To many of the tongue's inarticulate slips;
No less puzzled in retrospect by the reception
　　Of our misconduct by innocent girls and boys
Who saluted our embrace with vocal amusement,
　　So naughtiness was made innocuous by noise.
It seemed that one could get away almost with murder
　　If the crime were committed *coram publico,*
For we were regarded not so much as performing
　　An unnatural act as putting on a show,
In ostensible and ostentatious derision
　　Of the mores of more conventional romance.
This time our audience, abjuring imitation,
　　Continued childishly to chat and snack and dance.
Discovering the dilemma of the performer
　　Who overidentifies with his or her part,
My performance, which owed everything to nature,
　　I tried to attribute, transparently, to art.
I had never experienced, nor yet imagined,
　　Such, in the phrase from *Fidelio,* nameless joy.
The absurd antics, on the screen, of men and women,
　　Acquiring undreamt-of dimensions with a boy—
Not exactly undreamt-of: had I not awakened
　　Often from the vague impression of an embrace
With the object of my long-standing admiration
　　Whom fantasy inserted in a stranger's place,
And whose absence, inexplicable as the presence
　　At a private party of this likeable lout,
Prevented me perhaps from putting into practice

Perversities I now was finding out about?
The idea of doing such things with Don Wisdom
    Intensified my hypothetical disgust
At squandering on an indifferent acquaintance
    The treasures of love found in the junk shop of lust.
In addition to the venereal excitement
    Mere proximity was sufficient to provoke,
Suffused by a novel sensation of connivance
    As a participant in the amorous joke
Which like all such jokes became less and less amusing
    With every delicious moment it was prolonged,
I reluctantly forsook our ludicrous posture
    And the arms in which I made believe I belonged.
The whole business lasted no more than a few minutes.
    We stopped our fooling as soon as the laughter died.
The episode seemed immediately forgotten
    But for my agitation, which was hard to hide.
For the rest of the evening we kept our distance
    Till it was time to go, when gruffly he proposed
Seeing me home: although in different directions,
    Our routes lay closer together than I supposed.
Soon, as if to short-circuit our mutual shyness,
    He unexpectedly reached out and grabbed my hand,
Scratching my palm—this was "the electrician's handshake"
    Which, while shocked, I pretended not to understand.

At his insistence we took the sinister short-cut
    Through the ill-illumined labyrinth of the park,
Which I had been expressly forbidden to enter,
    For mysterious reasons, ever after dark.
As an omnivorous reader, I had devoured the
    Gothic extravagances of popular lore:
The overly familiar face outside the window—
    Where have you seen it, or something like it, before?
Insinuating fingers fumbling for admittance,
    Too insistent and sympathetic to ignore?
These bloodthirsty noctambulists' contagious passion
    Suggests another equivocal metaphor.
As victims multiply as rapidly as crosses
    Each inevitably becomes a predator.
The scenario owed to hoary superstition
    Less than to Victorian prejudice and art.

A rival in love, once, of Oscar Wilde, Bram Stoker
    Described Dracula as a dandified up-start.
The undead, the unconventional, the unmarried
    In respectable society have no part;
And those who retire at sunrise obscenely sated
    With every encounter risk a stake through the heart.

Holding hands, as innocuous and comforting as
    Holding someone or being held in someone's arms,
Gave me perhaps unrealistic reassurance
    Of protection from all supernatural harms.
That my protector was himself perfectly harmless
    In spite of or because of his frightening size,
His uncouth yet diffident and courteous courtship
    Led me at once hopeful and helpless to surmise.
Whistling in the dark, a figurative expression
    For a cheerful pretense that effectively cheers,
Might have heartened me, except that I could not whistle
    Any more than I could have quite defined my fears.
At that age the slightest difference in our ages
    Gapped larger than it was ever to do again:
From the perspective of fourteen, overgrown children
    Of fifteen and sixteen already looked like men.
Though only chronologically my senior
    By a year or two, he seemed of another sphere,
Like an inhabitant of an alien planet—
    But what, I kept wondering, was he doing here?
He saw me home unenlightened and unmolested,
    Whatever that means: it is one transitive verb
That loses a lot of its menace in translation:
    In Spanish, No Molestar means, Do Not Disturb.
Bidding me goodnight at the door to my apartment
    He asked if he could see me again the next day.
The prospect of tomorrow filled me with misgiving,
    But I nodded my acquiescence anyway.
"O.K." he mumbled, "I'll pick you up at eleven
    And show you over my old man's effing boat."
I figured that F stood for fishing, but could not fathom
    The implications of his promissory note.
I went to bed in a fog of diffuse excitement
    Which took solidity in an erotic dream,
A naked masquerade of stationary leap-frog
    And similar variations of the same theme.

DARYL HINE

The next morning, however, I was dressed and ready
    For this mystery excursion long before nine.
My father, whom I had told of the invitation,
    To my astonishment forbade me to decline:
"Go ahead. Do you good to get out a little.
    Teach you a thing or two to see over this ship."
Encouraging me to embark on fresh friendship,
    "Maybe he'll ask you along on a fishing trip."
How could my father, with his upright and old-fashioned,
    Even narrow-minded notions of discipline,
Urge a seemingly innocuous course of action
    That might result in what he must regard as sin?
Of course I had not told him the unexpurgated
    Story—what normal boy in my position would?
Nor could, nor can, I understand my hesitation,
    For what did I stand to gain as a goody-good?

While waiting I set up my easel in the bedroom,
    The only spot where I could hope to be alone.
In our crowded, compulsively tidy apartment
    There was no little corner I could call my own.
Presently my father went out to do the shopping
    Leaving me alone, which was quite all right with me;
Only those who have lived for some time in close quarters
    Know the precarious pleasure of privacy.
I was working on a murky, ambitious canvas
    Symbolic of something, but what I did not know,
Which combined the technical skill of Grandma Moses
    With the flamboyant fantasy of Gustave Moreau.
For once hereabouts a splendidly sunny morning
    Infiltrated the unlovely Venetian blinds
As I daubed away at my dismal composition,
    Distinctly—maybe indistinctly—of two minds.
What apprehension caused my ambivalent fidgets?
    From what did I hope for a last-minute reprieve?
For all my recent, and relative, liberation,
    I remained nonetheless relatively naive,
Ignorant of the names, let alone the descriptions,
    Of the overtures I was apprehensive of,
The advances I had retreated from already,
    Much more so the mechanics of making love.
How could anyone make that which is uncreated,
    Engendered by an exceptional act of grace?

Perversely again I prayed for the unexpected
        To arrive in my expected visitor's place,
Though I suspect my transcendental love of Wisdom
        Merely meant I admired the beauty of his face,
Which was taking shape, independent of volition
        Or effort on the canvas now before my eyes,
The first likeness I had achieved, an apparition
        And, like most apparitions, a complete surprise.
When interrupted by the irrelevant doorbell
        I found I had forgotten all about my date:
There is nothing like an absorbing occupation
        While one is waiting to make one forget to wait.
But Dick was leaning impatiently on the buzzer
        With an exuberance I hated to deflate.
As I opened the door he seemed to fill the doorway
        With his expansive presence and expanded chest,
Looking rather less prepossessing than last evening,
        Though as far as I could tell identically dressed.
He demanded with a broad leer if I were ready,
        Though it must have been obvious that I was not;
I lied: I had forgotten, besides, I was busy . . .
        He followed me inside uninvited. "With what?"
Recognizing his rival in the picture
        By its inadvertent verisimilitude,
He remarked, "Not bad, but you need a better model.
        How would you like me to pose for you—in the nude?"
It was, in retrospect, a kind of ultimatum,
        But prudence and prudery together forbade
Taking any notice of his immodest offer,
        So to my covert regret he stayed fully clad.
Again, not for the last time, I found myself playing
        The thankless part of the unhappy hypocrite,
And when I postponed our nautical expedition
        Sine die, Dick commented succinctly, "Shit!"
Dishonestly I pled parental disapproval,
        Which he (though God the Father has no Christian name)
On learning my surname acquiesced in, believing
        His principal and not my principles to blame.
That I should repent of this desperate, defensive
        Deception in the emptiness of time much less
Than of my perverse and obstinate refusal
        I could not then know, or did I already guess?
Such a lie must bring immediate retribution,

DARYL HINE

Whether or not I realized it at the time.
With a shrug Dick took his disappointed departure,
     So the punishment coincided with the crime.
He stalked out of my life for good or ill forever,
     As unpredictably as he had stumbled in,
If not quite naked with stocking feet in my chamber
     In the words of Wyatt, yet behovely as sin.

When he returned Fraser was furious to find me
     Still painting, and upbraided me at unfair length
For my lack of enterprise. In extenuation,
     I might have pled mortal frailty or moral strength,
Uncomfortably aware that I had been tempted
     Once again and, because unscathed by Cupid's skill,
Had again escaped. With chagrin I contemplated
     The trumpery, temporary triumph of will.
Had I not in my short-sighted thoughtlessness chosen
     Over the nonsense of life the essence of art?
As if a daubed canvas were any consolation
     For an unbroken hymen or a broken heart!
So, I was moved by that moving picture, The Heiress,
     And its prosy predecessor, Washington Square
Whose celibate, verbose, and expatriate author
     Had made the same choice, unhappily unaware
Of all of the future miracles of revision
     That would be inspired by this present despair.
From time to time and always at a certain distance
     I saw Dick again, often as not with his gang
On their bicycles, and we passed without a greeting
     But never, on my part at least, without a pang.

Richard Howard

Richard Howard (born 1929 in Cleveland, Ohio) is the author of many books of poetry, including *Fellow Feelings* (1976), *Misgivings* (1979), and *Lining Up* (1983). *Untitled Subjects* (1969) won the Pulitzer Prize. Howard is also the author of *Alone with America*, a major critical study of forty-one contemporary American poets, and a distinguished translator from the French, having published over 150 works, including books by Gide, Camus, DeGaulle, and Barthes. His complete *Les Fleurs du Mal* of Baudelaire received the 1983 American Book Award in translation.

AGAIN FOR HEPHAISTOS, THE LAST TIME

OCTOBER 1, 1973

> *. . . translate for me till I*
> *accomplish my corpse at last.*
> W. H. AUDEN

What do we share with the past?
Assurance we are unique,
even in shipwreck. The dead
take away the world they made
certain was theirs—they die
knowing we never can have it.

As each of *us* knows, for even
a nap is enough to confirm
suspicions that when we are not
on the scene, nothing else is.
Call it the comfort of dying:
you *can* take it all with you.

"The ship is sinking": Cocteau managed to stage his whisper
while a camera was "well trained" (according to Stravinsky)
on the televised deathbed in Paris some dozen years ago;

his sparrow had fallen one day before this master forger
(who was hardly your *miglior fabbro*, although you had translated
his tangle of true and false Ginifers into your own Tintagel)—

finding Piaf had "gone on," as she always did, ahead
of time and tonsillitis, how could *he* help finding, too,
the vessel on the rocks, the wreck within easy reach?

Predeceased, your gaudy predecessor in death gave up
the ship—high season for sinking: Harlequin Jean, escorted
or just flanked by MacNeice and Roethke, alien psychopomps.

Yours though were quite as unlikely, every bit as outlandish.
This weekend, waves of applause (prerogative of popes!)
broke in the wake of a coffin leaving Santa Maria

sopra Minerva—Magnani, with Pablo Neruda your peer
on Sunday's appalling front page, though scarcely your pal:
Verga you loved, but had you stayed up late enough to see

"Mamma Roma" in his *Lupa*? Even heard of her? Like most
performers—like Piaf—she was, I suspect, as absent
from your now immortal reckonings as Rod McKuen et al.

You were not very fond of volcanoes—in verse or voice either,
and to violent Anna preferred a predictable Donna Elvira
who could always repeat her crises on key, on cue, encore!

Cocteau, you conceded, though stagy, had the *lacrimae rerum* note,
but did *you*? The *Times*, this morning, declared you had failed to make,
or even make your way inside, "a world of emotion."

I wonder. Given your case, or given at last your encasement,
who knows? Only the poems, and to me at least they speak volumes:
your death makes a leap-day this fall, this autumn you would say.

But my *personal* knowledge is odd, my evidence suspect even:
on a club-car up to Cambridge, two freshmen scribbled a note—
"Are you Carl Sandburg?" "You've ruined," you wrote back,
    "mother's day."

Was that emotion? Was this—the time backstage at the Y
when impatient to read to the rustling thousands out front, you asked
(possessing no small talk—and with you I possessed no large)

why it was I no longer endured a difficult mutual friend.
"Because he calls everyone *else* either a kike or a cocksucker,
and since, Wystan, both he and I are . . . well, both of them . . ."

"My *dear*," you broke in, and I think you were genuinely excited,
"I never knew you were Jewish!" No, not a world of emotion—
say, for the time being, as you said, the emotion of a world.

> Only those poets can leave us
> whom we have never possessed.
> What did you leave me? The unsaid,
> mourning, hangs around me,
> desperate, not catastrophic,
> like a dog having a bad time.
>
> The difference, then, between
> your death and all those others
> is this: you did not take
> a certain world away, after
> all. After you, because of you,
> all songs are possible.

Langston Hughes

Langston Hughes (born 1902 in Joplin, Missouri, died 1967) was a major figure
of the intellectual and literary movement called the Harlem Renaissance. At
the age of nineteen, he published "The Negro Speaks of Rivers" in the na-
tionally known magazine *Crisis*, and in 1925 was awarded the First Prize for
Poetry by *Opportunity* magazine. From 1926, when Hughes published *The*

Weary Blues, his first book of poems, until his death, Hughes devoted his energies to writing poetry, short stories, essays, autobiography, song lyrics, humor, and plays. *The Langston Hughes Reader* was published in 1958, and *Selected Poems*, still the largest selection of his work, in 1959. Additional poems are available in *The Panther and the Lash: Poems of Our Times* (1967). Hughes's influence was enormous during his lifetime, and his work continues to inspire many writers to this day.

CAFÉ: 3 A.M.

Detectives from the vice squad
with weary sadistic eyes
spotting fairies.
        Degenerates,
        some folks say.

        But God, Nature,
        or somebody
        made them that way.

Police lady or Lesbian
over there?
        Where?

HARLEM

What happens to a dream deferred?

Does it dry up
like a raisin in the sun?
Or fester like a sore—
And then run?
Does it stink like rotten meat?
Or crust and sugar over—
like a syrupy sweet?

Maybe it just sags
like a heavy load.

Or does it explode?

TODAY

This is earthquake
Weather!
Honor and Hunger
Walk lean
Together.

STARS

O, sweep of stars over Harlem streets,
O, little breath of oblivion that is night.
  A city building
  To a mother's song.
  A city dreaming
  To a lullaby.
Reach up your hand, dark boy, and take a star.
Out of the little breath of oblivion
  That is night,
  Take just
  One star.

Will Inman

Will Inman, born 1923, Wilmington, North Carolina. Duke University, A.B., 1943. Worked in shipyard, tollgate, trade union, political party, meat and fish markets. Lived in Lower East Side New York 1956–1967. Poet-in-Residence, The American University, 1967. Taught English at American University and at Montgomery College (Maryland) for several years, then moved to Arizona 1973. Worked nine years with retarded adults in Tucson. Through

Pima College, taught at Rincon Branch of Arizona State Prisons. Retired, still writing strongly, 1986. Latest books: *A Way Through for the Damned* (Jelm Mtn. Press, 1983), *A Trek of Waking* (Landlocked Press, 1985), and *Brother Word* (Folio Productions, 1986). Currently leading a writing workshop with homeless men at the Tucson Shelter.

NO. 106 FROM *108 TALES OF A PO 'BUCKRA*

the dark brother touches me
with my own wanting:
I am all over
risen with his fingertips.

I ask him if he loves me:
he looks and says me nothing.
I frown . . . I command him to tell me
he loves me.
Mildly, as one looks at a child,
he looks at me
and says nothing.

Ten years pass.
He is married now, his wife
has returned him to himself
with a girlchild
and a boychild.

It is Thanksgiving Day: we
have shared dinner.

We ride in his car
side by side.
I have asked him nothing, but
quietly he affirms me:
"I told my wife
that, besides marriage
and the mystery of children,
I have one friend."

('*Buckra* is an American corruption of an African word, "Mbakara," meaning "boss man." A Po 'Buckra is a poor white.)

WILL INMAN   207

June Jordan

Poet, essayist, and political activist, June Jordan (born 1936, Harlem, U.S.A.) is also a playwright and professor of English at the State University of New York at Stony Brook. Recipient of numerous awards, internationally acclaimed, she is the author of sixteen books to date, including *Things That I Do in the Dark* (Beacon Press, 1980), *Civil Wars* (Beacon, 1980), *Passion* (Beacon, 1980), *On Call* (South End Press, 1985), and *Living Room* (Thunder's Mouth Press, 1985). Her poetry and prose have been published in English, Spanish, Arabic, Swedish, French, and Japanese.

POEM ABOUT MY RIGHTS

Even tonight and I need to take a walk and clear
my head about this poem about why I can't
go out without changing my clothes my shoes
my body posture my gender identity my age
my status as a woman alone in the evening/
alone on the streets/alone not being the point/
the point being that I can't do what I want
to do with my own body because I am the wrong
sex the wrong age the wrong skin and
suppose it was not here in the city but down on the beach/
or far into the woods and I wanted to go
there by myself thinking about God/or thinking
about children or thinking about the world/all of it
disclosed by the stars and the silence:
I could not go and I could not think and I could not
stay there
alone
as I need to be
alone because I can't do what I want to do with my own
body and
who in the hell set things up

like this
and in France they say if the guy penetrates
but does not ejaculate then he did not rape me
and if after stabbing him if after screams if
after begging the bastard and if even after smashing
a hammer to his head if even after that if he
and his buddies fuck me after that
then I consented and there was
no rape because finally you understand finally
they fucked me over because I was wrong I was
wrong again to be me being me where I was/wrong
to be who I am
which is exactly like South Africa
penetrating into Namibia penetrating into
Angola and does that mean I mean how do you know if
Pretoria ejaculates what will the evidence look like the
proof of the monster jackboot ejaculation on Blackland
and if
after Namibia and if after Angola and if after Zimbabwe
and if after all of my kinsmen and women resist even to
self-immolation of the villages and if after that
we lose nevertheless what will the big boys say will they
claim my consent:
Do You Follow Me: We are the wrong people of
the wrong skin on the wrong continent and what
in the hell is everybody being reasonable about
and according to the *Times* this week
back in 1966 the C.I.A. decided that they had this problem
and the problem was a man named Nkrumah so they
killed him and before that it was Patrice Lumumba
and before that it was my father on the campus
of my Ivy League school and my father afraid
to walk into the cafeteria because he said he
was wrong the wrong age the wrong skin the wrong
gender identity and he was paying my tuition and
before that
it was my father saying I was wrong saying that
I should have been a boy because he wanted one/a
boy and that I should have been lighter skinned and
that I should have had straighter hair and that
I should not be so boy crazy but instead I should
just be one/a boy and before that
it was my mother pleading plastic surgery for
my nose and braces for my teeth and telling me

to let the books loose to let them loose in other
words
I am very familiar with the problems of the C.I.A.
and the problems of South Africa and the problems
of Exxon Corporation and the problems of white
America in general and the problems of the teachers
and the preachers and the F.B.I. and the social
workers and my particular Mom and Dad/I am very
familiar with the problems because the problems
turn out to be
me
I am the history of rape
I am the history of the rejection of who I am
I am the history of the terrorized incarceration of
my self
I am the history of battery assault and limitless
armies against whatever I want to do with my mind
and my body and my soul and
whether it's about walking out at night
or whether it's about the love that I feel or
whether it's about the sanctity of my vagina or
the sanctity of my national boundaries
or the sanctity of my leaders or the sanctity
of each and every desire
that I know from my personal and idiosyncratic
and indisputably single and singular heart
I have been raped
be-
cause I have been wrong the wrong sex the wrong age
the wrong skin the wrong nose the wrong hair the
wrong need the wrong dream the wrong geographic
the wrong sartorial I
I have been the meaning of rape
I have been the problem everyone seeks to
eliminate by forced
penetration with or without the evidence of slime and/
but let this be unmistakable this poem
is not consent I do not consent
to my mother to my father to the teachers to
the F.B.I. to South Africa to Bedford-Stuy
to Park Avenue to American Airlines to the hardon
idlers on the corners to the sneaky creeps in
cars

I am not wrong: Wrong is not my name
My name is my own my own my own
and I can't tell you who the hell set things up like this
but I can tell you that from now on my resistance
my simple and daily and nightly self-determination
may very well cost you your life

UNTITLED

the snow
nearly as soft
as the sleeping nipple
of your left breast

Maurice Kenny

Maurice Kenny, Mohawk, poet-in-residence N.C.C.C., was born in northern New York in 1929. He is the author of two plays, *Buddies* and *Forked Tongues*, and editor of a number of anthologies, including *From the Belly of the Shark*, *A Rainbow of Poetry*, *Cycle Poems*, and *Wounds Beneath the Flesh*. Among recent collections of his own poems are *Dancing Back Strong the Nation* (revised edition, 1981), *The Mama Poems*, which received the American Book Award in 1984, and *Is Summer This Bear* (1985). In 1987, Kenny was Visiting Professor at the University of Oklahoma.

WINKTE*

And in their holiness made power
For the people of the Cheyenne Nation.
There was space for us in the village.

* Sioux word for male homosexual.

The Crow and Ponca offered deerskin
When the decision to avoid the warpath was made,
And we were accepted into the fur robes
Of a young warrior, and lay by his flesh
And knew his mouth and warm groin:
Or we married (a second wife) to the chief.
And if we fulfilled our duties, he smiled
And gave us his grandchildren to care for.

We were special to the Sioux, Cheyenne, Ponca
And the Crow who valued our worth and did not spit
Names at our lifted skirts nor kicked our nakedness.
We had power with the people!

And if we cared to carry the lance, or dance
Over enemy scalps and take buffalo
Then that, too, was good for the Nation,
And contrary to our stand we walked backwards.

Irena Klepfisz

Irena Klepfisz (born 1941, Warsaw, Poland) is the author of *Keeper of Accounts* (Sinister Wisdom Books, 1983) and *Different Enclosures: The Poetry and Prose of Irena Klepfisz* (Onlywomen Press, 1985), and the co-editor of *The Tribe of Dina: A Jewish Women's Anthology* (Sinister Wisdom Books, 1986). An activist in the Jewish and lesbian/feminist communities, she has lectured, written, and led workshops on feminism, office work and class, homophobia, Jewish identity, Yiddish culture, anti-Semitism, and the Middle East. A Ph.D. in English literature (University of Chicago, 1970), she is currently teaching creative writing and Women's Studies at Vermont College and translating Yiddish women writers.

DEATH CAMP

when they took us   to the shower   i saw
the rebbitzin   her sagging breasts   sparse
pubic hairs   i knew   and remembered
the old rebbe   and turned   my eyes away
i could still hear   her advice   a woman
with a husband   a scholar

when they turned   on the gas   i smelled
it   first   coming at me   pressed myself
hard to the wall   crying   rebbitzin   rebbitzin
I am here with you   and the advice you gave me
i screamed   into the wall   as the blood burst from
my lungs   cracking   her nails in women's flesh   i watched
her capsize   beneath me   my blood in her mouth   i screamed

when they dragged my body   into the oven   i burned
slowly at first   i could smell my own flesh   and could
hear   them grunt   with the weight of the rebbitzin
and they flung   her on top   of me   and i could smell
her hair burning   against my stomach

when i pressed through   the chimney
it was sunny   and clear   my smoke
was distinct   i rose quiet   left her
beneath

FROM THE MONKEY HOUSE AND OTHER CAGES

MONKEY II

The voices are those of female monkeys born and raised in a zoo.

1

to state each horror
would be redundant.   the objects
themselves suffice: a broken comb
an umbrella handle   a piece of blue
plastic   chipped pocket mirror.

the face is unfriendly.
i try to outstare it   but
it persists   moving

spastically   the eyes
twitching   open   shut
nose quivering   wrinkled fingers
picking at the ears.   i do not know

this stranger.

2

i have heard of tortures
yet remain
strangely safe.

but at night
i am torn by my own
dreams   see myself live
the grossest indignities   probes

and unable to rip myself from my flesh
i remain silent   not
uttering sound   nor moan   not
bothering to feel pain.

waking   in early light
alone   untouched
i cry over my safety.

3

when they first come
they screech with wildness
flinging themselves against the wall
and then against the bars.

some sit and cry for days
some   never recover and
die.
they are familiar
yet crap uncontrollably   plead
shiver and rock.   i refuse

to have anything to do with them
till they learn to behave.

4

at her arrival   she was
stunned and bruised.   she
folded up   refusing to eat

her mouth grim.   i staked
out my territory   recognizing
her fierceness   her strength.

but she weakened   grew sick
was removed without resistance
returned three days later
shaved patches on her arms.

later she told me: we create
the responses around us.

5

i remember the grasp of her claws
the vicious bite   the scar
still on my leg.   she was crazed

jabbering   then attacking
again.   and the sun seemed to fall away
into coldness   as i pressed myself
against the corner   the hardened sand
under my nails.   i began to gnaw
through concrete   my face raw.

they took her away
and when she came back
she did not look at me.

6

scatter yourself
i told her   moving
myself into the left

corner   where i sat
observing the movement
of her head.

          she nodded
seemed to sleep
then stood up   pointing
outside.   the leaves were
red.   it was a falling time
noisy   dry twigs cracking
off nearby trees.   i felt

content   watching myself
while she pointed   the leaves
red.

                    7

          and finally
she said   this is enough
and began to bang her head
against the wall   one thud

after another thud   she batted
herself beginning to bleed
throwing herself and falling.

they came   and tried to seize
her   while the sun vanished
and the trees   moved slowly

and everyone   so still
afraid to breathe: the moon
all fresh   and the birds
small balls of feathers.

i puked as they dragged her out:
tufts of fur on the stone floor.

                    8

when she died   i mourned
a silent mourning.
          and

216

the others asked
asked   asked
and poked at me.

there had been much between us
in gesture.   mostly i remember
her yellowed teeth   her attempt
at tameness.

9

there had been no sound:
just the motion of   our hands
our lips sucked in
toes pointed   outward.
it had been enough.

dizzy
with messages   i would lie
down   dream of different
enclosures.

Bill Kushner

Bill Kushner (born 1931 in New York City) is the author of two plays, *Magic Time* (1964) and *A Night for Ghosts* (1966), and two books of poems, *Night Fishing* (Midnight Sun, 1976) and *Head* (United Artists Books, New York, 1986). He says: "Writing as a way of calling out to one self in the dark. Writing as finding you there, hello. Who, me? Yes, writing telling who you me of this strange gay life: what's it like to be us, anyway, these days, those nights? Writing as a way to life! I speak with you, dear dead gay poets, speak to me! Writing as believing that words really do say something that mean something. On his deathbed my silent distant sometimes downright hostile father cried Hold me! to me! & so only 2 words once forever said helped heart's ease: Hold me!"

UP

This? it's my Lounge Lizard look, very
popular in the 20's when I was but a thought
whether Flying Down to Rio or crossing Mulberry
I am I suppose what I was always meant to be
a slight eccentric with a bit of a tic
a sort of a gay Mary Poppins so thank you dear
America you've got taste you've got style
& you know a good drag queen when you see one
she sure can talk & she thanks everybody & I'm
so happy that 2000 years ago sweet Jesus died
for me, including my girlfriend Judy up there
in Canada & like to thank my mother & my father
for putting up with my noise all these many years I
love & thank you all for the best performance by a male

2/28/84

Joan Larkin

Joan Larkin was born in Boston in 1939. Her published books of poetry are *Housework* (Out & Out Books, 1975) and *A Long Sound* (Granite Press, 1986). She helped to found Out & Out Books, a women's independent publishing company active from 1975 to 1981, and co-edited the anthologies *Amazon Poetry* (Out & Out, 1975) and *Lesbian Poetry* (Persephone, 1981) with Elly Bulkin. She lives in Brooklyn, has taught at Brooklyn College since 1969, and has taught poetry writing at Sarah Lawrence College, The Writers' Community (New York), and elsewhere. In 1987 she received NEA and New York State Foundation grants for poetry.

RHYME OF MY INHERITANCE

My mother gave me a bitter tongue.
My father gave me a turned back.
My grandmother showed me her burned hands.
My brother showed me a difficult book.
These were their gifts; the rest was talk.

I discovered my body in the dark.
It had a surprise in its little crack.
I started to say what I'd found in the dark,
but my mother gave me a dirty look
and my father turned a key in the lock.

I was left alone with the difficult book
and the stove that burned my grandmother's hands,
and while they muttered behind my back
I learned to read and to make my bread,
to eat my words and lie flat in my bed.

They took me to school where I learned to be cute:
I wore clean jumpers and washed my hands;
I put my hands up to cover my mouth;
I listened to everything everyone said
and kept what I could in my stuffed-up head.

I had weeping eyes and a chest that coughed,
a stomach that hurt, and a mouth that laughed
whether or not I felt good or bad.
I was always promoted to the next grade.
I graduated; I got laid.

I did what girls were supposed to do.
I wore a white dress; I was photographed;
my teeth were perfect, my knees were crossed.
I cleaned up the mess that the baby made.
I hope that my body's price is paid.

I'm giving the gifts back, one by one.
I'm tearing the pages of my past.
I'm turning my back. I'm turning them down.

I'm burning their strict house to the ground.
May I never want bread at their table again.

May I let go of these bitter rhymes;
and may this burial be my last
while I live in my body and learn from my bones
to make some less predictable sound.
Let this coffin of verses inherit my pain.

RAPE

After twenty years I want to call it that, but was it?
I mean
it wasn't all his fault, I mean
wasn't I out there on 8th Street,
wandering around looking for someone to fill the gap where my
        center would have been?
Didn't I circle the same block over & over until he saw me?
Wasn't I crying when he came along & said *Don't do that, cops see*
        me with a white girl crying—
I'm sorry. Didn't I say *I'm sorry,* & didn't I smile?
Didn't I walk with him, dumb, to the Hotel Earle,
didn't I drink with him in his room,
didn't I undress myself in the stare of a yellow bulb?
Didn't I drink—what was it I drank?
Didn't I drink enough to be numb for a long time?
Didn't I drink myself into a blackout?

Was it rape, if when I lay there letting him fuck me I started to feel
sore & exhausted & said *Stop,*
first softly, then screaming
Stop, over & over?
And if he was too drunk to hear me,
or if he heard me but thought, *Girls never mean it when they say stop,*
was that rape? Was it rape if he meant well
or was too drunk to hear me, was it rape
if he kept repeating *Girl, you can fuck*
& not really meaning any harm?

I think I remember that the room was green & black,
the small bulb dangling from a cord,
the bed filthy.

JOAN LARKIN

I don't exactly remember.
I know I had no pleasure, but lay there; I don't think he forced me.
It was just that he wouldn't stop when I asked him to.
He didn't take my money.
It may have been his booze I drank.
It may have been sort of a date.
He wrote his number on half a matchbook & said
Call Joe if you need him—I guess he was Joe.

Did I walk home?
Did I have any money?
Was it me who bought the booze?
Maybe I took a cab.
Was it 2:00 a.m., or safe daylight
when I climbed the five flights,
spent, feeling the tear tracks & pounded cervix,
the booze still coating me, my nerves not yet awake, stripped &
      screaming.

I climbed to my place, five flights,
somehow satisfied,
somehow made real by the pain.

Was it rape, then?

CLIFTON

I loved booze,
and booze and pills I loved more.
I still love them.
I still want them.
My wine, my Dexamil,
my after-dinner tall
tumbler of scotch,
my morning black espresso,
my Valium at work,
and more Valium.
It worked.
The Dexamil let me drink,
the drink kept me from feeling,
the Valium kept my hand from shaking.
The Dexamil let me drink

in the face of my psychiatrist saying,
I think you drink too much—
I think I won't see you if you drink.
In the face of fines,
in the face of swinging at a cop,
in the face of connecting with a two-by-four,
in the face of cops looking down at me in the middle of
    Amsterdam Avenue
in a Brooks Brothers suit, a briefcase,
in the *middle* of Amsterdam Avenue—
Where do you live, sir? We think you should go home.

I drank at Hanratty's for four reasons:
it's near where I live,
they cashed my checks,
they closed at one,
and they took me home.
At home, I would have another
scotch and a pill,
at 5:30 get up,
drink coffee, take a pill—
I had—I have—
a responsible job.
I was always first at my desk
and last to leave.
I never wanted to work.
I wanted someone else to take care of it all.

I don't know why I'm alive today.
I don't believe in God, I'm a strict Freudian.
When I stopped, I thought,
This is unspeakable deprivation.
I whined and cried.
I sat in the back eleven months
pitying myself. Home
from a dinner with board members,
with two glasses of wine, the first in a year—
I opened the half bottle of scotch
a guest had left. It was months under the sink.
Often I'd thought of it. Always,
I knew it was there.
I poured scotch into a tumbler,

JOAN LARKIN

and I couldn't drink it.
I couldn't. I thought, *I can't go through all that again.*

That was ten years ago.
My hair is gray. A doorman
with whom I left a package yesterday
described me to my friend as "distinguished."
Lots of things are the same.
Some things are changed, changing.
I love booze in my dreams.
I drink booze and take pills in my dreams.
I don't ask *Why
do I love alcohol?* Instead,
I have habits strict as the former ones,
meetings, books, service.
The dreams full of booze keep telling me what I am.

Late in my life,
in the numb elegance of this city,
I made a decision—
or the decision
shining in the soft, brutal darkness
took hold of me—
to live.
Often I am peaceful.
I never imagined that.

Michael Lassell

Michael Lassell was born in 1947 in New York City and now lives in Los Angeles. He holds degrees from Colgate University, California Institute of the Arts, and the Yale School of Drama; he works as a writer, editor, and photographer, although he'd rather be a movie star. Lassell's poetry and fiction have appeared in many periodicals, and his book of poems, *Poems for Lost and Un-*

lost Boys, won the Amelia Chapbook Award for 1985. A new collection of poems is forthcoming from Bhakti Books, Beverly Hills.

HOW TO WATCH YOUR BROTHER DIE

When the call comes, be calm.
Say to your wife, "My brother is dying. I have to fly
to California."
Try not to be shocked that he already looks like
a cadaver.
Say to the young man sitting by your brother's side,
"I'm his brother."
Try not to be shocked when the young man says,
"I'm his lover. Thanks for coming."

Listen to the doctor with a steel face on.
Sign the necessary forms.
Tell the doctor you will take care of everything.
Wonder why doctors are so remote.

Watch the lover's eyes as they stare into
your brother's eyes as they stare into
space.
Wonder what they see there.
Remember the time he was jealous and
opened your eyebrow with a sharp stick.
Forgive him out loud
even if he can't understand you.
Realize the scar will be
all that's left of him.

Over coffee in the hospital cafeteria
say to the lover, "You're an extremely good-looking
young man."
Hear him say,
"I never thought I was good enough looking to
deserve your brother."
Watch the tears well up in his eyes. Say,
"I'm sorry. I don't know what it means to be
the lover of another man."
Hear him say,
"It's just like a wife, only the commitment is

MICHAEL LASSELL

deeper because the odds against you are so much
greater."
Say nothing, but
take his hand like a brother's.

Drive to Mexico for unproven drugs that might
help him live longer.
Explain what they are to the border guard.
Fill with rage when he informs you,
"You can't bring those across."
Begin to grow loud.
Feel the lover's hand on your arm,
restraining you. See in the guard's eye
how much a man can hate another man.
Say to the lover, "How can you stand it?"
Hear him say, "You get used to it."
Think of one of your children getting used to
another man's hatred.

Call your wife on the telephone. Tell her,
"He hasn't much time.
I'll be home soon." Before you hang up say,
"How could anyone's commitment be deeper than
a husband and wife?" Hear her say,
"Please, I don't want to know all the details."

When he slips into an irrevocable coma,
hold his lover in your arms while he sobs,
no longer strong. Wonder how much longer
you will be able to be strong.
Feel how it feels to hold a man in your arms
whose arms are used to holding men.
Offer God anything to bring your brother back.
Know you have nothing God could possibly want.
Curse God, but do not
abandon Him.

Stare at the face of the funeral director
when he tells you he will not
embalm the body for fear of
contamination. Let him see in your eyes
how much a man can hate another man.

Stand beside a casket covered in flowers,
white flowers. Say,
"Thank you for coming" to each of several hundred men
who file past in tears, some of them
holding hands. Know that your brother's life
was not what you imagined. Overhear two mourners say,
"I wonder who'll be next."

Arrange to take an early flight home.
His lover will drive you to the airport.
When your flight is announced say,
awkwardly, "If I can do anything, please
let me know." Do not flinch when he says,
"Forgive yourself for not wanting to know him
after he told you. He did."
Stop and let it soak in. Say,
"He forgave me, or he knew himself?"
"Both," the lover will say, not knowing what else
to do. Hold him like a brother while he
kisses you on the cheek. Think that
you haven't been kissed by a man since
your father died. Think,

"This is no moment not to be strong." Fly
first class and drink scotch. Stroke
your split eyebrow with a finger
and think of your brother alive. Smile
at the memory and think
how your children will feel in your arms,
warm and friendly and without challenge.

TIMES SQUARE POEMS

1. DINO

This morning I clipped my fingernails
in case I ran into Dino again.
Dino's a stripper at the
Gaiety Burlesk on Forty-Sixth off
Broadway, the last of six dancers
four times daily and
well worth the wait.

There's only one way to
run into Dino
and it isn't by chance:
pay your six bucks at the door—
five if you've got a coupon from
The Village Voice—then
poke around in the dark with
the other fat fruits until
the lights come up and
decorum
goes down like
the Titanic.

Last night he
brought me off for
twenty-five bucks in
the small room behind the stage
while one finger of my
right hand
wormed into the hole in his
tight little ass.

I carried the smell of him
home with me—
talc, sweat and fear. I mean,
hygiene is one thing, but
I let him linger. I
wasn't about to
wash him off like
he'd never been there.
I owed him more than
the flower beds of a
worn-out youth or
the canned scent
housewives use to
freshen up
their porcelain.

2. THE GOING RATE

The going rate is
forty bucks, but
some of them will

do it for less.
Alberto did it for
thirty because I was
nice.

Tony said he'd go with me
for twenty, but
Tony's got a dollar sign
cut into the hair
at the back of his head, and
Tony is not
Alberto, although
it was sweet of him
to offer.

In the back room the
brown man slips off his
clothes, then
mine. There is no
kissing, of course,
nothing that might
leave a mark on
his skin. He is
more direct than
most people you'll run into
on a Thursday.

I come fast and apologize since
the semen gets on his shoe.
"Part of the work," he says
with an accented grin and
wipes it off, then me.

If you want to
get off with Alberto
bring cash
and believe when he says
"I like you" that he's
never said it before
and won't again
before sunrise.

3. STUD

His name is Jason; he's
Italian and twenty.
Actually, Jason is the name of
whoever is dancing third
because that's what
the sign says out front
(and these boys do have
a following).
He starts his second dance with
a hard-on that
softens in the
shuffle for
attention, but
it's never
lost for long.

Jason has a
lot of admirers.
Also a wife and child in
Puerto Rico.
Between shows—after a
private performance that
leaves him sapped
and sweaty—
he tries to call
San Juan on
the pay phone to see if
they came through the
hurricane.

Of course, the phones
are out, lines
down, signals dead.

He has the eyes of a Virgin and
pecs like the gifts of the Magi:
gold for wealth because he is
king of the roost;
frankincense because he is
the high priest of the
low in heart;

MICHAEL LASSELL   229

myrrh for cunning
because it heals my soul
just to look at him
and to know that
as long as there's money
there's a hairy chest
for my hand
somewhere in the world
and I'll never go
hungry again.

4. HOW TO FIND LOVE IN AN INSTANT

Sit as close to the stage as possible.
Look like you're one of the kind who's buying and
like you've got the wherewithal.
Look into his eyes.
Look into his lap.
Covet him as loud as you can without speaking.
Do not touch. Just worship silently.

Applaud; show
appreciation. At the end of the set
let him approach you in the lounge where
Boys Meet Boys. He will put
one hand on your left tit and one on the
tight bundle of your jeans and
offer a private session for forty bucks.
If you've got it, give it.
Don't dicker.

After you're both naked, he'll
rub his oiled body against yours.
You will be hard and hot and
grateful. He will be soft and bored
but attentive.

You will walk out into the night and no longer be
afraid of Forty-Second Street.
Now you are a part of it
and the locals can tell.
You will smile to have been accepted
and descend the subway stairs

MICHAEL LASSELL

knowing yourself better than ever
and better than ever
thinking yourself just fine.

Audre Lorde

Audre Lorde was born in 1934 in Harlem, New York. She has been called "an indispensable poet" by Adrienne Rich, "for the complexity of her vision, for her moral courage and the catalytic passion of her language . . ." Audre Lorde's third book, *From a Land Where Other People Live* (Broadside Press, 1973), was nominated for a National Book Award. Among her many other books of poetry are *Coal, The Black Unicorn,* and, most recently, *Our Dead Behind Us* (W. W. Norton, 1976, 1978, 1986). Further writing includes *The Cancer Journals,* a collection of original essays (Spinsters Ink, 1980); her autobiographical novel, *Zami: A New Spelling of My Name;* and *Sister Outsider,* essays and speeches (Crossing, 1984).

POWER

The difference between poetry and rhetoric
is being
ready to kill
yourself
instead of your children.

I am trapped on a desert of raw gunshot wounds
and a dead child dragging his shattered black
face off the edge of my sleep
blood from his punctured cheeks and shoulders
is the only liquid for miles and my stomach
churns at the imagined taste while
my mouth splits into dry lips
without loyalty or reason
thirsting for the wetness of his blood

as it sinks into the whiteness
of the desert where I am lost
without imagery or magic
trying to make power out of hatred and destruction
trying to heal my dying son with kisses
only the sun will bleach his bones quicker.

The policeman who shot down a 10-year-old in Queens
stood over the boy with his cop shoes in childish blood
and a voice said "Die you little motherfucker" and
there are tapes to prove that. At his trial
this policeman said in his own defense
"I didn't notice the size or nothing else
only the color." and
there are tapes to prove that, too.

Today that 37-year-old white man with 13 years of police forcing
has been set free
by 11 white men who said they were satisfied
justice had been done
and one black woman who said
"They convinced me" meaning
they had dragged her 4'10" black woman's frame
over the hot coals of four centuries of white male approval
until she let go the first real power she ever had
and lined her own womb with cement
to make a graveyard for our children.

I have not been able to touch the destruction within me.
But unless I learn to use
the difference between poetry and rhetoric
my power too will run corrupt as poisonous mold
or lie limp and useless as an unconnected wire
and one day I will take my teenaged plug
and connect it to the nearest socket
raping an 85-year-old white woman
who is somebody's mother
and as I beat her senseless and set a torch to her bed
a greek chorus will be singing in ¾ time
"Poor thing. She never hurt a soul. What beasts they are."

AUDRE LORDE

LOVE POEM

Speak earth and bless me with what is richest
make sky flow honey out of my hips
rigid as mountains
spread over a valley
carved out by the mouth of rain.

And I knew when I entered her I was
high wind in her forests hollow
fingers whispering sound
honey flowed
from the split cup
impaled on a lance of tongues
on the tips of her breasts on her navel
and my breath
howling into her entrances
through lungs of pain.

Greedy as herring-gulls
or a child
I swing out over the earth
over and over
again.

OUTLINES

I

What hue lies in the slit of anger
ample and pure as night
what color the channel
blood comes through?

A Black woman and a white woman
charter our courses close
in a sea of calculated distance
warned away by reefs of hidden anger
histories rallied against us
the friendly face of cheap alliance.

Jonquils through the Mississippi snow

you entered my vision
with the force of hurled rock
defended by distance and a warning smile
fossil tears   pitched over the heart's wall
for protection
no other women
grown beyond safety
come back to tell us
whispering
past the turned shoulders
of our closest
we were not the first
Black woman white woman
altering course to fit our own journey.

In this treacherous sea
even the act of turning
is almost fatally difficult
coming around full face
into a driving storm
putting an end to running
before the wind.

On a helix of white
the letting of blood
the face of my love
and rage
coiled in my brown arms
an ache in the bone
we cannot alter history
by ignoring it
nor the contradictions
who we are.

II

A Black woman and a white woman
in the open fact of our loving
with not only our enemies' hands
raised against us
means a gradual sacrifice
of all that is simple
dreams

AUDRE LORDE

where you walk the mountain
still as a water-spirit
your arms lined with scalpels
and I hide the strength of my hungers
like a throwing knife in my hair.

Guilt wove through quarrels like barbed wire
fights in the half-forgotten schoolyard
gob of spit in a childhood street
yet both our mothers once scrubbed kitchens
in houses where comfortable women
died a separate silence
our mothers' nightmares
trapped into familiar hatred
the convenience of others drilled into their lives
like studding into a wall
they taught us to understand
only the strangeness of men.

To give   but not beyond what is wanted
to speak   as well as to bear
the weight of hearing
Fragments of the word wrong
clung to my lashes like ice
confusing my vision with a crazed brilliance
your face   distorted into grids
of magnified complaint
our first winter
we made a home outside of symbol
learned to drain the expansion tank together
to look beyond the agreed-upon disguises
not to cry each other's tears.

How many Februarys
shall I lime this acid soil
inch by inch
reclaimed through our gathered waste?
from the wild onion shoots of April
to mulch in the August sun
squash blossoms   a cement driveway
kale and tomatoes
muscles etch the difference
between I need and forever.

When we first met
I had never been
for a walk in the woods.

III

light catches two women on a trail
together   embattled by choice
carving an agenda with tempered lightning
and no certainties
we mark tomorrow
examining every cell of the past
for what is useful   stoked by furies
we were supposed to absorb by forty
still we grow   more precise with each usage
like falling stars or torches
we print code names upon the scars
over each other's resolutions
our weaknesses   no longer hateful.

When women make love
beyond the first exploration
we meet each other   knowing
in a landscape
the rest of our lives
attempts to understand.

IV

Leaf-dappled the windows lighten
after a battle that leaves our night in tatters
and we two glad to be alive   and tender
the outline of your ear pressed on my shoulder
keeps a broken dish from becoming always.

We rise to dogshit   dumped on our front porch
the brass windchimes from Sundance stolen
despair offerings of the 8 A.M. News
reminding us we are still at war
and not with each other
"give us 22 minutes and we will give you the world . . ."
and still we dare

to say we are committed
sometimes without relish.

Ten blocks down the street
a cross is burning
we are a Black woman and a white woman
with two Black children
you talk with our next-door neighbors
I register for a shotgun
we secure the tender perennials
against an early frost
reconstructing a future we fuel
from our living   different precisions

In the next room a canvas chair
whispers beneath your weight
a breath of you between laundered towels
the flinty places that do not give.

V

Your face upon my shoulder
a crescent of freckle over bone
what we share   illuminates what we do not
the rest is a burden of history
we challenge
bearing each bitter piece to the light
we hone ourselves upon each other's courage
loving
as we cross the mined bridge   fury
tuned like a Geiger counter

to the softest place.

One straight light hair on the washbasin's rim
difference
intimate as a borrowed scarf
the children arrogant as mirrors
our pillows' mingled scent
this grain of our particular days
keeps a fine sharp edge
to which I cling like a banner

in a choice of winds
seeking an emotional language
in which to abbreviate time.

I trace the curve of your jaw
with a lover's finger
knowing the hardest battle
is only the first
how to do what we need for our living
with honor and in love
we have chosen each other
and the edge of each other's battles
the war is the same
if we lose
someday women's blood will congeal
upon a dead planet
if we win
there is no telling.

POLITICAL RELATIONS

In a hotel in Tashkent
the Latvian delegate from Riga
was sucking his fishbones
as a Chukwu woman with hands as hot as mine
caressed my knee beneath the dinner table
her slanted eyes were dark as seal fur
we did not know each other's tongue.

"Someday we will talk through our children"
she said
"I spoke to your eyes this morning
you have such a beautiful face"
thin-lipped Moscow girls translated for us
smirking at each other.

And I had watched her in the Conference Hall
ox-solid   black electric hair
straight as a deer's rein   fire-disc eyes
sweeping over the faces
like a stretch of frozen tundra
we were two ends of one taut rope

AUDRE LORDE

stretched like a promise from her mouth
singing the friendship song
her people sang for greeting
> *There are only fourteen thousand of us left*
> *it is a very sad thing   it is a very sad thing*
> *when any people   any people   dies*

"Yes, I heard you this morning"
I said   reaching out from the place where we touched
poured her vodka   an offering
which she accepted like roses
leaning across our white Russian interpreters
to kiss me softly upon my lips.

Then she got up and left
with the Latvian delegate from Riga.

Don Mager

Don Mager (born 1942 in Santa Rita, New Mexico) came out in 1972. Since then, he has been the founder of "Gayly Speaking," a radio show on WDET-FM in Detroit, and of Detroit's Gay Parents and Frontrunners organizations, as well as a writer for *Gay Liberator* (1972–74) and *Metro-Gay News* (1975–76). He was the first Executive Director of the Michigan Organization for Human Rights and is currently Co-Chair of the Gay-Lesbian Caucus of the Modern Language Association. His poems have appeared in such magazines as *Mouth of the Dragon* and *Christopher Street*. The excerpt here is from the title-poem of a forthcoming collection.

FROM *LETTERS FROM A MARRIED MAN*

8–6–86

Beloved,

What does it take to put a house in order?
Auden and Kallman kept theirs all those years
and Auden catalogued it, room by room, in poems
as if to meditate upon years shared
and through the celebration of mere rooms
to lift the sprawl of domesticity
into eloquence, even the bathroom and toilet
idealized. The literary grapevine has it,
though, that the place was almost a sty.
Grease caked onto the kitchen ceiling for years,
books stacked on books in every shelf's corner.
Maybe that's what makes a home: all the debris
of hours of shared meals, all the clutter
of half-completed projects in reading;
the pilings up, the fragments; expanse of time
pressing down upon one space, one site, one us;
put simply, all the shit that came down
between them spread right out for anyone to view
because secrets, closets, postures, poses
at last became dysfunctional and absurd.
Here, midst waiting and low-grade despair,
I've spent another day unpacking boxes
of our gathered "shit."
                    Let the meals be good here
but spare us grease upon our walls . . .
let the reading and writing here never attain
the last page, but spare us books
misplaced or unread . . . let the closets
keep storage only, not shame or sham . . .
let this site bear all that moves best between us . . .
but most, let your arrival—your possession—
your return home be not long—
                              be not long.

                              Love
                              Don

DON MAGER

Beloved,

Now as the season shifts poised on cooler nights
—late August—the early fleeting hints of fall—
which is surely the most glorious season of all—
I find I must not only locate us in a new space
—house, furnishings, neighborhood—sites of stores,
routes to schools—the mental maps and compass points
that hold daily routines together—I must also
locate us within a new time. Or rather,
I must begin to ease myself into a daily rhythm
such that when you come, there is a time
for you to move inside of to arrive back home—
all the way, completely back, rejoined.
I make it all right across mornings, noons
and evenings. Night remains a chaos.
Especially after the dogs are walked and shut in.
Now, secluded in our room, crickets at the window,
Marlowe's TV a dull hallway hum,
I confront the blankness of our large bed
almost like the blankness of this paper. Perhaps
I conjure you into the bed through the action
of filling paper with a flow of careful words—
scratching out, correcting, postponing the moment of lights out.
Something neither actual—you are not here I know—
nor make-believe fills both blank voids, bed and page.
My verbal masturbations are not narcissistic though
—an otherness, emphatically outside myself, is encountered—
nor are they sublimations, for actual union with you
is a point of arrival not of escape.
Yet neither are these sonnets merely verbal games.
A kind of consummation of the flesh transpires
through the seminal flow of ink across these pages . . .
and these miles . . . from my desire all the way to yours,
from yours to mine—
                              so, man, let's get on with it.

[#6]

"You rise from your prone length between my thighs,
your torso rises up before my gaze,

DON MAGER   241

your lithe and muscled frame erect before
my face looms high to fill the waiting air
—the space beneath which my desire holds still
—the space in which your stunning cock is poised.

Your hands raise up my neck to lift my lips
against your penis's lubricious tip.

I taste . . . I lick . . . I shape my lips to close
upon it but your hands pull up . . . the full
hard length of you in one long sudden pure
and unimpeded thrust drives past the gag's tight core . . .
As your lithe weight sinks down into my face
my limbs arch up, grow rigid with surprise."

[#7]

"The whole night's splendor of you—all this
is not me—inscribed inside the circle of
this time . . . the now, which always is the whole
of all that one can ever know of time . . .
this here . . . the point at which you fuse with me
is signified by cock and sucking mouth.

Synecdoche of each, your body is
enclosed within my body's orifice . . .

I hold you keen upon a threshold with
the pressure of my throat . . . your edge, for me,
drum of pulse, grows dervish and sublime . . .
the hole and whole of me engulfs the whole
of your ejaculate . . . the surges of
your semen astounds us . . . then the hush . . .
                                              the kiss."

The time that we will share here, beloved,
has three names. We will have routines
of finite days—jobs, chores—and the joy
of sun, wind, clouds—conversation, walks with the dogs.
We will also have times of sexual union—
hours that squeeze the whole cosmos of vast

DON MAGER

expanse of relativity and void into an instant
of pivotal, exacting, reciprocal, precise hush.
And, yes, we have the unspeakable breadth
of the full time taken to live out each's life;
one of us will bury the other in the end.
He who survives must one day transcend mourning
to survey all the years of joy that we have been.

Love
Don

Paul Mariah

Paul Mariah (born 1937 in Whittington, Illinois) is founder and on-going
editor of *ManRoot* magazine and ManRoot Books, which, since 1969, has pub-
lished works by a number of important gay male writers. Mariah has also been
a teacher, a project researcher/scheduler for a Kinsey study, a literary secretary
to poets Robert Duncan and Kay Boyle, and has written and lectured on the
oppression of prisoners in American penal institutions. Mariah's poems have
appeared in dozens of periodicals and anthologies, and *This Light Will Spread:
Selected Poems 1960–1975* (ManRoot Books) was published in 1978.

QUARRY/ROCK

I

O, Seeger, the night you tied the cabbie
to the tree
              and shot him, did you know
the shadow of the chair was waiting for you?
You, murderer, guillotined one,
You of the severed head,

You on death row for seven years,
You six feet seven taker of life
you with the death shrouded head.

One night you walking in line
to your cell, swung and touched
hands with your love, Stevie.
You two walking in line
to your cells, swung and touched
hands. Swung hands and touched
the only way you could say good-night
swung hands and touched.

Later, that same night Stevie
lying in his 6 by 9 cell
in the quiet one-man cell
in the quiet of his only home
his desires became rampant
wanting you wanting
wanting you touching him wanting

(O, Seeger, what have they done to Stevie?
What have they done to Stevie?)

(The County had said his voyeur eyes
were too blue and should be
put away until the color changed to grey)

wanting you wanting
wanting you touching him wanting

the broom became you
the broom became the strength of you
the broom became the anal worship of you
the broom became the regular stroke of you
the broom became the reality of you

until he fell off the bed
and broke
            the broom off, inside where
you were in the quiet of his night
he was visited by red horror
not withstanding, not waking

PAUL MARIAH

II

O, Seeger, the night you tied the cabbie
to the tree
          and shot him, did you
know . . .

that you would wait seven years
to be strapped in a chair?

that they would kill your love
in isolation, in lonely isolation?

that in the cubicle of a cell you
would want him, would want to love him?

It was the evening after you knew
Stevie had died that I heard

green tears whimper from your cell
and knew that in that severed head

you still had human tears.

(O, Seeger, what have they done to Stevie?
What have they done to Stevie?)

Later, when Stevie was taken
to pauper's field where dandelions
grow in reverence to the sun.

When his parents refused his body,
refused their son. It was then
I heard you rage like a wild tiger.

In the cold antigone of your dreams
I saw you in defiance go out
and bury the body. And in revenge
you took to the fields
looking for his parents
hiding in the forest of your dreams
in cabbie clothing.

O, Seeger, the night you tied the cabbie
to the tree
and shot him, did you know
you still had green tears?

CHRISTMAS 1962

Walker, a large two-hundred-fifty pound blackman, worked in the
prison laundry. He was a lake of black obsidian, almost six-feet tall,
solid man. He was rather slow with words, soft-spoken, demure. His
cheeks were as if a heavy-handed sculptor had scooped a fatted palm
into black clay and planketed it to form each cheek. When he was
excited he stuttered. His grey hair, black and kinky at the temples,
twitched with his cheeks and his cheek muscles when he broadened
his face into a smile. But when he was silent, he was broodingly
silent as if his tongue had been pierced by a fork and he was unable
to move it.

I remember one year my mother sent me five dollars for Christmas. I
spent most of it at the commissary buying cigarettes and supplies I
thought I needed. I had a few cents left over. So, I bought three
christmas cards. One for Walker.

The next day was bath day. In the morning between nine and ten
o'clock every one in the cellhouse was required to take a bath. I slipt
down the galley after my bath and put his card into his cell, tossed it
onto the single metal bunk.

Later that same morning, back at the laundry, he came over and put
his arms around me and hugged me. He held me hard. Tears formed
in his eyes and the salt crystals sparkled against his black cheeks as
they ran down his quiet laugh-lined face toward his chin. He looked
long at me and finally said, *"Thank you for remembering me. It is the
only christmas card I will get. You are the only one in the whole world
who will remember me this Christmas."* His Christmas consisted in
receiving one christmas card, and that from another convict. His
tears against my cheeks were the only gift he could afford to give.
That hulk of a loving blackman must have held me for five minutes
or more. That was all he could say, and all that he could have said.
He tied his arms around me. His tongue and body were unable to
move.

PAUL MARIAH

"All right you two break it up and get back to work 'r I'll report ya," Sneeze, the laundry guard yelled at us from his post at the front door. Walker and I disembraced. We returned to sorting the wet bundled clothing coming from the big swirling vats. Our vats of rehabilitation.

This is only one Christmas. There are others. How many are there that I have to remember like this? The River remembers and keeps count. Somehow, looking out from behind the bars onto the great Mississippi there seemed to be an answer with the wind and with the river. The rapt waters that kept me from going insane always spoke to me of the life outside, the life outside my life inside, the life outside that bars my mind, that blocks my mind. The bars.

O to see the river flow unbroken!

William Meredith

William Meredith (born 1919 in New York City) began his career as a poet when Archibald MacLeish selected *Love Letter from an Impossible Land* for the Yale Series of Younger Poets. That book as well as subsequent early works is largely concerned with his experiences in World War II and the Korean Conflict as a Navy pilot. Meredith has taught at various universities around the country, but for nearly thirty years has devoted himself to Connecticut College in New London, where he maintains his home. He has been awarded most of the major American prizes for poetry as well as the International Nikolai Vaptsarov Prize. He was Consultant in Poetry at the Library of Congress for several years, has served as a Literature Panelist at the National Endowment for the Arts, and has traveled to foreign countries for the Department of State as a visiting American artist. *Partial Accounts: New and Selected Poems* (Alfred A. Knopf) won the Pulitzer Prize in 1988. Since 1971 Meredith has shared his life with his friend Richard Harteis.

PARTIAL ACCOUNTS

I. SURGERY

When they needed a foreign part,
a valve which was not to be found
or spared elsewhere in his ample,
useful body, they chose a pig's valve.
This will be compatible, they reasoned,
with such pig-headed machinery
as has maintained a minor poet
for sixty-three years in America.

II. CONVALESCENCE

Once a week on Thursday there's a *souk*
or open market in Salé, the old Roman port
facing Rabat across the Bou Regreg.
At least one dentist always sets up shop—
a table of gun-metal teeth, formerly human.
One day I saw a woman have one pulled,
or saw as much as a queasy heart could watch.
The *chirurgien dentiste* was a small man,
authoritative, Berber I think.
His left foot was set gently on the woman's
shoulder, and when I last looked,
difficult, silent progress was being made.
A concept of necessary suffering, praise Allah,
is common to all civilizations.

Soon I will need to imagine again
what she was feeling, but for a few more days
that will not be necessary, a sensation
my body was too fastidious to wait for
hovers inside me. Even mortality
is briefly imaginable, like pain.
Arab sister, in your dark-robed dignity,
may we both be healed of our cures and live
painlessly forever, as our bodies urge.

TREE MARRIAGE

In Chota Nagpur and Bengal
the betrothed are tied with threads to
mango trees, they marry the trees
as well as one another, and
the two trees marry each other.
Could we do that some time with oaks
or beeches? This gossamer we
hold each other with, this web
of love and habit is not enough.
In mistrust of heavier ties,
I would like tree-siblings for us,
standing together somewhere, two
trees married with us, lightly, their
fingers barely touching in sleep,
our threads invisible but holding.

Photograph © 1988 by Layle Silbert

James Merrill

James Merrill (born 1926 in New York City) is the author of nine books of poems, which have won him two National Book Awards (for *Nights and Days* and *Mirabell*), the Bollingen Prize in Poetry (for *Braving the Elements*), and the Pulitzer Prize (for *Divine Comedies*). *From the First Nine: Poems 1946–1976*, a selection from these, was issued by Atheneum Publishers in 1982 with a companion volume, *The Changing Light at Sandover*, which included the long narrative poem begun with "The Book of Ephraim" (from *Divine Comedies*), plus *Mirabell: Books of Number* and *Scripts for the Pageant* in their entirety. The latter received the Book Critics Circle Award in poetry for 1983. He has also written two novels, *The (Diblos) Notebook* (1965) and *The Seraglio* (1957), and two plays, *The Immortal Husband* (first produced in 1955 and published in *Playbook* in 1956), and, in one act, *The Bait*, published in Artist's Theatre (1960).

DAYS OF 1941 AND '44

for David Mixsell

The nightmare shower room. My tormentor leers
In mock lust—surely?—at my crotch.
The towel I reach for held just out of reach,
I gaze back petrified, past speech, past tears.

Or Saturday night war games. Shy of the whole
Student body, and my own, I've hid
In the furnace room. His warning stokes my head:
This time, Toots, it's your pants up the flagpole!

And why, four-letter man, descend
To pick on me, in those days less than nothing,
A shaky X on panic's bottom line?

Imagine meeting now, here at the end—
You sheep-eyed, stripped of your wolf's clothing—
And seeing which came true, your life or mine.

At Silver Springs, that Easter break,
I'd noted "heavenly colors and swell fish"
—Mismarriage of maternal gush
To regular-guy. By evening: "Bellyache."

I was *fifteen?* Dear god. Page after page,
Fury and rapture, smudge and curlicue,
One ugly duckling waddled through
The awkward age.

A month of sundaes, gym excuses, play
("I got the part!!") and "long walk with S. J."
Locate the diarist away at school

Right after the divorce. Would brat-
tishness that ripe for ridicule
Ever be resorbed like baby fat?

"A lord of Life, a prince of Prose"—
Alliterations courtesy of Wilde.

Another year, with such as these to wield,
I won the Fourth Form Essay Prize.

In vain old Mr Raymond's sky-blue stare
Paled with revulsion when I spoke to him
About my final paper. "Jim,"
He quavered, "don't, *don't* write on Baudelaire."

But viewed from deep in my initial
Aesthetic phase, brought like a lukewarm bath to
Fizzy life by those mauve salts,

Paradises (and if artificial
So much the better) promised more than Matthew
Arnold. Faith rose dripping from the false.

My dear—yes, let that stand: you were my first
True hate. You whispering the sadist's glee.
You lounging, buried in my diary—
Each phrase a fuse. I wanted you to burst.

Your cubicle across from mine was bleak
As when school opened. Oh, *you* didn't need
Cushions, posters, cotton for nosebleed.
A mother caught by flash in Red Cross chic.

Or did you? Three more years and you would die,
For lack of them perhaps, in France, at war.
Word reached me one hot twilight. It was raining,

Clay spattering the barracks. I
Fell back onto my bunk, parched for decor,
With *Swann's Way*. Basic training . . .

I'd have my France at war's end. Over highballs
Back home, would show that certain of us *were* up
To the museums and cafés of Europe—
Those peeling labels!

Rich boy you called me. True, there'd be no turning
Back from the mixed blessings of a first-rate

Education exquisitely offset
By an inbred contempt for learning.

And true, when money traveled, talent stayed
Deep in the trunk, assuming it got packed.
Mine was a harmless figment? If you like.

Remember, though, how untrained eyes subtract
From the coin-glint of a summer glade
The adder coiled to strike.

The nothing you'd become took on a weight
No style I knew could lighten. The latrine
Mirrors that night observed what once had been
Your mortal enemy disintegrate

To multiabsent and bone-tired hoplite,
Tamed more than told apart by his dog-tags.
Up the flagpole with those rank fatigues
Bunched round his boots! Another night

Beneath unsimulated fire he'd crawl
With full pack, rifle, helmeted, weak-kneed,
And peeking upward see the tracers scrawl

Their letter of atonement, then the flare
Quote its entire red minefield from midair—
Between whose lines it has been life to read.

UP AND DOWN

*"The heart that leaps to the invitation of sparkling
appearances is the heart that would itself perform as handsomely."*
—JOHN H. FINLEY, JR., *FOUR STAGES OF GREEK THOUGHT*

1. SNOW KING CHAIR LIFT

Prey swooped up, the iron love seat shudders
Onward into its acrophilic trance.

What folly has possessed us? Ambulance!
Give me your hand, try thinking of those others'

Unhurt return by twos from June's immense
Sunbeamed ark with such transfigured faces,
We sought admission on the shaky basis
That some good follows from experience

Of anything or leaving it behind,
As now, each urchin street and park sent sprawling
By the mountain's foot—why, this is fun, appalling
Bungalows, goodbye! dark frames of mind,

Whatever's settled into, comfort, despair,
Sin, expectation, apathy, the past,
Rigid interiors that will not outlast
Their decorator or their millionaire,

Groaning of board and bed of ruses, oh
I've had it up to here, fiftieth story
Glass maze, ice cube, daybreak's inflammatory
Montage subsiding into vertigo

Till, with their elevations all on file,
Joys, now demolished, that I used to live in,
This afternoon I swear halfway to heaven
None housed me—no, not style itself—in style.

Risen this far, your ex-materialist
Signs an impetuous long lease on views
Of several states and skies of several blues
Promptly dismantled by the mover mist

—What's going on? Loud ceiling shaken, brute
Maker of scenes in lightning spurt on spurt—
How did those others, how shall we avert
Illuminations that electrocute!

Except that suddenly the danger's gone.
Huge cloudscapes hang in the sun's antechamber.
Somebody takes our picture, calls a number.
We've done it. Reached the heights and quit our throne.

While knowing better, now, than to repeat
Our sole anabasis, unless in rhyme,
I love that funny snapshot from a time
When we still thought we were each other's meat.

The very great or very fatuous
Complicate the pinnacles they reach,
Plant banners, carve initials, end a speech,
"My fellow Texans, let us pray . . ." Not us.

You merely said you liked it in that chill
Lighthearted atmosphere (a crow for witness)
And I, that words profaned the driven whiteness
Of a new leaf. The rest was all downhill.

Au fond each summit is a cul-de-sac.
That day at least by not unprecedented
Foresight, a Cozy Cabin had been rented.
Before I led you to the next chair back

And made my crude but educated guess
At why the wind was laying hands on you
(Something I no longer think to do)
We gazed our little fills at boundlessness.

2. THE EMERALD

Hearing that on Sunday I would leave,
My mother asked if we might drive downtown.
Why certainly—off with my dressing gown!
The weather had turned fair. We were alive.

Only the gentle General she married
Late, for both an old way out of harm's,
Fought for breath, surrendered in her arms,
With military honors now lay buried.

That week the arcana of his medicine chest
Had been disposed of, and his clothes. Gold belt
Buckle and the letter from President Roosevelt
Went to an unknown grandchild in the West.

Downtown, his widow raised her parasol

Against the Lenten sun's not yet detectable
Malignant atomies which an electric needle
Unfreckles from her soft white skin each fall.

Hence too her chiffon scarf, pale violet,
And spangle-paste dark glasses. Each spring we number
The new dead. Above ground, who can remember
Her as she once was? Even I forget,

Fail to attend her, seem impervious . . .
Meanwhile we have made through a dense shimmy
Of parked cars burnished by the midday chamois
For Mutual Trust. Here cool gloom welcomes us,

And all, director, guard, quite palpably
Adore her. Spinster tellers one by one
Darting from cages, sniffling to meet her son,
Think of her having a son—! She holds the key

Whereby palatial bronze gates shut like jaws
On our descent into this inmost vault.
The keeper bends his baldness to consult,
Brings a tin box painted mud-brown, withdraws.

She opens it. Security. Will. Deed.
Rummages further. Rustle of tissue, a sprung
Lid. Her face gone queerly lit, fair, young,
Like faces of our dear ones who have died.

No rhinestone now, no dilute amethyst,
But of the first water, linking star to pang,
Teardrop to fire, my father's kisses hang
In lipless concentration round her wrist.

Gray are these temple-drummers who once more
Would rouse her, girl-bride jeweled in his grave.
Instead, she next picks out a ring. "He gave
Me this when you were born. Here, take it for—

For when you marry. For your bride. It's yours."
A den of greenest light, it grows, shrinks, glows,
Hermetic stanza bedded in the prose
Of the last thirty semiprecious years.

I do not tell her, it would sound theatrical,
Indeed this green room's mine, my very life.
We are each other's; there will be no wife;
The little feet that patter here are metrical.

But onto her worn knuckle slip the ring.
Wear it for me, I silently entreat,
Until—until the time comes. Our eyes meet.
The world beneath the world is brightening.

Larry Mitchell

Larry Mitchell (born 1938 in Muncie, Indiana) reached the safety of New York City in 1960. In addition to *The Faggots and Their Friends Between Revolutions* (Calamus Books, 1977), Larry Mitchell is the author of several works of fiction, including *The Terminal Bar* (Calamus Books, 1983), *In Heat: A Romance* (Gay Presses of New York, 1985), and *My Life as a Mole and 4 Other Stories* (Calamus Books, 1988). His play, *Get It While You Can*, was produced by Theater for the New City in 1985. He teaches Sociology and Women's Studies at The College of Staten Island, The City University of New York.

FROM *THE FAGGOTS AND THEIR FRIENDS BETWEEN REVOLUTIONS*

The faggots and their friends now live in Ramrod. The leader of Ramrod is Warren-And-His-Fuckpole. He is the leader of Ramrod because he is the most paranoid and therefore the most vicious man in the land. Warren wants to know who the leader of the faggots is so he can rationalize with him. But the faggots have no leader. They have only dead heroes.

Ramrod is known to its neighbors for the fierceness of its weapons and the touchiness of its leaders. To support their violence, the rich men without color who own Ramrod send their tax collectors out to steal the people's work; they send their shifty-eyed ones out to sell the people machines which do not work and security which is not dependable: they send their thugs and goons out to take peacefulness away from the people. The more the rich men without color can steal from or take from or sell to the people, the more violence they can buy.

Ramrod is known to its neighbors for the elaborateness of its violence and its eagerness to use it.

*　*　*

WOMEN WISDOM

The strong women told the faggots that there are two important things to remember about the coming revolutions. The first is that we will get our asses kicked. The second is that we will win.

The faggots knew the first. Faggot ass-kicking is a time-honored sport of the men. But the faggots did not know about the second. They had never thought about winning before. They did not even know what winning meant. So they asked the strong women and the strong women said winning was like surviving, only better. As the strong women explained winning, the faggots were surprised and then excited. The faggots knew about surviving for they always had and this was going to be just plain better. That made ass-kicking different. Getting your ass kicked and then winning elevated the entire enterprise of making revolution.

*　*　*

The men spread disease among the faggots, one of the things they love most to do to those they despise. The men will only cure diseases they themselves suffer from.

Once the faggots were overtaken by a new mysterious weak feeling. They could hardly leave their houses, they turned a bright yellow, they became unhappy and death seemed near. The men called it a name, but refused to help anyone who had this state. The men said this state arose from an overuse of the cock, which the faggots knew was a lie.

So the faggots stayed in their beds in their houses, reading the classic love texts, dreaming of a soulful revolution, drinking the potions that the strong women made for them until they were cured.

*　*　*

SONS AND FATHERS

The faggots created a rite of cleansing. The faggots sit in a circle. The first faggot enters into a father's head while the second faggot becomes a son. Then they enact a part of that endless story. With a blink, the second faggot enters the father and the third faggot is born into a son. And another part of the endless story is revealed. Like a wind over sand, faggots are transformed from father to son to father to son. A father's hatred and a son's anger; a father's ambitions and a son's failures; a father's fantasies and a son's rebellion reenacted until the spell of dead generations is broken. With a scream of laughter the faggots see, and for a moment they love each other freely, fathers making love to sons, and sons making love to fathers.

* * *

The men love papers. They love to sign them, file them and move them around. They believe that certain papers are sacred and display them. They buy papers from each other and they lock papers up. They store them in huge underground hiding places so other men who are their enemies cannot have them. They make women sit endlessly in airless, tall buildings making new papers for them to write on and then send to other men to write on. And if enough men who the men think are important men sign a paper, it becomes either famous and is put on guarded display or it becomes important and is hidden away and gossiped and speculated about endlessly. All the men accumulate paper. But if a man can accumulate enough of the correct papers he can become powerful. Then he hires other men to watch over his correct papers. Most men never get hold of many correct papers. Still they hoard and protect the papers they do have hoping the market will change.

The fairies use their papers to start fires and to wrap up the trees in the winter.

The faggots throw their papers away every spring when they clean out the winter tribal odors.

The queens use their papers to wipe their asses with.

Honor Moore

Honor Moore was born in 1945 in New York City. Her poems have been widely published in periodicals and anthologies and on a cassette tape, *Take Hands: Singing and Speaking for Survival*, along with work by Margie Adam, Susan Griffin, and Janet Marlow (Watershed Foundation, 1984). Her first full-length collection of poetry, *Memoir*, the title poem of which appears here, was published in 1988 by Chicory Blue Press (Goshen, Connecticut). She is the recipient of a Creative Writing Fellowship in Poetry from the NEA (1981) and of a CAPS Fellowship (New York State Council on the Arts, 1975) for her first play, *Mourning Pictures*, which was produced on Broadway in 1974 and subsequently in San Francisco, Minneapolis, and London. She lives in Kent, Connecticut, where she is currently completing a biography of her grandmother, the painter Margarett Sargent.

FIRST TIME: 1950

In the back bedroom, laughing when you pull
something fawn-colored from your black
tight pants, the unzipped chino slit.
I keep myself looking at the big belt
buckled right at my eyes, feel the hand
riffle my hair: You are called Mouse, baby-

sitter trusted Wednesdays with my baby
brother. With me. I still see you pull
that huge bunch of keys from a pocket, hand
them to my brother, hear squeaking out back
Mrs. Fitz's clothesline as you unbelt,
turn me to you, my face to the open slit.

It's your skin, this thing, head, its tiny slit
like the closed eye of a still-forming baby:
As you stroke, it stiffens like a new belt—

your face gets almost sick. I want to pull
away, but you grip my arm: I tell by your black
eyes you won't let go. With your left hand

you take my chin. With your other hand
you guide it, head reddening, into my slit,
my five-year old mouth. In the tight black
quiet of my shut eyes, I hear my baby
brother shaking the keys. You lurch, pull
at my hair. I don't breathe, feel buckle, belt,

pant. It tastes lemony, musty as a belt
after a day of sweat. Mouth hurts, my hands
push, push at your hips. I gag. You let me pull
free. I open my eyes, see the strange slits
yours are; you don't look at me. "Babe, babee—"
You are moaning, almost crying. The black

makes your skin clam-white now, your jewel-black
eyes blacker. You buckle up the thick belt.
When you take back the keys, my baby
brother cries. You extend a shaking hand
you make kind. In daylight through the wide slit
an open shade leaves, I see her pull,

Mrs. Fitz pulling in her rusty, soot-black
line. Framed by the slit, her window, her large hands
flash, sort belts, dresses, shirts, baby clothes.

MEMOIR

For J. J. Mitchell, dead of AIDS 4/26/86

I first remember you in Paris, blaze
of a smile, eleven years ago. Today
Joan tells me you're dead, the first I've loved
dead of that disease. It was New Year's Eve.
We sat on St. Germain drinking, watching
a boy in a black and white, convict-striped
Edwardian bathing suit weave festive
traffic on a skateboard—you, wild with
talk and blond hair. We had run into you

HONOR MOORE

and Joe, and with you we walked to a dark
turreted flat on Ile St. Louis to meet
the silent, pale boy who was your lover.

I would not have said love then, didn't know
as we drank I watched your face to learn
what ignited your laugh: How might I live
to come to that? You lived outside Paris,
"in a forest" you said, at an old mill
with a famous woman painter. My mother
had died. The man I loved bored me. You had
drugs and you were homosexual. I
wouldn't have said I too had drugs, was
in my wine where you were in whatever
one drinks with a famous woman at the end
of her looks, or smokes with a quiet boy.

"He killed himself," you said, smoking on the street
years later in New York. I didn't say
I had become homosexual, and you
didn't say the boy's death had caused you much
aside from anger. But you got sober. Paul
said so Christmas Eve before he left us
to cook what he would serve at your bed.
And I got sober. Today when Joan
told me of your death, we both said, "but he was
in recovery." The young woman who
drank with you amazed at a boy on a skate
New Year's Eve never saw you grin sober,

but I have the image of Paul at St. Marks
days after your death, waving. I didn't
know what I was learning in how he lifted
his hand, but I have what the loss meant:
how his hat hid his eyes, how blond winter
grass hides a blue pond as I stop my car now
to speak a prayer for the dead. "Sober you can
do anything," you told Joan. Jimmy said
your last days the virus at your brain had you
in summer at the door on Fire Island
offering refreshment as guests arrived—
beautiful men, one after another.

Cherríe Moraga

Cherríe Moraga (born 1952, Los Angeles) is a Chicana poet, playwright, essayist, and editor. Her books include *Loving in the War Years: Lo Que Nunca Pasó Por Sus Labios* (poetry and prose, South End Press, Boston, 1983) and *Giving Up the Ghost* (theatre, West End Press, Los Angeles, 1986). She co-edited *This Bridge Called My Back: Writings by Radical Women of Color* with Gloria Anzaldúa (Persephone, 1981, republished by Kitchen Table) and *Cuentos: Stories by Latinas* with A. Gomez and M. Romo-Carmona (Kitchen Table, 1983). Moraga is an instructor of writing in Chicano Studies at the University of California, Berkeley. She is currently working on a play about *la familia chicana.*

FEED THE MEXICAN BACK INTO HER

para mi prima

what I meant to say to her as she reached
around the cocktail glass to my hand, squeezing it
saying, *it makes no difference to me.* what I meant to say
is that it must make a difference,
but then I did say that and it made
no difference, this difference
between us.

what I meant to say to her is I dreamed we were children. I meant to tell her how I took her thin brown hand in mine and led her to the grocery store—the corner one, like in l.a. on adams street, where I remember her poor and more mexican than ever. we both were. I meant to remind her of how she looked in her brother's hand-me-downs—the thin striped tee shirt, the suspenders holding up the corduroy pants, literally "in suspension" off her small frame.

I meant to sit her down and describe to her the love, the care with which I drew the money from my pocket—my plump pink hand, protective, counting out the change. I bought tortillas, chiles verdes. I meant to say, "Teresita, mi'jita, when we get home, I'll make you a meal you'll never forget."

Feed the Mexican back into her.

I meant to tell her how I thought of her as not brown at all, but black—an english-speaking dark-girl, wanting to spit the white words out of her—be black angry. I meant to encourage.

Teresita

there is a photograph of us
at seven, you are skinny
at the knees where the brown wrinkles
together black,
my hand like a bright ring around yours

we are smiling.

In the negative, I am dark
and profane/you light & bleached-boned
my guts are grey & black coals glowing.

I meant to say, *it is this fire you see*
coming out from inside me.

Call it the darkness you still wear
on the edge of your skin
the light you reach for
across the table
and into my heart.

"FOR YOU, MAMÁ . . ."

For you, mamá, I have unclothed myself before a woman
have laid wide the space between my thighs
straining open the strings held there
taut and ready to fight.

Stretching my legs and imagination so open
to feel my whole body cradled
by the movement of her mouth, the mouth
of her thighs rising and falling, her arms
her kiss, all the parts of her open
like lips moving, talking me into loving.

I remember this common skin, mamá
oiled by work and worry.
Hers is a used body like yours
one that carries the same scent
of silence   I call it home.

Robin Morgan

Robin Morgan (born 1941, Lake Worth, Florida) is a founder of this wave of U.S. feminism and has been an organizer/activist in the international women's movement for fifteen years. She compiled and edited *Sisterhood Is Powerful* (Random House, 1970) and *Sisterhood Is Global* (Anchor/Doubleday, 1984), has written several books of feminist theory, including *The Anatomy of Freedom* (Doubleday, 1982) and the forthcoming *The Sexuality of Terrorism* (Norton, 1988), and poetry, including *Monster* (Random House, 1972) and *Death Benefits* (Copper Canyon, 1981). The most recent of her ten books is her first novel, *Dry Your Smile* (Doubleday, 1987). She lives in New York City, where she is completing a second novel and a fifth book of poems.

ON THE WATERGATE WOMEN

Maureen Dean, wearing persimmon summer silk,
sits smiling, silent, in the Senate Hearing Room.
Her eyelids droop. She must not doze.
She bolts upright.
But if she cannot doze, she finds she *thinks*.
She is the second wife.

The first says that he never lied.
The musings of the second are inadmissible.

Martha Mitchell, Cassandra by extension,
nurses the bruises from her beatings,
nurses her mind from the forced commitments,
waits at home, alone, with the terror that all her truths
will be seen as comic relief.

Dita Beard
has disappeared,
clutching the heart she was permitted to keep
alive, in payment for her scandal's death.

Rose Mary would
if she could, but she can't;
lips sealed by loyalty (for which, read: fear),
a faintly ridiculous scapegoat
as any Good Friday girl could have predicted.

The Committee wives watch their husbands on TV,
alone, preferably, so they can smile to themselves
at the righteous purity of such judges.

All the secretaries hunch at their IBM's,
snickering at the keys.
What they know could bring down the government.

The maids, the governesses, the manicurists,
the masseuses avert their eyes.
What they know could bring down the family.

The mistresses wait for their phones to ring.
Afraid to miss the call, they hurry
through their vomiting.

None of these witnesses would be believed.
Some do not believe themselves.

And Dorothy, Mrs. Howard Hunt, tucked into her coffin,
could hardly testify
to the cash, nestled in her lap like a rapist,
to the plane's dive through a bleached spring sky,

the taste of arsenic on her teeth,
the enormous dazzling wisdom that struck all her braincells
at the impact.
Her silence should bring down the nation.

But all the while, one woman, sitting alone
in rooms and corridors thick with deceit;
familiar, by now, with an unimaginable weariness,
having smiled and waved and hostessed her only life
into a numbness that cannot now recall
even the love
which was once supposed to make all this worthwhile—

having slept out summer in a wintry bed,
having borne children who were neither of them sons,
having, for years, stood at attention
so close to power, so powerless—

not, oh not
Thelma Catherine Patricia Ryan Nixon

blamed by the Right for her careful stupidity
blamed by the Middle for her cultivated dullness
blamed by the Left for her nonexistent influence
blamed by most men for being unbeautiful
blamed by some women for being broken
blamed by her daughters for their father
blamed by her husband for her cherished mis-memory of him
        as a young Quaker—

not, oh not
Thelma Catherine Patricia Ryan Nixon

who, as a young girl, loved Scarlatti,
who wanted to become an actress playing Ibsen,
who lost her own name somewhere along the way,

who now sits alone in some oversized chair,
watching with detached interest
how her sedated visions do their best
to picket before so many defilements.

This is no melodrama.
Here is no histrionic pain.

This quality of grief
could bring down
mankind.

FROM "THE HALLOWING OF HELL"

And blessed be the women who get you through:
the woman who lets you stay in her apartment,
the woman who takes you out for a drink,
the woman who guides you through the House of Mirrors
    in Copenhagen's Tivoli,
the woman who walks you through the Belvedere
    gardens of maroon-stalked orange gladioli,
the woman who loans you money,
the woman who has fresh Kleenex,
the woman who offers to chart your horoscope,
the woman who writes a stranger a letter about her poems,
the woman who sells your jewelry for you,
the woman who feeds your cats when you're gone,
the woman who makes you laugh,
the woman who tempts you to a superficial movie,
the woman who sees through Aquinas,
the woman who gives you a ream of 20-pound bond paper,
the woman who always seems to have an extra concert ticket,
the woman who prays for you,
the woman who writes her own books,
the woman who insists you keep a set of her keys,
the woman who gets you a poetry reading,
the woman who rings up to see how it's going,
the woman who loans you a book,
the woman who loves a man and is going through the same thing,
the woman who loves a woman and is going through the same thing,
the woman who gives you an inflatable travel pillow,
the woman you can show a first draft to,
the woman who cries with you,
the woman who makes you eat something,
the woman who gives you work to do,
the woman who reminds you to be fair,
the woman who helps you face answering letters,
the woman who talks about light,
the woman who falls in love with you
    but remains your friend,

the woman you yourself once loved above all women—
    weaned before her time, who hates you for that
    weaning now—blessed be her freeing vengeance even;
blessed be all the love like waves of light
    of all the others.
Blessed, blessed be the women who get you through.

Carl Morse

Carl Morse (born 1934 in Skowhegan, Maine) is the author of three books of poems, including *The Curse of the Future Fairy*, as well as the translator of a biography of Paul Verlaine and the essays of André Maurois. An editor with several major publishers, he was for a number of years Director of Publications for The Museum of Modern Art, New York. Morse's lyrics and speeches for theater have been performed throughout Europe and the United States. In recent years Morse has presented Open Lines, New York—a national series of readings by profeminists, lesbians, and gay men. A selection of his poems appears in *Three New York Poets* (GMP, London, 1987). He is currently completing the full-length performance piece *Impolite to My Butchers*.

DREAM OF THE ARTFAIRY

One day over the course of a week or so,
all the art ever made by fairies
became invisible to straights,
starting with the Sistine Chapel.
It was mid-July, and thousands of riled-up visitors
demanded an apocalypse or their money back,
although it was noticed certain persons
continued to point and giggle at the ceiling
—for the fairies could still see perfectly well.

Then the Last Supper went.
And some noted art historians tried to get back their vision
by clumsily attempting a gross indecency or two,
and traffic in forged fairy papers became a nightmare.
But nothing worked
—including the ethically dubious practice
of tempting real fairies to simulate
the shapes of the Elgin marbles.

And then to indelible effect
a Tchaikovsky symphony disappeared
in the middle of Avery Fisher Hall,
but for a piping fairy here and there
who could still read the music on the page
and one panicky but determined violin.

And the bins of Sam Goody bulged
with the unsold silent discs of Broadway hits,
and hum-along fairies ruled the Met,
and Take-a-fairy-to-Tanglewood clubs were formed,
in case any Brahms or Ravel was played,
and the first Easter passed without even one *Messiah.*

And then in the classroom of our days
the fairy voices died—in mid-pronunciation. So:

—I taste a liquor never brewed
   from tankards _____ ___ _____,
—The mass of men lead lives ___ _____

_____,
—A rose is a rose ___ __ _____,
—They told me to take a streetcar _____ _____,
—Out of the cradle _____ _____,
—Call me _____,
—Oh, Mama, just look at me one minute as though you really saw
   me . . . Mama! Fourteen years have gone by!   —I'm dead!
   —You're a grandmother, Mama   — . . . I married George
   Gibbs, Mama!   —Wally's dead, too. —Mama! His appendix
   burst on a camping trip to Crawford Notch. We felt just terrible
   about it, don't you remember?   — . . . But, just for a moment
   now we're all together   —Mama, just for a moment let's all be
   happy   — . . . Let's _____ ___ _____ _____!*

* If you filled in any of the above, even in your head, you may be a gifted fairy.

And the publishers failed when so many books
went blank in mid-fulfillment,
and no-one but fairies passed their bar exams.

At last only Clifton Webb kept making love
to the hole where Garbo used to be,
and a touchdown pass in the closing game
never reached its tight end on the screen,
and all hell really broke loose in the land.

And the Good Fairy saw that it was bad,
or at least not so hot,
and that a sense of justice can go a long way.
So she kicked the transmitter
and the straights woke up restored.
And the earthfairies didn't mind so much,
since they had more time to draw
—and interpreting isn't the best of jobs,
no matter how you get paid.

look at one another (Thornton Wilder)
Ishmael (Herman Melville)
endlessly rocking (Walt Whitman)
named Desire (Tennessee Williams)
is a rose (Gertrude Stein)
of quiet desperation (Henry David Thoreau)
scooped in pearl (Emily Dickinson)

FAIRY STRAIGHTTALK

—to *Jerry Falwell, to Jesse Helms, to Ed Meese, to Phyllis Schlafly, to John Paul II, to William F. Buckley, Jr., to Rupert Murdoch, to Warren E. Burger*
—*and to the couple who stared with deliberate contempt, disgust, and loathing at four gay men in my neighborhood restaurant on April 8, 1983 (five days after Easter, three days after Passover)*

—letting us know for certain you didn't want that kind of Jew
    spreading cancer in *your* restaurant
    as if they owned the place,
    even asking for more bread,

CARL MORSE

almost biting off your lipstick
in your haste to
slam on your fur and exit with a ramrod back.

May the next AIDS donor
to spit down your throat
be your son and heir,
yes, the married one who never forgets
your cake or smile.
May he be one of the three-piece men
who daily get faggots to gulp their loads
in bushes and gyms and picture shows,
in the front seats of out-of-town coupe de villes
and the back seats of full-service Burgerpits,
and in everyone's stockroom after five.
May you presoak the Pampers of such a tyke,
and may he get tagged by your friendly guard
who will send you duplicate restroom snaps
to paste on the page with the cap and gown
and the bride and sweethearts who must bear
your history and genes,
as well as a super-color-eight
of junior on your bedroom wall
moaning *suck it, suck it, suck it*
before zipping up quick and thanking you
as he exits the dump or parkway lot
heading home for a nourishing warm-up dish
and helping the kids with homework math.
And may every faggot he ever traded
kisses, cocks, and caresses with
show you their assholes in their dreams.

As for you, sir, training half your back
and undercurled sneer and lip on us,
may your gate be guarded by a muscle flit,
may your flag be folded by an anthem queer,
may a service pansy lead your prayers,
may a paper faggot deliver to your door,
may a spelling fairy promote your kids,
may a navigation faggot steer your flight,
may your call be routed by a switchboard queer,
may a justice fairy adopt your case,
may a thirsting faggot fill your mug,

may your car be inspected by a wrench fairy,
may a hammer faggot build your house,
may a power pervert buzz your station,
and may a federal finkfaggot target *your* population
for a nationwide screen test.

—And when you have your straight, white heart attack,
may your eyes, rolling wildly about the ward,
find only a lifetime lesbo nurse for help,
and a bedpan fairy and oxygen aide,
and a really pissed-off healthfaggot
with the nitroglycerin bottle
at an unreachable distance from the bed,
holding the cap down tight.

And may thus you recover the signal range
of how much a regular kiss can do,
how many clubmates have Herpes Two,
and what you produced in the dream of the girl
who didn't want only a football fuck,
while "fooling around" in the pop-up tent,
not hiding a hard-on in the pool,
but beating the shit out of any guy,
or woman or child who has the cool
to look in your eye,
or ask you why.

On the basis of your table manners alone,
I think it best we not compare
breeding or education,
since only one of us seems to know
that, unlike fairies,
Nazis are made not born.

SCENES OF CHILDHOOD

for my sister

The fairies are taken into the world
the way children are taken from women,
their fears taken from the limbs of their brothers,
their flight taken from the roofs of their fathers,

CARL MORSE

their sight taken from the breasts of their mothers,
their hopes taken from the eyes of their sisters,
and they eat their own placentas.

No, we can't share all the kisses and slaps
of the modern screen
—but the shade, yes,
window, yes, and the rain
—and a cold glass of life
handed down from the sink;
also the secret doors of food,
the alarm of being dressed for snow,
the boot that stays tied all day,
the introduction to the bus.

What's so odd about letting me near your kids?

Yet we often agreed
on privacy,
cheerleading,
fashion,
the stars,
and no one left out of the Valentine box;
also to comfort our rained-on dolls,
pretending their faces were still O.K.

We share the teatowel over the bread,
the crumbs under the rack,
the uneven slice;
we share the serrated edge.

By a glance during study hall let you know
when your skirt was good
and please not to care
when the shape of your lipstick spelled despair
wishing you could see him nude
and trying to shave
himself   himself   himself

We are the women the Men invent
when they can't get it up for your easy ass.
You are burning my jack-off porn
for the good of the middle class.

CARL MORSE   273

Night after night I set out to undress
the men I walked home on the silver screen,
and one by one I tried to compress
his own big love between my legs,
like marriage in a mezzanine.

Ever watch a fag hit a dance floor high?
            break a three-way tie?
            be the funny guy?
Ever watch a dyke look a stud in the eye?
We know how to make short visits work.

As the silent dates arrive for you,
the obedient fairies brush their teeth
and improve their nails
and work on their phoney scrapbooks.
They don't have to be punished to make them lie,
and they beg to be fucked when scared to die.

After decades of serving as dangerous Other,
I relax with you and my tribal brother.
The facts have found us sane, mature,
the kids grown up, the house secure.
We clink our glasses and make them fizz.
He tells me how tight your pussy still is.

As the rescued princess begins to sweep,
the fairies are watching the woods for the witch,
at the gate,
on the back of the stove,
by the crib,
in the unmown grass as you ride by,
also standing in line,
crying over a book,
and planning their own escape.

CARL MORSE

Eileen Myles

Eileen Myles (born 1949, Cambridge, Massachusetts) has published the poetry collections *A Fresh Young Voice from the Plains* (Power Mad, New York, 1981) and *Sappho's Boat* (Little Caesar, Los Angeles, 1982) and a book of stories, *Bread & Water* (Hanuman, New York, 1987). A third poetry collection, *The Real Drive*, is forthcoming from Semiotext(e). Myles says, "I came to New York from Boston in '74 to be a poet. I read all the New York School poets and went to workshops and millions of readings at St. Marks. I did a magazine called *dodgems* in the '70s. Was very active in the East Village poets community. I like to memorize my poems now and look at the audience. I wish they were a bunch of Russians."

A WOMAN LIKE ME

for Rose Lesniak

Wanna hear something really funny?
The urge to write a poem
That looks like this:
Is gone.
Behold the blank napkin on the bar
My Love.
O!
This bartender named Marilyn
Has just neatly placed
Six candles in Six Rocks Glasses.
She is not a priest
As the good pope tells us
There are no woman priests.
Ah! Thank God who isn't
Listening to women.
Ostracizing us
Is endearingly political

& it's time for *the revolution.*
Nothing very newsy
Just the toppling of the patriarchy
The shooting of the pope in
Chicago or Washington
By a lesbian.
A lesbian like me.
Here we have the reason
Why all the napkins are Pretty & Pure.
There's this lunatic with a gun
Running loose
& she's not inclined
To sit on a napkin.
& here she goes reminiscing:
I had a date & I wore a dress
In *1969*
& this guy & I
Walked down to the Charles
& so I could sit down
He unfolded his handkerchief
& placed it on the grass
So I could sit down with
My dress & my little heels &
Really a little *ribbon*
Tying part of my long-hair
Back
& I just looked at him &
I looked at the napkin
& all the World Turned inside my
Stomach
& I placed my ass on that napkin
& my eyes crossed & I looked
At the big buildings
Of the Harvard Business School
On the other side of the river.
I could shoot the pope.
Last night I got drunk on champagne
& walked into a glass door
Looking for my lover
Though I'm not blaming her
That my nose is wide & hurts.
Full moon last night
In Taurus. I drank tons

276   EILEEN MYLES

Of champagne
Then I was sitting in
An all-night coffee shop
Eating my cheeseburger
When this black guy
Presiding
Over a group made
Some tiny statement
About the typical white female
So she said to him:
O, according to the
Average black male?
Two statistics addressing
One another
A little silence—nothing much.
O I really wonder
If I shouldn't go
To the hospital with this nose.
(I could hardly go without it
But that's hardly
The point. My nose hurts
And I feel sick
And nothing, nothing's new.)

*   *   *

Last night by the champagne table
Rose is talking to this older french woman
Who says she's entirely celibate
& has decided for life & then
I get introduced to the woman
Who's decidedly cruising me.
Makes me think about the pope again
He maintained his stand on celibacy
—the big flirt. You know how
That works don't you? I mean
You know how easy it is for married
Men to get laid. "I'm discreet."
I love you, you're so unique.
And *undemanding.* So later
I'm putting my arms around this
Celibate woman. I'm crazy
About integrity. That's

Why I'd like to shoot the pope.
And actually the guy
Who placed me on a napkin
Had only a few weeks earlier
Plowed a volkswagen
Into a telephone pole. I was
In that volkswagen. With
My friend Sally & this
Napkin guy & that volkswagen
Were all in cape cod.
So this guy starts taking
Me on dates & placing me on napkins
& finally he told me how
The accident *really* happened.
That's what history means to
A woman like me. There
Were so many women in the room
Last night. I loved it—
I hardly danced. I danced
Slow once with my lover
And another high school dance
Collapsed inside my head.
That's the beauty of a lesbian.
Each one of us undoes history
A little bit & that's a lot.
Do you know we are the new
Nation? Do you know we are
The Anti-Christ? That's what
It means. Both her & I
Decided that. Independently
Then we told each other &
In the happy shock it was true.
Do you know what it's like
When two women make love
Under a full moon? The
Light comes in waves.
Debussy had his fauns
In the afternoon
And it's really very lovely.
And I even wrote a
Poem to the sun once.
In the grand male tradition.
I used to think the thing to do

Was to be a woman doing
All the things that poets do.
Talking to the sun & all that shit.
"Hello—this is a woman speaking."
When I told her I was planning
To shoot the pope—she said
"And in that moment,
You would know what it was like
To be a man." One such recognition
Would stop history I think.
The day seems to be lightening up.
I was going to ask him if
He needed more light—he's
Reading the Sunday Times in bed
But now the sky is brighter
& it's flowing into here.
Earlier we were in the bar
And she asked me how it
Was and I said, *well*
She asked me if I still love
Her . . . *and*   "Of course
I still love you"   I'll
Always love her and her face
Brightened. Whose? The one
I was talking to. In the bar
We were all popping Zoom
And then we went to the dance
In the room where all
The women were. Still are I bet.
That's why you should always
Leave early. I remember
—a full room. And a full
Moon—where is she, where
Is she—*Slam.* Right into glass.
Couple of years ago I was going
Up to the podium to read *Me*
And I walked smack into a mirror.
Imagine. I wrote *Me* when I
Was yelling at her and now she's
My very best friend. We seem
To know one another's minds.
She was drunk
Too last night. But anyhow so

I went home & she was in
Bed & stroked my nose. And here
I am today. Just arrived.
Smoked my last cigarette again
So here I am at the crux again
Blam   the place where it always starts.

Suniti Namjoshi

Suniti Namjoshi was born in Bombay, India, in 1941. She has lived in Canada since 1969 and is an associate professor of English literature at the University of Toronto. Her books include *Feminist Fables* (Sheba, London, 1981), *From the Bedside Book of Nightmares* (Fiddlehead, 1984), *The Conversations of Cow* (The Women's Press, London, 1985), *Flesh and Paper* with Gillian Hanscombe (Ragweed, PEI, Canada, 1986), and *The Blue Donkey Fables* (The Women's Press, London, 1988). She has collaborated with Gillian Hanscombe in producing works of several poets, accompanied by improvised music, for Jezebel Tapes and Books.

FROM *THE TRAVELS OF GULLIVER*
(revised edition)

And I fell in love with a woman so tall that
when I looked at her eyes I had to go star-gazing.

Tall treasure-houses, moon-
maidenly silence . . . Someday I'll teach you
to smile on me. She sways, sighs,
turns in her sleep. Did a feather fall?
Thor's hammer blow makes no effects.
I'm told that it's unnatural
to love giantesses.

In the mornings small dogs bark.
Giantesses strut, fell trees like toothpicks,
while we just stand there, gaze up
their thighs, foreshortened, of course,
but astonishingly pretty.

One day she picked me up off the floor and set
me on her nipple. I tried to ride, but consider my
position—indubitably tricky.

To sleep forever in my fair love's arms,
to make of her body my home and habitation . . .
She keeps me about her like a personal worm.
She is not squeamish.

       Once,
the giddy and gay were gathered together.
Then she brought me out, bathed me
and kissed me. She put me in a suit
of powder blue silk and set me to sail
in a tepid cup of tea. There
I fought out the storm of their laughter.
I performed valiantly.

I love to hear her laugh,
    would not see her grieve,
but a teacup of brine would have seemed
more seemly. I could sail in such a cup,
be swayed by her sighs.

She gluts me on the milk
    of healthy giantesses;
"Poor little mannikin,
    will nothing make you grow?"
I grow. I am growing. You should
    see me in her dreams.

Harold Norse

Harold Norse, born in 1916 in New York and raised there, spent fifteen years in Europe and Morocco and now lives in California. He has taught at Cooper Union, San Jose State, and other colleges. Author of twelve books of poems, many of them collected first in *Hotel Nirvana: Selected Poems 1953–1973* (City Lights, 1974) and then in *Carnivorous Saint: Gay Poems 1941–1976* (Gay Sunshine, 1977), Norse has been a National Book Award nominee and is the recipient of a National Endowment Grant and other honors. His novella *Beat Hotel* (Atticus) appeared in 1983. Of his latest collection, *Harold Norse: The Love Poems*, *Booklist* wrote: "A major collection of gay literature." Norse's *Memoirs* will soon be published by William Morrow.

I'M NOT A MAN

I'm not a man. I can't earn a living, buy new things for my
family. I have acne and a small peter.

I'm not a man. I don't like football, boxing and cars.
I like to express my feelings. I even like to put an arm
around my friend's shoulder.

I'm not a man. I won't play the role assigned to me—the role
created by Madison Avenue, Playboy, Hollywood and Oliver
Cromwell. Television does not dictate my behavior. I am under
5 foot 4.

I'm not a man. Once when I shot a squirrel I swore that I would
never kill again. I gave up meat. The sight of blood makes me
sick. I like flowers.

I'm not a man. I went to prison resisting the draft. I do not
fight back when real men beat me up and call me queer. I dislike
violence.

I'm not a man. I have never raped a woman. I don't hate blacks.
I do not get emotional when the flag is waved. I do not think
I should love America or leave it. I think I should laugh at it.

I'm not a man. I have never had the clap.

I'm not a man. Playboy is not my favorite magazine.

I'm not a man. I cry when I'm unhappy.

I'm not a man. I do not feel superior to women.

I'm not a man. I don't wear a jockstrap.

I'm not a man. I write poetry.

I'm not a man. I meditate on peace and love.

I'm not a man. I don't want to destroy you.

San Francisco, 1972

WE BUMPED OFF YOUR FRIEND THE POET

*Based on a review by Cyril Connolly, "Death in Granada,"
on the last days of García Lorca,* The Sunday Times
(London), May 20, 1973.

> We bumped off your friend the poet
> with the big fat head this morning
>
> We left him in a ditch
> I fired 2 bullets into his ass
> for being queer
>
> I was one of the people
> who went to get Lorca
> and that's what I said to Rosales
>
> My name is Ruiz Alonso
> ex-typographer
> Right-wing deputy

alive and kicking
Falangist to the end

Nobody bothers me
I got protection
the Guardia Civil are my friends

Because he was a poet
was he better than anyone else?

He was a goddam fag
and we were sick and tired
of fags in Granada

The black assassination squads
kept busy
liquidating professors
doctors lawyers students
like the good old days of the Inquisition!

General Queipo de Llano
had a favorite phrase
"Give him coffee, plenty of coffee!"

When Lorca was arrested
we asked the general what to do
"Give him coffee, plenty of coffee!"
this meant finish him

We took him out in the hills and shot him
I'd like to know what's wrong with that
he was a queer with Leftist leanings

Didn't he say
I don't believe in political frontiers?

Didn't he say
I'm a brother to all men?

Didn't he say
The capture of Granada in 1492
by Ferdinand and Isabella
was a disastrous event?

HAROLD NORSE

Didn't he call Granada *a wasteland
peopled by the worst bourgeoisie in Spain?*

a queer communist poet!

General Franco owes me a medal
for putting 2 bullets up his ass

San Francisco, 26. vi. 73

YOU MUST HAVE BEEN A SENSATIONAL BABY

1

I love your eyebrows, said one.
the distribution of your bodyhair
is sensational. what teeth, said two.
your mouth is like cocaine, said three.
your lips, said four, look like sexual organs.
they are, I said.
as I got older features thickened.
the body grew flabby. then
thin in the wrong places. they
all shut up or spoke about life.

2

a pair of muscular calves
drove me crazy today.
I studied their size, their shape,
their suntanned hairiness. I spoke
to the owner of them. are you
a dancer? I asked. oh no,
I was born with them, he said.
you must have been a sensational baby,
I said. he went back to his newspaper,
I went back to his calves.
he displayed them mercilessly.
he was absolutely heartless.
men stole secret looks at them.
women pretended he was a table.
they all had a pained expression.

he went on reading the Sports Page.
his thighs were even more cruel
thrust brutally from denim shorts.
the whole place trembled with lust.

San Francisco, 1973

Frank O'Hara

Frank O'Hara (born 1926 in Baltimore, died 1966) grew up in Massachusetts, was a sonarman third class on the destroyer USS *Nicholas* (1944–46), graduated from Harvard in 1950, and received an M.A. from the University of Michigan and the Hopwood Award in Creative Writing in 1951. He worked at The Museum of Modern Art and was an editorial associate of *Art News*. His first book, *A Winter City and Other Poems* (Tibor de Nagy Gallery, New York, 1952) was followed by *Meditations in an Emergency* (Grove Press, 1957), *Odes* (Tiber Press, 1960), *Lunch Poems* (City Lights Books, 1964), and *Love Poems* (Tibor de Nagy, 1965). O'Hara died as the result of injuries sustained in an automobile accident in 1966. *The Collected Poems* was issued by Knopf in 1972, and *The Selected Poems* in 1974.

ODE: SALUTE TO THE FRENCH NEGRO POETS

From near the sea, like Whitman my great predecessor, I call
to the spirits of other lands to make fecund my existence

do not spare your wrath upon our shores, that trees may grow
upon the sea, mirror of our total mankind in the weather

one who no longer remembers dancing in the heat of the moon may
  call
across the shifting sands, trying to live in the terrible western world

here where to love at all's to be a politician, as to love a poem
is pretentious, this may sound tendentious but it's lyrical

which shows what lyricism has been brought to by our fabled times
where cowards are shibboleths and one specific love's traduced

by shame for what you love more generally and never would avoid
where reticence is paid for by a poet in his blood or ceasing to be

blood! blood that we have mountains in our veins to stand off
        jackals
in the pillaging of our desires and allegiances, Aimé Césaire

for if there is fortuity it's in the love we bear each other's differences
in race which is the poetic ground on which we rear our smiles

standing in the sun of marshes as we wade slowly toward the
        culmination
of a gift which is categorically the most difficult relationship

and should be sought as such because it is our nature, nothing
inspires us but the love we want upon the frozen face of earth

and utter disparagement turns into praise as generations read the
        message
of our hearts in adolescent closets who once shot at us in doorways

or kept us from living freely because they were too young then to
        know
what they would ultimately need from a barren and heart-sore life

the beauty of America, neither cool jazz nor devoured Egyptian
        heroes, lies in
lives in the darkness I inhabit in the midst of sterile millions

the only truth is face to face, the poem whose words become your
        mouth
and dying in black and white we fight for what we love, not are

HAVING A COKE WITH YOU

is even more fun than going to San Sebastian, Irún, Hendaye,
        Biarritz, Bayonne
or being sick to my stomach on the Travesera de Gracia in
        Barcelona
partly because in your orange shirt you look like a better happier St.
        Sebastian
partly because of my love for you, partly because of your love for
        yoghurt
partly because of the fluorescent orange tulips around the birches
partly because of the secrecy our smiles take on before people and
        statuary
it is hard to believe when I'm with you that there can be anything as
        still
as solemn as unpleasantly definitive as statuary when right in front of it
in the warm New York 4 o'clock light we are drifting back and forth
between each other like a tree breathing through its spectacles

and the portrait show seems to have no faces in it at all, just paint
you suddenly wonder why in the world anyone ever did them
                                                        I look
at you and I would rather look at you than all the portraits in the
        world
except possibly for the *Polish Rider* occasionally and anyway it's in
        the Frick
which thank heavens you haven't gone to yet so we can go together
        the first time
and the fact that you move so beautifully more or less takes care of
        Futurism
just as at home I never think of the *Nude Descending a Staircase* or
at a rehearsal a single drawing of Leonardo or Michelangelo that
        used to wow me
and what good does all the research of the Impressionists do them
when they never got the right person to stand near the tree when
        the sun sank
or for that matter Marino Marini when he didn't pick the rider as
        carefully
as the horse
                it seems they were all cheated of some marvellous
        experience
which is not going to go wasted on me which is why I'm telling you
        about it

FRANK O'HARA

ODE TO JOY

We shall have everything we want and there'll be no more dying
        on the pretty plains or in the supper clubs
for our symbol we'll acknowledge vulgar materialistic laughter
        over an insatiable sexual appetite
and the streets will be filled with racing forms
and the photographs of murderers and narcissists and movie stars
        will swell from the walls and books alive in steaming rooms
        to press against our burning flesh not once but interminably
as water flows down hill into the full-lipped basin
and the adder dives for the ultimate ostrich egg
and the feather cushion preens beneath a reclining monolith
        that's sweating with post-exertion visibility and sweetness
        near the grave of love
                        No more dying

We shall see the grave of love as a lovely sight and temporary
        near the elm that spells the lovers' names in roots
and there'll be no more music but the ears in lips and no more wit
        but tongues in ears and no more drums but ears to thighs
as evening signals nudities unknown to ancestors' imaginations
and the imagination itself will stagger like a tired paramour of ivory
        under the sculptural necessities of lust that never falters
        like a six-mile runner from Sweden or Liberia covered with gold
as lava flows up and over the far-down somnolent city's abdication
and the hermit always wanting to be lone is lone at last
and the weight of external heat crushes the heat-hating Puritan
        whose self-defeating vice becomes a proper sepulchre at last
        that love may live

Buildings will go up into the dizzy air as love itself goes in
        and up the reeling life that it has chosen for once or all
while in the sky a feeling of intemperate fondness will excite the
        birds
        to swoop and veer like flies crawling across absorbed limbs
that weep a pearly perspiration on the sheets of brief attention
and the hairs dry out that summon anxious declaration of the organs
        as they rise like buildings to the needs of temporary neighbors
        pouring hunger through the heart to feed desire in intravenous
                ways
like the ways of gods with humans in the innocent combination of
        light

and flesh or as the legends ride their heroes through the dark to
    found
great cities where all life is possible to maintain as long as time
    which wants us to remain for cocktails in a bar and after dinner
    lets us live with it
                No more dying

Peter Orlovsky

Peter Orlovsky (born 1933 in New York City) is the author of *Dear Allen: Ship will land Jan 23, 58* (Beau Fleuve Series No. 5, Intrepid Press, Buffalo, 1971), *Lepers Cry* (Phoenix Book Shop, New York, 1972), and *Clean Asshole Poems & Smiling Vegetable Songs* (City Lights Books, 1978). From the mid-50s a lover and companion of poet Allen Ginsberg, Orlovsky traveled with Ginsberg to Mexico City, Morocco, Paris, and India, etc., often reading and singing together. Important sources for Orlovsky's life include the interview with Winston Leyland and Charley Shively in *Gay Sunshine Interviews*, Volume I (Gay Sunshine Press, 1978) and the Ginsberg/Orlovsky volume *Straight Hearts' Delight: Love Poems and Selected Letters, 1947-1980* (Gay Sunshine Press, 1980). Of himself, Orlovsky wrote in 1960: "This summer got to like flies tickleing nose & face. I demand piss be sold on the market, it would help people to get to know each other. I.Q. 90 in school, now specialized I.Q. is thousands."

SOME ONE LIKED ME WHEN I WAS TWELVE

When I was a kid in summer camp,
around 13teen & one night I lay asleep
in bunglow bed with 13teen other boys,
when in comes one of the camp councilors
who is nice fellow that likes ya, comeing to
my bed, sits down & starts to say: now you
will be leaving soon back to Flushing & I may never see you
again—but if theres ever aneything I

can do to help ya let me know, my farther is
a lawyer & I live at such & such a place
& this is my adress—I like you very much—
& if yr ever alone in the world come to me.
So I loked at him getting sad & tuched &
then years latter like now, 28, laying on
bed, my hunney-due mellon Allen sleeping next to me
—I realize he was quear & wanted my
flesh meat & my sweetness of that age—
that we just might of given each other.

April 1962, Bombay

LEPERS CRY

When in Banaras
India in 1961 Summer I was
flooded on my morphine mattress.
So a bit shyly fitting for me to
go see how the poor sick
week thin no legs no hands no
fingers, only stubbs of joints
with the finger bones pokeing thru.
A bit like pigs feet in clean store jars.
Only these were the Lowest of
the Low of India the Leppers
or a fraction of the fractions
in this one small Lane near

Dasadsumad Ghat—this, maybe
32 yr old woman rapped in pure dirt
Burlap string strip around waist—whear
the Tips of her Toes should be were
her bone Toe stubs protruding out
still infessted with active
Leprocy growing by eating
away the flesh that surrounds
her extremites—she
could only crall on her rear
she can not walk and to
eat she has to use her rotten
sore Lepper fingers—

I gave some helpfull Indian soul
to go get her a new fresh Clean
sarrie a few ruppies
and began to help her change
her apparel when there to
my Eyes on her Left behind
I saw a 4 inch ring of open—
saw infection full of magots
cralling and happiley alive—I
was so supprised I dident know
what to do for a second—then
I hide tailed it to a doctor
in his office a bit across the street

asking him what to do
No I asked him to come down and examin
this street Lepper & that I would pay
him good for his expert servace—
He said he had to stay in his office
and told me to get some
Hydrogen Peroxide—cotton and
I think some sulpher ointment
to first clean out the infection
& kill the maybe, 30 or 50 maggots
in her side above the thigh—you
know that big round mussle
that is divided into two sphears.

Well on her Left sphear (ass)
played these maggots and as I
poured the Hydrogen Peroxide—I had to
turn her over on her side—the
maggots became more alive and
active & danced into the air
above her side more. It was
difficult to get all the maggots out
so after a few
pourings and cotton cleanings I
covered it with sulpher ointment of
I dont quite remember because its
been 10 years ago and I have

been so scattered fingers to write
This real sad tail—which is
another discusting disease in its self,
and Toped it with 5 × 5 inch compress pads—
and had some one bring her some
food and a clean mat for her to
sit on—for all this took place
in the poor beggers sick alley decked
with watery shit plops and I
finally got into the swing of
cleaning it up with my hands—that
the first problem was to clean up
all this free Floating Shit splashings all about

(I even went to Water Pipe Commissioner local office
to see if they would install a water forcet at
this disentary dispensing spot, but no luck.)
and it was on the next day I saw
her again and this Time I looked
on her right side behind and there
was another maggot soupe dish
big and eaten down
to her thigh bone I saw the
muscles getting eaten & sucked thin
jucey human sore magget puss—
have you ever smelt magot
puss on the body of a poor Human
Being—dont bother—it may make
you vommit—keep away—
Let the Prows attend the Nose.

I just dident expect to see the same
horrible infested condition on the
exact opposite side of her body—
I was now more suprissed and
taken aback—and now I Looked
into her eyes & she had very
dark olive calm eyes peasefull sweet sad
eyes that seemed to tell me
I am okay—its nice of you
to have some food brought to me
and I want to thank you

but I dont know yr Language
so I say silently with my

eyes—I gave her friends
food money for a varried diet
for a week & told them to get
her yougart & they got some
& spoon fed her—
and then I disappeared for a week
or a month and I saw her
again—in a bigger Square—up
above Dasadsumed Ghat—she—I
saw her from a distance of about
70 feet—(or someone else looking like her)
she was on her back—
in rigamaroartus I could Tell
by the ways her knees

& arms were sticking up into the
air—it looked like—I forgot her
name—I think I asked
or I forgot—I steared away
I could see the problem of
Burreying her or Burning her at
the Funeral Pire at Manikarneka Ghat—
it was—I figured
the proper Government Banaras workers job
would come and gather her up—
I was sad to see her end this way,
I dident think she would go so soon.
what fooled me was her calm eyes,

living so peasefulley
above her hip woe—
her hip infection
and then I thought that maybe me
by killing the maggots
it opened the Blood Veins
or something to cause premature
death—its all so sad—and
now to this day I feel all
the more Lazzey & Dumb

PETER ORLOVSKY

and all the more domb & Lazzey
Lazzey Bastard of a selfish
Human Creap Sleep

Halloween Night, 1971

(1977: read in NY Times was it Leprosy may be caused by eating too much of one food like gulping rice over decades)

Charles Ortleb

Charles Ortleb (born 1950 in Elizabeth, New Jersey) is the founder and publisher of *Christopher Street* magazine, the *New York Native*, and *TheaterWeek*. A selection of his poems appears in *Three New York Poets* (GMP, London, 1987).

SOME BOYS

When some boys
offer to dance
you can see how innocently
their cocks hang in their pants.
Pendulously, as they say,
connoting
horses, barns, liquor, hay.

some boys open up their shirts
and the beauty almost hurts.

some boys even undress in
rooms cluttered with Dylan on.

Some boys are evil.
They lure boys into deeper statements.
They take showers together,
they eat flowers together
and call each other studs.

Some boys, though, do take to sex like apes and monsters and their
     fathers.
They get hair-raising erections.
Pools of smegma collect near their beds.
Discarded condoms build up in their backseats
and dead pubic insects fall from their groins into
patches of vaseline.

The meat of rough alleys hangs in their underwear.
The kind of meat you pull out of the pants of muggers.
The meat in its American juice that lays in jeeps and B42s
I mean the meat
of all soldier boys who will bomb the hell out of heaven,
the meat
of all those high school cadets
masturbating in the twilight as though they were landing a 747.

MILITEROTICS

Sexuality grows out of the barrel of a gun
          —HOMAGE TO JANCSO

     In Vietnam
     eels live in the water
     until they are stuffed
     into the vaginas of the opposition.
     Do not think of the women.
     Think of the eel:
     bloodstained, hungry,
     staring out of
     the cunt
     having completed
     a political journey.

     In Chile the opposition
     dream from cattle cribs
     that they have not been
     castrated
     and forced to eat
     their own erections.

CHARLES ORTLEB

As young boys
they stripped each other
naked, tied each other up
in their basements
and then the beatings began.
The beatings have not ended.
On the last day of the world
there will be one of these beatings.

Normandy was erotic.
Pearl Harbor was erotic.
Hiroshima was erotic,
but too quick, like
premature ejaculation.

Let's play animals and
guards, someone says
in the echo of time,
in the holocaustic maleness.

Chile,
Cuba,
Lawrence, Kansas,
Dallas, Texas
force and sexuality
go together
like men with men
on horses,
like whips with marriages.
Force seeks sexuality,
sexuality seeks
out force.
There is all you need to know.

How well you coordinate
it all
almost symphonically.
You speak, cry,
pull out your hair
and hemorrhage at the
same time.

II

What do you do in a room
full of torturers but
begin the show.

I seek
the perfect solitude of
having a jail full of
naked men to throw
into the sea
one at a time
or to retain one
for sleepless nights,
spontaneous pummelling.

I must find a way
to fuck you that
begins and ends
with the words
yes, sir.

To love: to promise
a prisoner that you will be even
worse to him
tomorrow.
To say it mellifluously.

You can
encompass all of a man's
sperm
through electric shock
and cattle prod.
Sometimes during initiations
in Kansas, naked 18-year-olds
are taken from the locker rooms,
stuffed into Volkswagons
and driven into cornfields
for good old-fashioned
gang rapes.
Even the Mafia is erotic:
to be in a
sauna with

your father and
to be asked
how you want a
specific man destroyed.
In or out of his underwear.

III

Orders:

Order a wife to go down
on her son in front of her son's teachers.
Order a mother to masturbate
her baby in front of her mother.
Order a mother to castrate her
political teenage son with a
potato knife.
Order mothers to stick sharpened
pencils up your daughters' asses.
Order that all communication be
translated into sexual terms.
Order that all men must be fucked
ten times a day by their fathers.
Order that all pain be suspected
of having sexual origin.
Order that all shitting be done
in open-air theaters with Greek choruses.

Build
museums of mutilated
freaks to demonstrate
the male sensibility.

Reward civil artists
for humiliation captured
in rococo
and Baroque.

Panorama of problems.
Panorama of naked men.
Whether to starve them
before you humiliate them
or humiliate them

before you starve them.
Generals,
consult management experts.

When a young girl is
stripped and tied to a pole
in an alley
let the artists
capture
that confused look in the
face of the gang
the look of
what to do first.

IV

This is the do not be bitter
part of history,
the part the church sponsors,
the part where they line them up
and make them fuck each other
and then punish them and
ridicule them for fucking each
other and then make them do it
again . . . not in circles, but in
rich spirals, forever and ever
in a vertical movement
into heaven.

When a father beats
his son behind the barn
he must take off his belt
and from then on
it's lust.
In the cries of the son,
nude where he lays,
nations form.

V

Juan Mirabel.
You ask what turns men on.
You do, Juan Mirabel.

When your dress is
torn from your thighs
they flay your skin
and bounce your head
in the stadium
in soccer
the national sport of Chile.
But if you save up a little money
for a weapon,
if you tell
another man
to take off
his clothes and
you are holding
a gun . . .
you are a political genius.

John Doe.
You ask what turns men on.
You do, John Doe.
When, in a small
Dallas County jail
they have the power
to strip you down
and examine the folds
of your ass
for nuclear weapons
nightly after dinners
with their wives
when they're burping,
when it's more fun
than stretching.

John Doe, Juan Mirabel,
if they let you wear
pajamas,
if they do not
immediately
change your name,
If they give you
your knuckle for
your last toothbrush
the day you die,

bite into bone,
John Doe and Juan Mirabel.
You turn men on.
You always will.

METAPHOR AS ILLNESS

Listen to the phone calls they do not
make: "Hello mommy, I hurt myself
erotically. Please come to New York Hospital."
The doctors do what little they have time for, they're
all yuppied-out and tired of what
sin does to the bodies of other people
who don't own co-ops.
We must learn to eroticize our wounds.
The new love means getting it up
for things that are falling apart.

ON FINDING OUT THAT THE ONE YOU SLEPT WITH THE NIGHT BEFORE WAS MURDERED THE NEXT DAY

I got his name and phone
number
but then the name
appeared in the *Times* the
next day as a body.

True, that's all he
had been the night
before, and true, both
I and the murderer
had entered him, one
by a hole that was there,
and one by a hole that
had to be made.

And maybe both I and
the murderer, as we
entered his body, were
both equidistant from

the core of his love.

or maybe there really
was no quarry of
love there at all,
no rock of love, no
ballast or bullshit, just
the perfect trick,
a convenient victim.

Or he must have felt
something. Either I or
the murderer must
have moved him a
little before the police
moved him.

I like to imagine
his childhood—his
mother processing his
nakedness and how
from the first strange
spoonful of his babyfood
and from the chill of his
first anal thermometer
you just never know
how many people are
going to get in.

Pat Parker

Pat Parker (born 1944, Houston, Texas) has published five books of poetry about being black, female, and gay: *Child of Myself* (Shameless Hussy Press, 1972), *Pit Stop* (The Women's Press Collective, 1973), *Womanslaughter* and

Movement in Black (Diana, 1978), and Jonestown and Other Madness (Fire-brand, 1985). A dynamic reader, she has performed her work alone and in concert across the country. Until recently, she was director of the Oakland Feminist Women's Health Center. She lives in Pleasant Hill, California, with her lover and two children.

"WHERE WILL YOU BE?"

Boots are being polished
Trumpeters clean their horns
Chains and locks forged
The crusade has begun.

Once again flags of Christ
are unfurled in the dawn
and cries of soul saviors
sing apocalyptic on air waves.

Citizens, good citizens all
parade into voting booths
and in self-righteous sanctity
X away our right to life.

I do not believe as some
that the vote is an end,
I fear even more
It is just a beginning.

So I must make assessment
Look to you and ask:
Where will you be
when they come?

They will not come
a mob rolling
through the streets,
but quickly and quietly
move into our homes
and remove the evil,
the queerness,
the faggotry,
the perverseness

from their midst.
They will not come
clothed in brown,
and swastikas, or
bearing chest heavy with
gleaming crosses.
The time and need
for ruses are over.
They will come
in business suits
to buy your homes
and bring bodies to
fill your jobs.
They will come in robes
to rehabilitate
and white coats
to subjugate
and where will you be
when they come?

Where will we *all be*
when they come?
And they will come—

they will come
because we are
defined as opposite—
perverse
and we are perverse.

Every time we watched
a queer hassled in the
streets and said nothing—
It was an act of perversion.

Everytime we lied about
the boyfriend or girlfriend
at coffee break—
It was an act of perversion.

Everytime we heard,
"I don't mind gays
but why must they

be blatant?" and said nothing—
It was an act of perversion.

Everytime we let a lesbian mother
lose her child and did not fill
the courtrooms—
It was an act of perversion.

Everytime we let straights
make out in our bars while
we couldn't touch because
of laws—
It was an act of perversion.

Everytime we put on the proper
clothes to go to a family
wedding and left our lovers
at home—
It was an act of perversion.

Everytime we heard
"Who I go to bed with
is my personal choice—
It's personal not political"
and said nothing—
It was an act of perversion.

Everytime we let straight relatives
bury our dead and push our
lovers away—
It was an act of perversion.

And they will come.
They will come for
the perverts

& it won't matter
if you're
        homosexual, not a faggot
        lesbian, not a dyke
        gay, not queer
It won't matter
if you

own your business
have a good job
or are on S.S.I.
It won't matter
if you're
> Black
> Chicano
> Native American
> Asian
> or White

It won't matter
if you're from
> New York
> or Los Angeles
> Galveston
> or Sioux Falls
It won't matter
if you're
> Butch, or Fem
> Not into roles
> Monogamous
> Non Monogamous
It won't matter
if you're
> Catholic
> Baptist
> Atheist
> Jewish
> or M.C.C.

They will come
They will come
to the cities
and to the land
to your front rooms
and in *your* closets.

They will come for
the perverts
and where will
you be
When they come?

PROLOGUE FROM "LEGACY"*

for Anastasia Jean

There are those who think
or perhaps don't think
that children and lesbians
together can't make a family
that we create an extension
of perversion.

They think
or perhaps don't think
that we have different relationships
with our children
that instead of getting up
in the middle of the night
for a 2 AM and 6 AM feeding
we rise up and chant
'you're gonna be a dyke
you're gonna be a dyke.'

That we feed our children
lavender Similac
and by breathing our air
the children's genitals distort
and they become hermaphrodites.

They ask
'What will you say to them
what will you teach them?'

Child
that would be mine
I bring you my world
and bid it be yours.

---

* 'Anything handed down from, or as from an ancestor to a descendant.'

PAT PARKER

MY BROTHER

for Blackberri

I

It is a simple ritual.
Phone rings
Berri's voice
low, husky
'What's you're doing?'
'Not a thing,
you coming over?'
'Well, I thought I'd
come by.'
A simple ritual.
He comes
we eat
watch television
play cards
play video games
some nights
he sleeps over
others
he goes home
sometimes
he brings a friend
more often
he doesn't.
A simple ritual.

II

It's a pause that alerts me
tells me this time
is hard time
the pain has risen
to the water line
we rarely verbalize
there is no need.

Within this lifestyle
there is much to undo you.

Hey look at the faggot!
When I was a child
our paper boy was Claude
every day
seven days a week
he bared the Texas weather
the rain that never stopped
walked through the Black section
where sidewalks had not
yet been invented
and ditches filled with water.
Walk careful Claude
across the plank
that served as sidewalk
sometime tips into the murky water
or heat
wet heat
that covers your pores
cascades rivulets of
stinging sweat down your body.
Our paper boy Claude
bared the weather well
each day he came
and each Saturday at dusk
he would come to collect.

My parents liked Claude.
Each Saturday Claude polite
would come
always said thank you
whether we had the money
or not.
Each Saturday
my father would say
Claude is a nice boy
works hard
goes to church
gives his money to his mother
and each Sunday
we would go to church
and there would be Claude
in his choir robes

PAT PARKER

til the Sunday
when he didn't come.

Hey look at the faggot!

Some young men howled at him
ran in a pack
reverted to some ancient form
they took Claude
took his money
yelled faggot
as they cast his body
in front of a car.

III

How many cars have you dodged Berri?
How many ancient young men have you met?
Perhaps your size saved you
but then you were not always this size
perhaps your fleetness
perhaps
there are no more ancient young men.

Ah! Within this lifestyle
we have chosen.
Sing?
What do you mean
you wanna be a singer?
Best get a good government job
maybe sing on the side.
You heard the words:
Be responsible
Be respectable
Be stable
Be secure
Be normal, boy.

How many quarter-filled rooms
have you sang your soul to
then washed away with
blended whiskey?

I told my booking agent one year
book me a tour
Blackberri and I
will travel this land
together
take our Black Queerness
into the face
of this place and say

Hey, here we are
a faggot & a dyke, Black
we make good music
& write good poems
We Be—Something Else.

My agent couldn't book us.
It seemed my lesbian audiences
were not ready for my faggot
brother
and I remembered
a law conference
in San Francisco
where women
women who loved women
threw boos and tomatoes
at a woman who dared
to have a man in her band.

What is this world we have?
Is my house the only safe place
for us?
And I am rage
all the low-paying gigs
all the uncut records
all the dodged cars
all the fear escaping
all the unclaimed love
so I offer my bosom
and food
and shudder
fearful of the time
when it will not be
enough

fearful of the time
when the ritual
ends.

Kenneth Pitchford

Kenneth Pitchford (born 1931 in Moorhead, Minnesota) was a member of the Flaming Faggots in the founding year of gay liberation (1969), an editor of *Double-F: a magazine of effeminism*, and author, with Steven Dansky and John Knoebel, of "The Effeminist Manifesto." His works of poetry include *The Blizzard Ape* (Scribners, 1958), *A Suite of Angels* (Chapel Hill, 1967), *Color Photos of the Atrocities* (Atlantic–Little, Brown, 1973), *The Contraband Poems* (Templar Press, 1976), and a new collection, *Dedications* (1987; on offer). Pitchford is also the translator of *The Sonnets to Orpheus of Rainer Maria Rilke* (Purchase Press, 1981), and the author of a novel, *The Brothers* (Lippincott), and a play, *The Wheel of the Murder*, which was produced by Joseph Papp at The New York Public Theater. Pitchford has taught poetry workshops at the New School, New York University, and St. Clement's Poetry Festival. He lives in New York.

SURGERY

So now just suppose that someone wanted to know
if faggots are men—a fair question.
Would I then trot out all the masculinists I have known
who are homosexual
and show how they did and do and will oppress women and
are certainly male supremacist, no less than I,
or should that be no more?—which is not even to speak
of hideous straight men with their most of the most.
And then should I apologize
about how long we've existed and haven't had any
consciousness to speak of

but have allowed them to kill Oscar Wilde with that longdrawnout
        torture
from which he died
and have allowed them to keep on using J. Edgar Hoover against us
without anyone's avenging that suffering life from
the death-brain they clamped over him as a child,
not to speak of Hart Crane, and here fill in your long
list of faggots murdered by the hatred of straight men,
and how Andy Warhol can make millions only by
showing how disgusting faggots are.
If he showed anything else—how beautiful, how usual, how human—
no dough.
No, faggots aren't not men. It's just that they
tried to cut something out of us very early on,
and sometimes succeeded, sometimes failed,
and they have counted ever since on the quarrel that got set up
between those they damaged and those who escaped what they meant
to do (whatever other damages got done escaping that one).
And I care so much about the part of me they wanted to kill
that I will risk any death to continue cherishing that part—
listen how it sings along in forbidden music and poetry,
listen how it sings inside a man when, stroking another man's brow,
he even experiments with meaning it for a full minute.
When they came with their knife, I lied as sincerely as I knew how,
saying Oh yes, I *do* hate girls and dolls and singing and picking
flowers and drawings and dancing,
and they went away and didn't cut *that* out of me,
although they beat me up every time
they caught it ulping out of me afterwards.
I don't really want this body or any other,
I don't know who I might hope could hold my hand and
walk half a block with me without needing to say anything.
But if it isn't you, my fellow faggot hearing or reading this, then
I'm in a bad way, because faggots *are* men, or else they'd have killed us,
and who else am I to share that knowledge with
if not you? learning to love
in each other The Other no other way.
And I want to have that taste in my mouth before they catch me
        and lock me
away (sanatorium/crematorium): my own warm
blood welling up arrogant and fanatic from having told
the last unutterable truth about how I know they've already failed
and are going to die and how all that will be left afterwards

KENNETH PITCHFORD

will be wild gigantic whorls of purple-green fingerpaint colors
dancing as though to an effeminist étude,
my very atoms indestructibly subversive
of everything they did to me.
The only way they might have succeeded is if
they could have cut out of my body
the whole universe infolded there under amnion like
a bud or a tumor.
No wonder they failed.
They wouldn't even know what the universe looks like, much
less how to spell it.

Ralph Pomeroy

Ralph Pomeroy (born 1926 in Evanston, Illinois) is an artist, curator, and a
writer on art. His poetry collections include *Stills & Movies* (Gesture Press,
1961) and *The Canaries As They Are* (Charioteer, 1964). A third book, *In the
Financial District* (Macmillan, 1968), won the Illinois Sesquicentennial Poetry
Prize. Since 1979, Pomeroy has been the associate director of Forum Gallery,
New York City, where he is also Lecturer on Modern Painting at the New York
School of Interior Design.

A TARDY EPITHALAMIUM FOR E. AND N.

You are proof that it can happen
and that it should.
There is as little hysteria
attached to your household
as to that of the most "normal" couple.

Because you are outlaw lovers though
I must salute you only with initials.
I hate this.

After eight years you still seem examples of clarity:
clear about looking at one another,
clear about getting up in the morning,
clear about people in relation to you,
clear about me when I arrive for dinner,
drink,
end up drunk.

All three writers, whenever we get together
we carp about careers and such.
We do this for some time, eating delicious
meals meanwhile, "keeping it down" because of
the nosey neighbors (who express their
contempt by making love or fighting
with their shades up).

At regular intervals we seem—like deer
perked-up to the sense of something—
to stop and see the joke of it all,
and laughter comes barging in and takes over.

I, sooner or later, grow jealous of you
and begin to realize that I have to get up and go,
alone,
while you get to stay with each other.

This makes me blue and close to tearful
and defiant even. So I kiss you both gingerly
and head resolutely for the subway,
or resolutely for the bars.

Grateful for you
all the same.

1969

Minnie Bruce Pratt

Minnie Bruce Pratt (born in Selma, 1946) was raised in Alabama and lives in Washington, D.C. Her published collections of poetry are *The Sound of One Fork* (Night Heron, 1981) and *We Say We Love Each Other* (Spinsters/Aunt Lute, 1985); other poetry appears in *Conditions, New England Review/Breadloaf Quarterly, Sinister Wisdom,* and elsewhere. She co-authored, with Elly Bulkin and Barbara Smith, *Yours in Struggle: Three Feminist Perspectives on Anti-Semitism and Racism.* She teaches Women's Studies at the University of Maryland and at George Washington University; she is a former member of the *Feminary* editorial collective, a member of the D.C. lesbian-feminist action group LIPS, and the mother of two teenage sons.

WAULKING SONG: TWO

Waulking tunes are sung by groups of Hebridean women as they work woolen cloth with their hands and feet to strengthen its weave. The women measure their task by the number of songs needed to complete the work, rather than by minutes or hours. Each waulking song has a narrative which may be altered by the lead singer, as well as a unique refrain so ancient that the meaning of its syllables has been lost. The refrains below may have been sung by women at work as much as a thousand years ago.

I

É hó hì ura bhì,
Ho ro ho, ì, o ho ro ho.

At first she would not answer
when I asked what was wrong.

Then she told what had happened
in that afternoon when she went to work.

Ho ro ho ì, ó ho ro ho,
É hó hì ura bhì.

Later she gave me the shirt to mend,
a thin K-Mart cotton

with lines of yellow blue and red
running from grey to brighter plaid.

É hó hì ura bhì,
Ho ro ho ì, o ho ro ho.

She had worn it the winter we met.
Under the lines I felt her heart beat.

Many times I had held her and felt
her heart beating beneath that thin cloth.

Ho ro ho ì, ó ho ro ho,
É hó hì ura bhì.

II

Ì u ru rù bhi u o,
Hó í abh o.

In the summer haze she had gone to work.
The man with the knife stopped her.

He shoved her from the door to the straggling hedge.
He jerked at her shirt and ripped the seams.

Chalain éileadh ò hi o,
Ro ho leathag.

He cut the buttons off one by one.
He raped her and tried to cut her throat.

He tried to cut her throat. And he did.
The red of her blood crossed the plaid of her shirt.

Ì u ru rù bhi u o,
Hó í abh o.

He asked if she liked it.
When she would not say yes,

he glinted the knife and he laughed.
He laughed and he left. She lay in the dust,

smoked a cigarette, got up,
went home to her trailer, took a bath.

She washed the shirt, put it away,
and looked to see what else was torn.

Chalain éileadh ò hi o,
Ro ho leathag.

III

O ho i hì ò,
Hao ri o hù ò.

We swore his knife would not part us,
yet fear divided us with many blades.

She did not want me to touch her,
to feel semen and dirt on her skin.

When I moved suddenly, she saw
the sun flash on the knife blade.

She wanted to know where
my hands were at all times.

When I slept with my arm around her,
she dreamed he had her pinned down

and woke night after night saying *no*,
night after night saying *no*.

She feared that I would not touch her,
would not touch, and that I would.

Hao ri o hù ò,
Ro ho i o hì ò.

I wanted the red mark to peel
off her throat like a band-aid

so she would be her self
without this pain: unscarred, unchanged,

not a woman who could have been
dead behind a QuickStop store

a line of ants running from her neck
a woman her friends would not touch.

Ro ho i o hì ò,
O ho i o hì ò.

After three months we wanted her
over it, to be done with dying

while she heard her rape each time
a rock cracked under feet behind her

as she crossed an empty parking lot.
I heard her death each time

a friend spoke the word *rape*
as matter-of-fact as the evening news.

O ho i o hì ò,
Hao ri o hù ò.

That winter, on weekends, when we shared a bed,
we shared bad dreams. We twisted in sheets.

Some nights she heard her voice cry out
and woke herself, breath tearing her throat.

Some nights I felt her shake beside me,
caught in the hedge in December wind.

Before I touched her, I called her name
to wake her before his hand could reach.

We held hands as we talked in the dark.

The shirt lay folded, unmended, in my drawer.

Hao ri o hù ò,
Ro ho i o hì ò.

IV

O ho ì ù ó,
Air fair all ill ó ho.

It has been three years; the shirt
was mended, not thrown away.

We rise at dawn to dress for work.
I touch her bare arm. She is alive.

Her heartbeats rush under my fingers.
Her flesh is solid, not crumbled to dust.

Air fair all ill ó ho,
Ro ho hao ri rì ó.

Under my hands, her shoulders spread,
broad, an outcrop of limestone,

under her skin, layers of muscle,
from heft and lift, the weight of her work.

She has made herself strong, enough
to knock a man down, enough

to tell me one night what his hands
had done, the exact, secret wounds.

Ro ho hao ri rì ó,
O ho ì ù ó.

I wanted my hands to be rain for her
to wash away all hurt, the trace of blood.

I did what I could. I took out the shirt,
sewed the buttons back on, one by one,

sewed over each seam, twice, by hand.
He would not ruin what we had made.

O ho ì ú ó,
Air fair all ill ó ho.

She wore the shirt, walked alone to her job.
She would not live in tatters and shreds.

But some afternoons he got his death:
when we heard of a nurse off work, the men,

blackberry vines in an empty lot;
a woman raped at the Gulf station,

stabbed through both eyes with a screwdriver
so she would not see to find him later.

Air fair all ill ó ho,
Ro ho hao ri rì ó.

Then we could not bear witness to our life.
We bought beer and drank to become like stone,

no live woman or dead in our touch.
We cried out with the voice of falling rocks.

We fell asleep, dead weight, in each other's arms,
but always we swore that we would wake up.

Ro ho hao ri rì ó,
O ho ì ù ó.

It has been three years: I wake before dawn
in the dark. I think of the mended shirt.

It still hangs in her closet, the pattern
of red blue yellow lines seamed together.

Her scar has faded to a thin white line.
I can touch her breast. I can feel her heart beating.

He has not ruined what we have made.

At dawn we will rise to dress for work.

O ho ì ù ó,
Air fair all ill ó ho.

V

Hao ri o hù ò,
Ro ho i o hì ò.

When she got to work at five til 8
this morning, a woman named Millie was shot

in the parking lot as she left her car.
The man with the gun watched her blood

disappear into the asphalt. Her boss,
other women watched from a doorway.

At first she asked for help. The man
left to rape a woman in the next street.

In emergency she fought with nurses
who held her to the cart, said *Lie down.*

She said *I know I'm dying. I want*
to sit up. And she did, before she died,

while they were saying *Be quiet, you'll be better.*
She was a secretary, three months pregnant.

Ro ho i o hì ò,
O ho i o hì ò.

Do you want me to be quiet? You are tired
of the words *blood, rape, death.*

So am I. I had ended these lines
at the last refrain, but this morning I heard

about Millie. I remembered again your blood
in the dirt, your stomach exposed to the knife.

I want to keep harm from you. I want
to clothe and protect you with my arms.

I look at my hands that held needle and thread.
We resist by whatever means we can.

At work your arm has thrust, your hand
has hefted two feet of steel pipe

over a counter at the man who threatened.
You say *Next time I fight back even if I die.*

Your hands are not quiet; your voice is angry.
I love you because you have refused to die.

O ho i o hì ò,
Hao ri o hù ò.

This poem is for you, to pin to the mended shirt,
like the paper slip you find in a new pocket,

#49, but you know it's a woman,
all day folding sleeves around cardboard.

At work almost dead on her feet,
she folds the plaid thin fabrics.

She thinks of what her hands make at home.
When she leaves the line, the machines are silent.

Her steps make a poem to the rhythm of her heart,
like a poem for you, to pin to the mended shirt.

Hao ri o hù ò,
Ro ho i o hì ò.

THE CHILD TAKEN FROM THE MOTHER

I could do nothing: nothing. Do you
understand? Women ask: *Why didn't you—?*
like they do of women who've been raped.
And I ask myself: Why didn't I? Why

didn't I run away with them? Or face
him in court? Or—

                              ten years ago I
answered myself: No way for children to live.
Or: The chance of absolute loss. Or:

I did the best I could. It was not
enough. It was about terror and power.
I did everything I could: not enough.

This is not the voice of the guilty mother.

Clumsy with anger even now, it is a voice
from the woman shoved outside, one night, as words
clack into place like bricks, poker chips.

Like the lawyer: *It's a card game. You were too
candid. They know what's in your hand.*
I look down. My hands dangle open and empty
in the harsh yellow light. Strange men,
familiar, laugh and curse in the kitchen, whisky,
bending over cards. Or is it something held down
on the table? Someone says: *Bull Dog Bend.*
Someone says: *The place of the father in the home.*

My mother's voice: *Those women have never held
a little baby in their arms.* In the old window,
a shadow. Two hands, brick and mortar, seal
the house, my children somewhere inside. The youngest
has lost his baby fat, navel flattened, last
of my stomach's nourishing.
                              You say: *Do something.*
You say: *Why is this happening?*
                              My body. My womb.
My body of a woman, a mother, a lesbian.
                              And here,
perhaps, you say: *That last word doesn't belong.*

Woman, mother: those can stay. Lesbian: no.
Put that outside the place of the poem. Too
slangy, prosy, obvious, just doesn't belong.

*Why don't you: Why didn't you: Can't you
say it some other way?*

        The beautiful place
we stood arguing, after the movie, under blue-white
fluorescence: two middle-aged women in jeans,
two grown boys, the lanky one, the tactful one,
bundled in a pause before cold outside, to argue
the significances: bloody birth, the man cursing
a woman in the kitchen, dirt, prayer, the place
of the father, the master, the beatings, black and
white, home lost, continents, two women
lovers glimpsed, the child taken from the mother
who returns.

        No one says: *This is about us.* But
in the narrow corridor, stark cement block walls,
we become huge, holding up the harsh images,
the four of us loud, familiar.

        Other movie-
goers squeeze past, light their cigarettes,
glance, do not say even to themselves: *Children
and women, lovers, mothers, lesbians. Yes.*

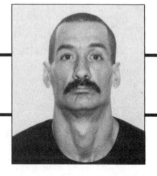

J. M. Regan

J. M. Regan (born 1947 in Manhattan) is a former chef and a former writing instructor at City University of New York. Educated at CUNY and at Georgetown, Regan is currently Program Director at an educational center for the elderly on Manhattan's Upper West Side. A number of his poems have appeared in *The James White Review*.

PARTIAL LUETIC HISTORY OF AN INDIVIDUAL AT RISK

In the Downtown Tombs of long long ago
    I learned how
to roll tobacco,
and eat stew with my fingers
    like a Hindu,
and survive getting raped all day by murderers.
In return I earned an eternally positive sera,

and became a natural host, a host-plant
    the drowned feed from,
a stand in the water my doctor flails
    the seed-pods from—
with his polyclinic hands and seas of hair
    I nearly disappear under,
how I sprout and flower flower
for my sky-blue and Mediterranean doctor.

He sneaks looks at me like a dirty picture.
When I was small and caught men watching me
    like that,
I thought they hated me.
But now I'm big and think better.
I think I'm protected.

It's not ALL bad, it's not ALL bad,
he keeps promising—
as though *good* or *bad* had a single thing
    to do with it!
and, *Did I hurt you?*—the pick in the duct.
I don't know.

Are you still suicidal? —prob-
    ing my swollen groin.
It's an option, doc.
While the cringing vein, sick of invasion,
reluctant to give up more blood,
drips drips drips into the rubber tube.

My Jewish doctor loves me truer,
sitting rigid at the bare Care Center

like a gaunt tree,
and the air of a bored whore,
one eye on her watch,
one hand in her snatch,

one face a nest of snakes to shock
   me into shape—
inescapably stable, like iron.
They held a razor to my neck.
The world, she says, *is full of irritation.*
Our hour's up.

Two decades later now I've got
   stigmata,
I'm going holy:
tongue and palate cancers, gummatous
   change
engage my way of tasting tasting, my way
   with speech.
It's grown unruly.

It's exploding my bones.
Find me a spontaneous cure! the kind
   that purifies the lives of saints
and drives the sun to leave its prints
in every leaf, and each brief bird,
and even in the marrows of the stones.

Adrienne Rich

Adrienne Rich, born 1929 in Baltimore, Maryland, is widely acknowledged as a major American poet whose vision and work have transforming power in her readers' lives. She has published eleven volumes of poetry, including *Diving*

into the Wreck, The Dream of a Common Language, A Wild Patience Has Taken
Me This Far, and Your Native Land, Your Life (W. W. Norton, 1973, 1978,
1981, 1986). Among her prose works are Of Woman Born; On Lies, Secrets and
Silence; and Blood, Bread, and Poetry (Norton 1976, 1979, 1986). She lives in
Santa Cruz, California, with the writer Michelle Cliff.

TWENTY-ONE LOVE POEMS

I

Wherever in this city, screens flicker
with pornography, with science-fiction vampires,
victimized hirelings bending to the lash,
we also have to walk . . . if simply as we walk
through the rainsoaked garbage, the tabloid cruelties
of our own neighborhoods.
We need to grasp our lives inseparable
from those rancid dreams, that blurt of metal, those disgraces,
and the red begonia perilously flashing
from a tenement sill six stories high,
or the long-legged young girls playing ball
in the junior highschool playground.
No one has imagined us. We want to live like trees,
sycamores blazing through the sulfuric air,
dappled with scars, still exuberantly budding,
our animal passion rooted in the city.

II

I wake up in your bed. I know I have been dreaming.
Much earlier, the alarm broke us from each other,
you've been at your desk for hours. I know what I dreamed:
our friend the poet comes into my room
where I've been writing for days,
drafts, carbons, poems are scattered everywhere,
and I want to show her one poem
which is the poem of my life. But I hesitate,
and wake. You've kissed my hair
to wake me. *I dreamed you were a poem,*
I say, *a poem I wanted to show someone . . .*
and I laugh and fall dreaming again
of the desire to show you to everyone I love,

to move openly together
in the pull of gravity, which is not simple,
which carries the feathered grass a long way down the upbreathing air.

III

Since we're not young, weeks have to do time
for years of missing each other. Yet only this odd warp
in time tells me we're not young.
Did I ever walk the morning streets at twenty,
my limbs streaming with a purer joy?
did I lean from any window over the city
listening for the future
as I listen here with nerves tuned for your ring?
And you, you move toward me with the same tempo.
Your eyes are everlasting, the green spark
of the blue-eyed grass of early summer,
the green-blue wild cress washed by the spring.
At twenty, yes: we thought we'd live forever.
At forty-five, I want to know even our limits.
I touch you knowing we weren't born tomorrow,
and somehow, each of us will help the other live,
and somewhere, each of us must help the other die.

IV

I come home from you through the early light of spring
flashing off ordinary walls, the Pez Dorado,
the Discount Wares, the shoe-store. . . . I'm lugging my sack
of groceries, I dash for the elevator
where a man, taut, elderly, carefully composed
lets the door almost close on me. —For god's sake hold it!
I croak at him. —Hysterical,—he breathes my way.
I let myself into the kitchen, unload my bundles,
make coffee, open the window, put on Nina Simone
singing Here comes the sun. . . . I open the mail,
drinking delicious coffee, delicious music,
my body still both light and heavy with you. The mail
lets fall a Xerox of something written by a man
aged 27, a hostage, tortured in prison:
My genitals have been the object of such a sadistic display
they keep me constantly awake with the pain . . .
Do whatever you can to survive.

ADRIENNE RICH

You know, I think that men love wars . . .
And my incurable anger, my unmendable wounds
break open further with tears, I am crying helplessly,
and they still control the world, and you are not in my arms.

V

This apartment full of books could crack open
to the thick jaws, the bulging eyes
of monsters, easily: Once open the books, you have to face
the underside of everything you've loved—
the rack and pincers held in readiness, the gag
even the best voices have had to mumble through,
the silence burying unwanted children—
women, deviants, witnesses—in desert sand.
Kenneth tells me he's been arranging his books
so he can look at Blake and Kafka while he types;
yes; and we still have to reckon with Swift
loathing the woman's flesh while praising her mind,
Goethe's dread of the Mothers, Claudel vilifying Gide,
and the ghosts—their hands clasped for centuries—
of artists dying in childbirth, wise-women charred at the stake,
centuries of books unwritten piled behind these shelves;
and we still have to stare into the absence
of men who would not, women who could not, speak
to our life—this still unexcavated hole
called civilization, this act of translation, this half-world.

VI

Your small hands, precisely equal to my own—
only the thumb is larger, longer—in these hands
I could trust the world, or in many hands like these,
handling power-tools or steering-wheel
or touching a human face. . . . Such hands could turn
the unborn child rightways in the birth canal
or pilot the exploratory rescue-ship
through icebergs, or piece together
the fine, needle-like sherds of a great krater-cup
bearing on its sides
figures of ecstatic women striding
to the sibyl's den or the Eleusinian cave—
such hands might carry out an unavoidable violence

with such restraint, with such a grasp
of the range and limits of violence
that violence ever after would be obsolete.

VII

What kind of beast would turn its life into words?
What atonement is this all about?
—and yet, writing words like these, I'm also living.
Is all this close to the wolverines' howled signals,
that modulated cantata of the wild?
or, when away from you I try to create you in words,
am I simply using you, like a river or a war?
And how have I used rivers, how have I used wars
to escape writing of the worst thing of all—
not the crimes of others, not even our own death,
but the failure to want our freedom passionately enough
so that blighted elms, sick rivers, massacres would seem
mere emblems of that desecration of ourselves?

VIII

I can see myself years back at Sunion,
hurting with an infected foot, Philoctetes
in woman's form, limping the long path,
lying on a headland over the dark sea,
looking down the red rocks to where a soundless curl
of white told me a wave had struck,
imagining the pull of that water from that height,
knowing deliberate suicide wasn't my métier,
yet all the time nursing, measuring that wound.
Well, that's finished. The woman who cherished
her suffering is dead. I am her descendant.
I love the scar-tissue she handed on to me,
but I want to go on from here with you
fighting the temptation to make a career of pain.

IX

Your silence today is a pond where drowned things live
I want to see raised dripping and brought into the sun.
It's not my own face I see there, but other faces,

ADRIENNE RICH

even your face at another age.
Whatever's lost there is needed by both of us—
a watch of old gold, a water-blurred fever chart,
a key. . . . Even the silt and pebbles of the bottom
deserve their glint of recognition. I fear this silence,
this inarticulate life. I'm waiting
for a wind that will gently open this sheeted water
for once, and show me what I can do
for you, who have often made the unnameable
nameable for others, even for me.

X

Your dog, tranquil and innocent, dozes through
our cries, our murmured dawn conspiracies
our telephone calls. She knows—what can she know?
If in my human arrogance I claim to read
her eyes, I find there only my own animal thoughts:
that creatures must find each other for bodily comfort,
that voices of the psyche drive through the flesh
further than the dense brain could have foretold,
that the planetary nights are growing cold for those
on the same journey, who want to touch
one creature-traveler clear to the end;
that without tenderness, we are in hell.

XI

Every peak is a crater. This is the law of volcanoes,
making them eternally and visibly female.
No height without depth, without a burning core,
though our straw soles shred on the hardened lava.
I want to travel with you to every sacred mountain
smoking within like the sibyl stooped over his tripod,
I want to reach for your hand as we scale the path,
to feel your arteries glowing in my clasp,
never failing to note the small, jewel-like flower
unfamiliar to us, nameless till we rename her,
that clings to the slowly altering rock—
that detail outside ourselves that brings us to ourselves,
was here before us, knew we would come, and sees beyond us.

XII

Sleeping, turning in turn like planets
rotating in their midnight meadow:
a touch is enough to let us know
we're not alone in the universe, even in sleep:
the dream-ghosts of two worlds
walking their ghost-towns, almost address each other.
I've wakened to your muttered words
spoken light- or dark-years away
as if my own voice had spoken.
But we have different voices, even in sleep,
and our bodies, so alike, are yet so different
and the past echoing through our bloodstreams
is freighted with different language, different meanings—
though in any chronicle of the world we share
it could be written with new meaning
we were two lovers of one gender,
we were two women of one generation.

XIII

The rules break like a thermometer,
quicksilver spills across the charted systems,
we're out in a country that has no language
no laws, we're chasing the raven and the wren
through gorges unexplored since dawn
whatever we do together is pure invention
the maps they gave us were out of date
by years . . . we're driving through the desert
wondering if the water will hold out
the hallucinations turn to simple villages
the music on the radio comes clear—
neither *Rosenkavalier* nor *Götterdämmerung*
but a woman's voice singing old songs
with new words, with a quiet bass, a flute
plucked and fingered by women outside the law.

XIV

It was your vision of the pilot
confirmed my vision of you: you said, *He keeps
on steering headlong into the waves, on purpose*

ADRIENNE RICH

while we crouched in the open hatchway
vomiting into plastic bags
for three hours between St. Pierre and Miquelon.
I never felt closer to you.
In the close cabin where the honeymoon couples
huddled in each other's laps and arms
I put my hand on your thigh
to comfort both of us, your hand came over mine,
we stayed that way, suffering together
in our bodies, as if all suffering
were physical, we touched so in the presence
of strangers who knew nothing and cared less
vomiting their private pain
as if all suffering were physical.

(THE FLOATING POEM, UNNUMBERED)

Whatever happens with us, your body
will haunt mine—tender, delicate
your lovemaking, like the half-curled frond
of the fiddlehead fern in forests
just washed by sun. Your traveled, generous thighs
between which my whole face has come and come—
the innocence and wisdom of the place my tongue has found there—
the live, insatiate dance of your nipples in my mouth—
your touch on me, firm, protective, searching
me out, your strong tongue and slender fingers
reaching where I had been waiting years for you
in my rose-wet cave—whatever happens, this is.

XV

If I lay on that beach with you
white, empty, pure green water warmed by the Gulf Stream
and lying on that beach we could not stay
because the wind drove fine sand against us
as if it were against us
if we tried to withstand it and we failed—
if we drove to another place
to sleep in each other's arms
and the beds were narrow like prisoners' cots
and we were tired and did not sleep together

and this was what we found, so this is what we did—
was the failure ours?
If I cling to circumstances I could feel
not responsible. Only she who says
she did not choose, is the loser in the end.

XVI

Across a city from you, I'm with you,
just as an August night
moony, inlet-warm, seabathed, I watched you sleep,
the scrubbed, sheenless wood of the dressing-table
cluttered with our brushes, books, vials in the moonlight—
or a salt-mist orchard, lying at your side
watching red sunset through the screendoor of the cabin,
G minor Mozart on the tape-recorder,
falling asleep to the music of the sea.
This island of Manhattan is wide enough
for both of us, and narrow:
I can hear your breath tonight, I know how your face
lies upturned, the halflight tracing
your generous, delicate mouth
where grief and laughter sleep together.

XVII

No one's fated or doomed to love anyone.
The accidents happen, we're not heroines,
they happen in our lives like car crashes,
books that change us, neighborhoods
we move into and come to love.
Tristan und Isolde is scarcely the story,
women at least should know the difference
between love and death. No poison cup,
no penance. Merely a notion that the tape-recorder
should have caught some ghost of us: that tape-recorder
not merely played but should have listened to us,
and could instruct those after us:
this we were, this is how we tried to love,
and these are the forces they had ranged against us,
and these are the forces we had ranged within us,
within us and against us, against us and within us.

XVIII

Rain on the West Side Highway,
red light at Riverside:
the more I live the more I think
two people together is a miracle.
You're telling the story of your life
for once, a tremor breaks the surface of your words.
The story of our lives becomes our lives.
Now you're in fugue across what some I'm sure
Victorian poet called the *salt estranging sea.*
Those are the words that come to mind.
I feel estrangement, yes. As I've felt dawn
pushing toward daybreak. Something: a cleft of light—?
Close between grief and anger, a space opens
where I am Adrienne alone. And growing colder.

XIX

Can it be growing colder when I begin
to touch myself again, adhesions pull away?
When slowly the naked face turns from staring backward
and looks into the present,
the eye of winter, city, anger, poverty, and death
and the lips part and say: *I mean to go on living?*
Am I speaking coldly when I tell you in a dream
or in this poem, *There are no miracles?*
(I told you from the first I wanted daily life,
this island of Manhattan was island enough for me.)
If I could let you know—
two women together is a work
nothing in civilization has made simple,
two people together is a work
heroic in its ordinariness,
the slow-picked, halting traverse of a pitch
where the fiercest attention becomes routine
—look at the faces of those who have chosen it.

XX

That conversation we were always on the edge
of having, runs on in my head,
at night the Hudson trembles in New Jersey light

polluted water yet reflecting even
sometimes the moon
and I discern a woman
I loved, drowning in secrets, fear wound round her throat
and choking her like hair. And this is she
with whom I tried to speak, whose hurt, expressive head
turning aside from pain, is dragged down deeper
where it cannot hear me,
and soon I shall know I was talking to my own soul.

XXI

The dark lintels, the blue and foreign stones
of the great round rippled by stone implements
the midsummer night light rising from beneath
the horizon—when I said "a cleft of light"
I meant this. And this is not Stonehenge
simply nor any place but the mind
casting back to where her solitude,
shared, could be chosen without loneliness,
not easily nor without pains to stake out
the circle, the heavy shadows, the great light.
I choose to be a figure in that light,
half-blotted by darkness, something moving
across that space, the color of stone
greeting the moon, yet more than stone:
a woman. I choose to walk here. And to draw this circle.

1974–1976

YOM KIPPUR 1984

I drew solitude over me, on the long shore.
—ROBINSON JEFFERS, "PRELUDE"

*For whoever does not afflict his soul throughout
this day, shall be cut off from his people.*
—LEVITICUS 23:29

What is a Jew in solitude?
What would it mean not to feel lonely or afraid

far from your own or those you have called your own?
What is a woman in solitude: a queer woman or man?
In the empty street, on the empty beach, in the desert
what in this world as it is can solitude mean?

The glassy, concrete octagon suspended from the cliffs
with its electric gate, its perfected privacy
is not what I mean
the pick-up with a gun parked at a turn-out in Utah or the Golan
        Heights
is not what I mean
the poet's tower facing the western ocean, acres of forest planted to
        the east, the woman reading in the cabin, her attack dog
        suddenly risen
is not what I mean

Three thousand miles from what I once called home
I open a book searching for some lines I remember
about flowers, something to bind me to this coast as lilacs in the
        dooryard once
bound me back there—yes, lupines on a burnt mountainside,
something that bloomed and faded and was written down
in the poet's book, forever:
Opening the poet's book
I find the hatred in the poet's heart: . . . *the hateful-eyed*
and human-bodied are all about me: you that love multitude may have
        them

Robinson Jeffers, multitude
is the blur flung by distinct forms against these landward valleys
and the farms that run down to the sea; the lupines
are multitude, and the torched poppies, the grey Pacific unrolling its
        scrolls of surf,
and the separate persons, stooped
over sewing machines in denim dust, bent under the shattering skies
        of harvest
who sleep by shifts in never-empty beds have their various dreams
Hands that pick, pack, steam, stitch, strip, stuff, shell, scrape,
        scour, belong to a brain like no other
Must I argue the love of multitude in the blur or defend
a solitude of barbed-wire and searchlights, the survivalist's final
        solution, have I a choice?

ADRIENNE RICH   339

To wander far from your own or those you have called your own
to hear strangeness calling you from far away
and walk in that direction, long and far, not calculating risk
to go to meet the Stranger without fear or weapon, protection
        nowhere on your mind
(the Jew on the icy, rutted road on Christmas Eve prays for another
        Jew
the woman in the ungainly twisting shadows of the street: *Make
        those be a woman's footsteps*; as if she could believe in a
        woman's god)

Find someone like yourself. Find others.
Agree you will never desert each other.
Understand that any rift among you
means power to those who want to do you in.
Close to the center, safety; toward the edges, danger.
But I have a nightmare to tell: I am trying to say
that to be with my people is my dearest wish
but that I also love strangers
that I crave separateness
I hear myself stuttering these words
to my worst friends and my best enemies
who watch for my mistakes in grammar
my mistakes in love.
This is the day of atonement; but do my people forgive me?
If a cloud knew loneliness and fear, I would be that cloud.

To love the Stranger, to love solitude—am I writing merely about
        privilege
about drifting from the center, drawn to edges,
a privilege we can't afford in the world that is,
who are hated as being of our kind: faggot kicked into the icy river,
        woman dragged from her stalled car
into the mist-struck mountains, used and hacked to death
young scholar shot at the university gates on a summer evening
        walk, his prizes and studies nothing, nothing availing his
        Blackness
Jew deluded that she's escaped the tribe, the laws of her exclusion,
        the men too holy to touch her hand;   Jew who has turned
        her back
on *midrash* and *mitzvah* (yet wears the *chai* on a thong between her
        breasts) hiking alone

ADRIENNE RICH

found with a swastika carved in her back at the foot of the cliffs
    (did she die as queer or as Jew?)

Solitude, O taboo, endangered species
on the mist-struck spur of the mountain, I want a gun to defend you
In the desert, on the deserted street, I want what I can't have:
your elder sister, Justice, her great peasant's hand outspread
her eye, half-hooded, sharp and true
And I ask myself, have I thrown courage away?
have I traded off something I don't name?
To what extreme will I go to meet the extremist?
What will I do to defend my want or anyone's want to search for her
    spirit-vision
far from the protection of those she has called her own?
Will I find O solitude
your plumes, your breasts, your hair
against my face, as in childhood, your voice like the mockingbird's
singing *Yes, you are loved, why else this song?*
in the old places, anywhere?

What is a Jew in solitude?
What is a woman in solitude, a queer woman or man?
When the winter flood-tides wrench the tower from the rock,
    crumble the prophet's headland, and the farms slide into the
    sea
when leviathan is endangered and Jonah becomes revenger
when center and edges are crushed together, the extremities crushed
    together on which the world was founded
when our souls crash together, Arab and Jew, howling our loneliness
    within the tribes
when the refugee child and the exile's child re-open the blasted and
    forbidden city
when we who refuse to be women and men as women and men are
    chartered, tell our stories of solitude spent in multitude
in that world as it may be, newborn and haunted, what will solitude
    mean?

1984–1985

Muriel Rukeyser

Muriel Rukeyser (1913–1980) was born and died in New York City. Her first book, *Theory of Flight,* received the Yale Younger Poets Award (1935), and in 1940 Louis Untermeyer called her "the most inventive and challenging poet of her generation." Fourteen volumes are gathered in her *Collected Poems* (McGraw-Hill, 1978). Her interest in science and its connection to art led her to write biographies of Willard Gibbs and Thomas Hariot; she also wrote prose studies, children's books, and a play, and translated the work of Bertolt Brecht and other poets. A lifelong activist for radical social change, she was arrested during the second Scottsboro trial in Alabama, traveled to Spain during the Civil War, and fought against American involvement in Vietnam and against the spread of nuclear power.

ST. ROACH

For that I never knew you, I only learned to dread you,
for that I never touched you, they told me you are filth,
they showed me by every action to despise your kind;
for that I saw my people making war on you,
I could not tell you apart, one from another,
for that in childhood I lived in places clear of you,
for that all the people I knew met you by
crushing you, stamping you to death, they poured boiling
    water on you, they flushed you down,
for that I could not tell one from another
only that you were dark, fast on your feet, and slender.
    Not like me.
For that I did not know your poems
And that I do not know any of your sayings
And that I cannot speak or read your language
And that I do not sing your songs
And that I do not teach our children
        to eat your food

or know your poems
or sing your songs
But that we say you are filthing our food
But that we know you not at all.

Yesterday I looked at one of you for the first time.
You were lighter than the others in color, that was
    neither good nor bad.
I was really looking for the first time.
You seemed troubled and witty.

Today I touched one of you for the first time.
You were startled, you ran, you fled away
Fast as a dancer, light, strange and lovely to the touch.
I reach, I touch, I begin to know you.

LOOKING AT EACH OTHER

Yes, we were looking at each other
Yes, we knew each other very well
Yes, we had made love with each other many times
Yes, we had heard music together
Yes, we had gone to the sea together
Yes, we had cooked and eaten together
Yes, we had laughed often day and night
Yes, we fought violence and knew violence
Yes, we hated the inner and outer oppression
Yes, that day we were looking at each other
Yes, we saw the sunlight pouring down
Yes, the corner of the table was between us
Yes, bread and flowers were on the table
Yes, our eyes saw each other's eyes
Yes, our mouths saw each other's mouth
Yes, our breasts saw each other's breasts
Yes, our bodies entire saw each other
Yes, it was beginning in each
Yes, it threw waves across our lives
Yes, the pulses were becoming very strong
Yes, the beating became very delicate
Yes, the calling   the arousal
Yes, the arriving   the coming

Yes, there it was for both entire
Yes, we were looking at each other

THE SPEED OF DARKNESS

I

Whoever despises the clitoris despises the penis
Whoever despises the penis despises the cunt
Whoever despises the cunt despises the life of the child.

Resurrection music,   silence,   and surf.

II

No longer speaking
Listening with the whole body
And with every drop of blood
Overtaken by silence

But this same silence is become speech
With the speed of darkness.

III

Stillness during war, the lake.
The unmoving spruces.
Glints over the water.
Faces, voices.   You are far away.
A tree that trembles.

I am the tree that trembles and trembles.

IV

After the lifting of the mist
after the lift of the heavy rains
the sky stands clear
and the cries of the city risen in day
I remember the buildings are space
walled, to let space be used for living

I mind this room is space
this drinking glass is space
whose boundary of glass
lets me give you drink and space to drink
your hand, my hand being space
containing skies and constellations
your face
carries the reaches of air
I know I am space
my words are air.

V

Between   between
the man : act   exact
woman : in curve   senses in their maze
frail orbits, green tries,   games of stars
shape of the body speaking its evidence

VI

I look across at the real
vulnerable   involved   naked
devoted to the present of all I care for
the world of its history leading to this moment.

VII

Life the announcer.
I assure you
there are many ways to have a child.
I bastard mother
promise you
there are many ways to be born.
They all come forth
in their own grace.

VIII

Ends of the earth join tonight
with blazing stars upon their meeting.

These sons,   these sons
fall burning into Asia.

IX

Time comes into it.
Say it.   Say it.

The universe is made of stories,
not of atoms.

X

Lying
blazing beside me
you rear beautifully and up—
your thinking face—
erotic body reaching
in all its colors and lights—
your erotic face
colored and lit—
not colored body-and-face
but now entire,
colors   lights   the world thinking and reaching.

XI

The river flows past the city.

Water goes down to tomorrow
making its children   I hear their unborn voices
I am working out the vocabulary of my silence.

XII

Big-boned man young and of my dream
Struggles to get the live bird out of his throat.
I am he am I?   Dreaming?
I am the bird am I?   I am the throat?

A bird with a curved beak.
It could slit anything, the throat-bird.
Drawn up slowly.   The curved blades, not large.
Bird emerges   wet   being born
Begins to sing.

XIII

My night awake
staring at the broad rough jewel
the copper roof across the way
thinking of the poet
yet unborn in this dark
who will be the throat of these hours.
No.   Of those hours.
Who will speak these days,
if not I,
if not you?

THEN

When I am dead, even then,
I will still love you, I will wait in these poems,
When I am dead, even then
I am still listening to you.
I will still be making poems for you
out of silence;
silence will be falling into that silence,
it is building music.

Michael Rumaker

Michael Rumaker (born 1932 in Philadelphia) has published a number of novels, including A Day and a Night at the Baths and My First Satyrnalia (Grey Fox Press, 1979 and 1981). He has recently completed a new novel, Pagan Days. His poems have appeared in numerous periodicals and anthologies. Rumaker teaches at City College of New York and at Rockland Community College, Suffern, New York.

THE FAIRIES ARE DANCING ALL OVER THE WORLD

The fairies are dancing all over the world
    In the dreams of the President
        they are dancing
  although he dares not mention this at cabinet meetings
In the baby blood of the brandnew
    they are dancing O most rapturously
and over the graves of the fathers and mothers
      who are dead
and around the heads of the mothers and fathers who are not dead
    in celebration of the sons and daughters
      they've given the earth
The fairies are dancing in the paws and muzzles
    of dogs larking in the broad field next to the church
The fairies have always danced in the blood of the untamed
      in the muscular horned goat
      and the shining snake
    in the blood of Henry Thoreau
      and most certainly Emily Dickinson
And they skip in the blood of the marine recruit
    in his barracks at night
      his bones aching with fatigue and loneliness
    and pure dreams of women
        and his goodbuddy in the next bunk
They are most lovely in the eyes of the black kid
     trucking in front of the jukebox
      at the local pizzeria,
more timorous in the eyes of his white friend
    whose hips are a bit more calcified
with hereditary denunciation of the fairies
    May the fairies swivel his hips
On sap green evenings in early summer
      the fairies danced under the moon in country places
    danced among native american teepees
and hung in the rough hair of buffalos racing across the prairies
      and are dancing still
      most hidden
      and everywhere
In some, only in the eyes
  in others a reach of the arm
    a sudden yelp of joy

    MICHAEL RUMAKER

reveals their presence
The fairies are dancing from coast to coast
   all over deadmiddle America
        they're bumping and grinding on the Kremlin walls
     the tap of their feet is eroding all the walls
      all over the world as they dance
In the way of the western world
     the fairies' dance has become small
   a bleating, crabbed jerkiness
but there for all that,
   a bit of healthy green in the dead wood
       that spreads an invisible green fire
  around and around the globe
encircling it in its dance
  of intimacy with the secret of all living things
The fairies are dancing even in the Pope's nose
     and in the heart of the most stubborn macho
  who will not and will not
    and the fairies will
      most insistently
   because he will not
In the Pentagon the fairies are dancing
    under the scrambled egg hats
   of those who see no reason why youths should live to old age
The fairies bide their time and wait
    They dance in invisible circlets of joy
     around and around and over the planet
They are the green rings unseen by spaceships
   their breath is the earth of the first spring evening
They explode in the black buds of deadwood winter
      Welcome them with open arms
    They are allies courting in the bloodstream
   welcome them and dance with them

Kate Rushin

Kate Rushin (born 1951, Syracuse, New York) grew up in Lawnside and Camden, New Jersey. She has a B.A. in Theatre and Communications (Oberlin, 1973) and has taught poetry workshops for adults and children. In 1978, Rushin was in residence at Cummington Community of the Arts and received fellowships from the Fine Arts Work Center, Provincetown, and the Massachusetts Artists' Foundation. Her work appears in *Home Girls* (Kitchen Table, 1983), *This Bridge Called My Back* (Persephone, 1981), and *Sojourner*. She belongs to the National Coalition of Black Lesbians and Gays, Boston Women's Community Radio, and New Words Bookstore collective.

THE BRIDGE POEM

I've had enough
I'm sick of seeing and touching
Both sides of things
Sick of being the damn bridge for everybody

Nobody
Can talk to anybody
Without me
Right?

I explain my mother to my father my father to my little sister
My little sister to my brother my brother to the white feminists
The white feminists to the Black church folks the Black church folks
To the ex-hippies the ex-hippies to the Black separatists the
Black separatists to the artists the artists to my friends' parents . . .

Then
I've got to explain myself
To everybody

I do more translating
Than the Gawdamn U.N.

Forget it
I'm sick of it

I'm sick of filling in your gaps

Sick of being your insurance against
The isolation of your self-imposed limitations
Sick of being the crazy at your holiday dinners
Sick of being the odd one at your Sunday Brunches
Sick of being the sole Black friend to 34 individual white folks

Find another connection to the rest of the world
Find something else to make you legitimate
Find some other way to be political and hip

I will not be the bridge to your womanhood
Your manhood
Your human-ness

I'm sick of reminding you not to
Close off too tight for too long

I'm sick of mediating with your worst self
On behalf of your better selves

I am sick
Of having to remind you
To breathe
Before you suffocate
Your own fool self

Forget it
Stretch or drown
Evolve or die

The bridge I must be
Is the bridge to my own power
I must translate
My own fears

Mediate
My own weaknesses

I must be the bridge to nowhere
But my true self
And then
I will be useful

Assotto Saint

Assotto Saint (born 1957 in Haiti) is the author of several theater pieces on black gay men. His first, *Risin' to the Love We Need*, won numerous awards and was produced in a number of cities across the United States. *New Love Song* had its premiere in the spring of 1988. He is currently working on an opera, *Nuclear Lovers*, with Jaan Urban, his lover, who has composed the score for all of Saint's theater pieces and with whom he founded the band Xotika. Assotto Saint is one of five black gay poets whose writings are represented in *Tongues Untied* (GMP, London, 1987).

TRIPLE TROUBLE

AN EXORCISM

"Cops Lock Up Gay Sex Den"
"Long Island Grandma Dead of AIDS"
"Bachelors Forcing Sex Ed on Kids"
　　　　　　　—headlines, *The New York Post*

Last July 4th, like every July 4th for four years,
Nile ground ginger roots and lime rind, spooned
brown sugar in a cup of Cockspur rum he gulped.
Carrying on his head

all the front pages
        of The New York Post for the past year
all the front pages
        with sorry stories
all the front pages
        with mad headlines
which had struck and hurt his eyes, he climbed
the stairs of his abandoned building on Eighth
Street between B & C. In the center of the cement
rooftop, he heaped the papers on which he
gracefully stripped. He rubbed greek-imported
olive oil over his body to catch more heat.
Staring straight at the sun
        Nile waited to hear the voice
staring straight at the sun
        Nile waited to feel the beat
staring straight at the sun
        Nile waited till his teeth clacked
with a shriek so hot it set the heap on fire. Round
and round the flames he ran, talking in tongues.
Then, on the roof's edge, he perched in arabesque
like an eagle ready for flight. High above his
head, he lifted his arms. In his fluttering fingers,
the sun shattered. The universe stood still while
Nile smiled. An empowering mystery, the past
passed on from generations, all the joy of life
reflected. So slowly his body bent far forward.
Long supple arms opened low
to pay homage
to surrender in prayer
to offer himself
        a black queen   dancing with shadows
            at high noon
triple trouble that's brutal chasing America's evil
        spirits away.

Susan Saxe

Susan Saxe was born in 1949 in Hartford, Connecticut, and raised in Albany, New York. She graduated from Brandeis University in 1970. *Notes from the first year*, a collection of poems written while she was "underground" (1970 to 1975), was published in 1976. While in prison (1975 to 1982) for politically motivated actions, she initiated several model services to address the needs of incarcerated women and their children. After her release, she worked in reproductive rights and disability rights advocacy and completed a master's degree from Antioch University. She currently works for a human services agency.

QUESTIONNAIRE

from "Notes from the First Year"

There is unfeminine, (but oh, so Female)
sureness in my hands,
checking "No." to every question
in the Harris poll, Reader's Digest,
    Mademoiselle.
I am an outlaw, so none of that applies to me:
I do not vote in primaries, do not wish to increase
    my spending power, do not take birth control
    pills.
I do not have a legal residence, cannot tell you
    my given name or how (sometimes very) old
    I really am.
I do not travel abroad, see no humor in uniforms,
    and my lips are good enough for my lover
    as they are.
Beyond that, no one heads my household, I would not
    save my marriage if I had one, or anybody else's
    if I could.

I do not believe that politicians need me, that Jesus
    loves me, or that short men are particularly sexy.
Nor do I want a penis.
What else do you have to offer?

1971

Ron Schreiber

Ron Schreiber was born in Chicago in 1934 and raised in Dayton, Ohio. He
has lived in Connecticut, Japan (with the U.S. Army), New York City,
Amsterdam, Somerville, and, now, Cambridge, Massachusetts. In 1969,
Schreiber edited the anthology *31 New American Poets* (Hill and Wang). He is
one of the editors of *Hanging Loose* magazine and press. His own collections of
poetry include *False Clues, Tomorrow Will Really Be Sunday* (Calamus Books,
1978 and 1984), and a new book, *John,* recently published by Hanging Loose
Press & Gay Presses of New York.

"AN ALARMING NEW DEVELOPMENT"

Heterosexuals can get AIDS too
—not just the smaller "high risk

groups," but what doctors & newscasters
call "all of us." All of *them,*

say the Haitians, all of *them,*
say the queers. If *they (all of us)*

can get it too, then maybe they
will begin to take it seriously:

that most people in the world
have been high risk groups for

years & years; maybe now "the majority
of Americans" is beginning to feel

at risk—their jobs, their planet,
& (now) even "our" disease is reaching

them. "Welcome," we will tell them,
"we were wondering how long it

would take for you to come out
as members of the species. It's not

easy here, but if you learn to behave
yourselves & stop trying to kill

the rest of us, we have room for you,
& we will try to teach you how to

survive while you're dying."

THE HOUSE IS OLD

I sit in another house whose character is
just now forming as we live here &
dust & scrub & clean & wash windows or
just live together now our enemies have gone

—*enemies* because that's what friends become
sometimes when they leave us or we leave them
& cast one another out of our lives like
leaves cluttering the lawn, the grass gone too.
—because we are sometimes difficult to live with.

we gossip sometimes & tear one another into
tiny rags we wear in preference to warm clothing
—furs & scruffy rugs made into hair boas
like snakes to wrap around us in the dark.

—*enemy* is not a word of hate. it's what we call
our lovers when we don't love them any more
now they've rejected us. we live here.
we think of the other house.

the house is old.
it's like an old person we are getting to know
for the first time. or the second.
above the house a hawk dives

down for a mouse beside the pond, beside
the garden, the rosa rugosa, the
blackberries. beside the house where
the faggots live with their friends.

James Schuyler

James Schuyler (born 1923 in Chicago) grew up in Washington, D.C., and East Aurora, New York. After serving in the Navy during World War II, he moved to New York City and worked for the Voice of America before leaving for a few years' sojourn in Italy. He returned to New York in the early 1950s, became an associate editor of *Art News*, and worked at The Museum of Modern Art. Schuyler's poetry collections include *Freely Espousing* (Doubleday, 1969; reissued, Sun, 1979), *The Crystal Lithium* (Random House, 1972), *Hymn to Life* (Random House, 1974), the Pulitzer Prize–winning volume *The Morning of the Poem* (Farrar, Straus and Giroux, 1980), and *A Few Days* (Random House, 1985). He is also the author of three novels, including (with John Ashbery) *A Nest of Ninnies*. Schuyler's *Collected Poems* were published by Farrar, Straus and Giroux in 1988.

GROWING DARK

The grass shakes.
Smoke streaks, no,
cloud strokes.
The dogs are fed.
Their licenses
clank on pottery.

The phone rings.
And is answered.
The pond path
is washed-out grass
between green
winter cover.
Last night in
bed I read.
You came to
my room and
said, "Isn't
the world
terrible?" "My
dear . . ." I
said. It could be
and has been
worse. So
beautiful and
things keep getting
in between. When
I was young I
hurt others. Now,
others have hurt
me. In the night
I thought I heard
a dog bark.
Racking sobs.
Poor guy. Yet,
I got my sleep.

TOM

They told me, Heraclitus,
they told me you were dead.

A key. The door. Open
shut. "Hi, Jim." "Hi,
Tom." "How didja sleep?"
"I didn't. And you?" "A
log." Blond glory, streaked,
finger-combed, curling
in kiss curls at the nape.

A kiss, like bumping fore-
heads. A god, archaic Greek
Apollo in a blue down
jacket. Fifteen degrees
no snow. Tom hates that;
me too. "French toast?"
"Of course." With apple-
sauce. The *Times*, the
obits, a great blues singer
has been taken from us
and a businessman. OJ,
coffee with milk, lecithin
to control mouth movements,
a side effect of Thorazine.
At the stove Tom sings the
release of his rock song,
"Manhattan Movie." His voice
is rich, true, his diction
perfect. I'm so in love
I want to die and take
my happiness to heaven!
No. To be with Tom, my
assistant, three hours
a day four days a week.
(Tom likes "assistant"
I
prefer "secretary."
No sweat: "Ain't no
flies on the lamb
of God." Ahem. Phlegm.)
Tom's eyes are "twin
compendious blue oceans in
which white sails and
gulls wildly fly." We'll
never make it. Tom's
twenty-eight, I'm fifty-
six: he isn't Proust's
"young man born to love
elderly men." He loves E.
an eighteen-year-old
poet, whose mother feels
concern at Tom's two-
year pursuit (they only

lately made it). I'm
going to tell her how
lucky her son is, if he
is to have a homosexual
episode (or be one, as
I think he is, pretty
boy), to have a lover so
kind, so loving, so
witty—that thrash-about
laugh—I've said it
and I will. At Number
One Fifth Avenue I tell
E., "You should un-
reservedly make love
to Tom and be cosy and
tender." "I'm sorry, I
don't feel that way
about him." Later
he tells Tom,
"We had a man-
to-man talk." Sad.
I only care about Tom's
happiness. "He's not
very sexually oriented.
Here." The French toast
and applesauce are
delicious. We settle down
to read: he, a Ross
Macdonald, me *Phineas
Redux*. How superb is
Mme. Goesler when she
repudiates the Duke of
Omnium's bequest of priceless
pearls and diamonds and
a fortune (she already
has one) so they will
go to Lady Glencora, the
rightful heir, and no one
can ever say her three years'
tenderness to the dying
man was motivated. In
Tom's book a corpse is
found in corrupt upper-

JAMES SCHUYLER

middle-class L.A., where
he comes from. Beauty.
We might some
day shower
together, wash
each other's back.
Travelling share a bed.
Flesh on flesh,
a head pillowed
on an arm. Touch.
Running from a cab to
the deli, the energy
(graceful) of youth.
Thomas Paul Carey of
Sherman Oaks, California,
who writes and sings
his own rock songs, the
son and grandson of two
great movie actors, the
two Harry Careys. Love
is only and always beautiful.

SLEEP

(from "The Payne Whitney Poems")

The friends who come to see you
and the friends who don't.
The weather in the window.
A pierced ear.
The mounting tension and the spasm.
A paper-lace doily on a small plate.
Tangerines.
A day in February: heart-
shaped cookies on St. Valentine's.
Like Christopher, a discarded saint.
A tough woman with black hair.
"I got to set my wig straight."
A gold and silver day begins to wane.
A crescent moon.
Ice on the window.
Give my love to, oh, anybody.

Vickie Sears

Vickie L. Sears (born 1941, San Diego) is a Cherokee/Spanish/English writer, feminist therapist, and teacher living in Seattle. Her poetry and fiction appear in *A Gathering of Spirit* (Sinister Wisdom Books, 1984), *Gathering Ground* (Seal Press, 1984), *The Things That Divide Us* (Seal Press, 1985), *Calyx*, and *Backbone*. She has recently contributed a chapter on sexual abuse to a women's studies text, two chapters to a book about lesbian relationships, and two articles on ethics for a text to be published by members of the Feminist Therapy Institute. She is writing a novel.

PUBESCENCE AT 39

Went to dinner with her thursday.
liked what i heard
saw.
sorted out all day friday
wanted to be sure i interpreted her correctly
agonized in case i hadn't.
spent saturday worried about what the rules might be.
how long did i wait?
what shall/should i say?
waited to confirm with my therapist.
then decided to call.
that was wednesday.
a first date phone call
i sweated
my palms bled fluid.
what if she said "no" or worse "yes"?
she did!
now what?
by thursday night i had set up a fire in the fireplace
waiting for a monday match.

friday, at 1:30 in the morning,
i began to clean house
washed the sheets
just in case
put out a towel set
took it down
put it back
three times
finished at 5:30 am
slept on the couch,
to keep the sheets clean
slept there all weekend.
saturday found me buying as wide an assortment of
vegetarian food as i knew
carted it down the stairs
put it away to seem all natural in my meat eating environment
stood back to admire the stock
panicked
how do i cook this?
went to the bookstore for a cookbook
subgums and glutinous
didn't sound good.
put flowers all around
made a tape 120 minutes long.
just in case.
sunday i took the towels down
put them back up and down
three more times.
got the theatre tickets monday.
if i hadn't would she have wanted to be with me anyway?
like a woody allen script
i'm ready for this
first date.

Aaron Shurin

Aaron Shurin (born 1947 in New York City) has published five books of poetry, including *The Night Sun* (1976), *Giving Up the Ghost* (1980), and *The Graces* (1983), and a new booklet of prose, *Elsewhere* (1988). He has written for the theatre (*Line Drawing*, 1978) and dance ("Closer," text for Joe Goode, 1985), and his critical/theoretical writings have appeared in numerous publications, including the anthologies *Code of Signals* (1983) and *Gay Spirit* (1987). Since 1982 he has taught courses in Gay/Lesbian Studies and creative writing at New College of California and San Francisco Community College.

EXORCISM OF THE STRAIGHT/MAN/DEMON

You are just the kind of man
   who has always   sucked me
into loving him.   The kind
unable
to feed me love back.

You stuff me   with your need
and say it is my need.   You stick
   your hardness in my face
      and say it is my softness.
It IS my softness.   Go away.
I have no more openings
for hardness.

Straight man in me   who I never wanted.
Power spoon-fed me   that I despise.
      to lord over
    to judge   and not listen
   to thrust, not pull
  to be hard   and never   yield.
Look out!   I expel you.

And warn you not to   shove yourself
into the hands of my mouth.
See how hard your cock is?
That's how strong my jaw is.
    That's how fierce my heart is   and my love.

    My hate is not
from angry love   but from anger.
Not for who you are   but how you treat me.
Filling my need to be loved
    with your own need   to conquer love.

Man   Man   I call your name
in throwing you out.

    And reclaim my formlessness.
    And re-interpret my desires.
    And receive the world as made for me.

Spirit!   I bend to you.
    I cross/I bow
I deny the demon   and cry for his expulsion:

Obaob   Abniob   Baiax   Ousiri
                                        Spirit
who is alive in me   witness
this casting away.
The old threats   are leaving me.
I am living.

1971

Anita Skeen

Anita Skeen (born 1946, Charleston, West Virginia) is an associate professor of English at Wichita State University, teaching in the M.F.A. Program in Creative Writing and the Women's Studies Program. She has developed courses in journal writing, women's autobiography, and Canadian literature (in conjunction with a Canadian Studies faculty research grant from the Canadian Embassy). Her poems have appeared in *Ms.*, *Woman Poet: The Midwest*, *Sinister Wisdom*, *13th Moon*, *Prairie Schooner*, *New Letters*, *Nimrod*, and other journals. Her first collection of poetry is *Each Hand a Map* (Naiad, 1986).

WOMEN WHO COOK

When, this incredible thing, the principal of the junior high,
surprised by a blast from an M-1A rifle, slumps
a few feet from his office door, or the woman
out jogging in the Saturday morning snow, jubilant
as confetti, gets beaten and raped, or the son
does not recover from the ache in his side, we are left,
hands fumbling in pockets for more
than just words.

    The doorbell rings. A woman appears, offering
    an aluminum pan wrapped in foil. *I wanted to make something*
    chocolate, she says, *but there isn't anything chocolate*
    I can make really well. A later hour, another ring:
    She made you these rolls, he says, extending the sack
    like a drowned cat. Still later, a glass dish
    held out like a crystal ball: *We had this extra ham,*
    she says. *We thought you could use it now.*

I remember February's worst blizzard since 1912
when my grandmother, who made cornbread when Stevie's mother

did not return from the trip and blackberry cobbler
when Earle stayed down in the mine, chose
to die. A four-wheel drive took the body
and brought beans. Friends plowed through snow
with potato salad and stew. Wherever I turned,
I was handed a dish. My hands steamed for days.

Some of us women still bake, she says, *when we don't know
what else to do.* I take the butterscotch pie, meringue
frothy and deep as that February snow, and turn toward the kitchen,
thinking of women who turn on their stoves, take down their bowls.
I lift this gift, this tangible sorrow, to the shelf.
Right now, in this town, a woman beats eggs, each stroke
a blow against something out there, something
only a neighbor away.

Linda Smukler

Linda Smukler, born in 1954 in Cleveland, Ohio, was the 1986 winner of the Katherine Anne Porter Short Fiction Prize sponsored by *Nimrod* magazine. Her poetry and fiction have appeared in *Conditions, Ikon, The New England Review/Breadloaf Quarterly, Semiotext(e) USA,* and other periodicals. She has just completed her first novel, *Tales of a Lost Boyhood.*

THE SHOWER

my voice is thin   I stand in the shower   what's that I ask   I am at the
level of that   what is it?   a penis he says   men have them   I stand
there watching it   I don't have one   girls don't have one   he holds it
for me touch it   can I touch it?   long and skin thick over something
hard   thicker than all my fingers   it moves under them   it's not a part
of him   does he take it off when he puts on his clothes?   we are taking
a shower   he is holding it to show me underneath   this is the scrotum
he says   like two eggs   what's all that raised over them?   touch it

veins he says   hairy   he is very black hairy there   I am pink   it feels like a lie   what does it do? it's something men do   my face is no taller   I am pink and he is hairy black hair   against the wall are knobs to make the water go hot and cold   my back is against them   he tells me not to be scared and rubs his fingers through my hair   curly head he says it's just the difference between boys and girls   he is not a boy he is my father   boys are on t.v.   a boy is a friend of Lassie and rescues things   boys are me   smooth like me   he is still showing me   the shower walls are there   knobs like a gate I can't go through   I have to stand in the middle   I have to see him   the water protects me   falling between us   like rain falls   make it hotter I tell him   scared makes me cold   time to wash he says   no I say   first I'll wash you then you can wash me he says   no   I don't want to wash   I want to sit down in the water   the hot makes my heart beat too fast   he has the wash cloth he is washing me anyway   soaping my back   the thing hangs down on me as he bends over to scrub   it's sticking up   brushing back and forth along my shoulder   I pull away   I'm almost done he says   stand still and let me wash your legs   I have to pee   his legs are hairy too   I've seen them before   what's wrong?   he tickles me in the ribs with the wash cloth   it is rough and orange   more will come if I pull away   my serious little girl what's wrong?   he tickles more   I am laughing   no I try to pull away   be careful or you'll slip   he holds me and tickles me all over   I can't get past the water or the walls   he drops the soap   my feet lift off the ground   he holds me by the shoulder   I laugh and cry he can't tell if I am laughing or crying   I am going to pee   he pokes me in the stomach he is laughing   that penis thing   shaking as he laughs   had enough?   now let me wash you   I can't hold it   I am peeing   I bend down to get the soap to hide that I am peeing   he doesn't notice   the water runs too hard   I hand him the soap   I am done peeing   he washes up my legs   feet first up into my crotch washing me because I am dirty   washing the pee away   he washes me a long time   moving the washcloth and soap back and forth   I stand on my own   staring at the dark tiles   at the water beading and falling by its own weight   far away I hear him whistling   he echoes in the walls O.k. you're done he says it's my turn   I tell him to turn the water hotter   I'm getting cold   it's not cold he says   yes it is   he turns the water hotter to please me   he hands me the wash cloth and points to his stomach   here first he says   I wash his stomach reaching out and above the thing below   good he says and pulls me to him   my arms around him   the thing is in my face   my neck   he tells me to wash his back   he holds me there   I am choking I can barely move my arms you have to wash harder than that to get me clean   I try to wash harder   his legs are shaking   his knees around my own   I am choking   I try to say I'm done   he calls down to me   what? not letting go   I drop the washcloth and grab his hips and push away   the thing springs out after me   it's following me   I turn away and try to open the door handle   I can't reach it   I look at him   I'm done I say again   you're done?   but I'm not half as clean as you he says   I have to go   I'm cold he stares at me and says   I guess your daddy is just going to have to get clean himself   there's a towel for you outside on the rack   be careful and don't slip   he opens the shower door for me and closes it when I'm out   outside I am surprised the rest of the bathroom is still there   it is white and steamy   the mirror is covered with fog   I pretend I am hidden in the steam   I pull the towel to me and hold it to my belly   it is tired from the pee being forced out of me   I hear my daddy singing and look through the glass door of the shower to see his shadow washing himself   he sounds happy   he stops singing   I can see the pink outline of his hands   not hairy now   washing the thing   penis   he washes and is silent   it must take a long time to get clean   then I hear his breath and suddenly he shouts like he has hurt himself   his breath is fast like he is getting mad   he will come after me   I made him turn it up   I throw the towel up over my head and run out of the room   the water got too hot   I made him turn it up

May Swenson

May Swenson, born in 1919 and educated in Logan, Utah, has made her career mainly in the New York City area and now lives in Sea Cliff, Long Island. She has contributed to numerous national and literary magazines, some of her short stories have been anthologized, and a play, *The Floor*, was produced at the American Place Theatre, New York City. Nine books of her poems have been published since 1954, the newest titled *In Other Words* (Knopf, 1987). The most recent award to her work is a MacArthur Foundation Fellowship.

POET TO TIGER

THE HAIR

You went downstairs
saw a hair in the sink
and squeezed my toothpaste by the neck.
You roared. My ribs are sore.
This morning even my pencil's got your toothmarks.
Big Cat Eye cocked on me you see bird bones.
Snuggled in the rug of your belly
your breath so warm
I smell delicious fear.
Come breathe on me rough pard
put soft paws here.

THE SALT

You don't put salt on anything
so I'm eating without.
Honey on the eggs is all right
mustard on the toast.
I'm not complaining I'm saying I'm
living with *you.*
You like your meat raw
don't care if it's cold.
Your stomach must have tastebuds
you swallow so fast.
Night falls early. It's foggy. Just now

I found another of your bite marks in the cheese.
I'm hungry. Please
come bounding home
I'll hand you the wine to open
with your teeth.
Scorched me a steak unsalted
boil my coffee twice
say the blessing to a jingle on the blue TV.
Under the lap robe on our chilly couch
look behind my ears "for welps"
and hug me.

THE SAND

You're right I brought a grain
or two of sand
into bed I guess in my socks.
But it was you pushed them off
along with everything else.

Asleep you flip
over roll
everything under
you and off
me. I'm always grabbing
for my share of the sheets.

Or else you wake me every hour with sudden
growled I-love-yous
trapping my face between those plushy
shoulders. All my float-dreams turn spins
and never finish. I'm thinner
now. My watch keeps running fast.
But best is when we're riding pillion
my hips within your lap. You let me steer.
Your hand and arm go clear
around my ribs your moist
dream teeth fastened on my nape.

A grain of sand in the bed upsets you or
a hair on the floor.
But you'll get
in slick and wet from the shower if I let
you. Or with your wool cap
and skiing jacket on
if it's cold.
Tiger don't scold me
don't make me comb my hair outdoors.
Cuff me careful. Lick don't
crunch. Make last what's yours.

THE DREAM

You get into the tub holding *The Naked Ape*
in your teeth. You wet that blond
three-cornered pelt lie back wide
chest afloat. You're reading
in the rising steam and I'm
drinking coffee from your tiger cup.
You say you dreamed
I had your baby book
and it was pink and blue.
I pointed to a page and there
was your face with a cub grin.

You put your paws in your armpits
make a tiger-moo.
Then you say: "Come here
Poet and take
this hair
off me." I do.
It's one of mine. I carefully
kill it and carry
it outside. And stamp on it
and bury it.

In the begonia bed.
And then take off my shoes
not to bring a grain
of sand in to get
into our bed.
I'm going to
do the cooking
now instead
of you.
And sneak some salt in
when you're not looking.

FOUR-WORD LINES

Your eyes are just
like bees, and I
feel like a flower.
Their brown power makes
a breeze go over
my skin. When your
lashes ride down and
rise like brown bees'
legs, your pronged gaze
makes my eyes gauze.
I wish we were
in some shade and
no swarm of other
eyes to know that
I'm a flower breathing
bare, laid open to
your bees' warm stare.
I'd let you wade
in me and seize
with your eager brown
bees' power a sweet
glistening at my core.

Kitty Tsui

Kitty Tsui was born in the Year of the Dragon in the City of Nine Dragons, grew up in Hong Kong and England, immigrated to Gold Mountain in 1968. Actor, community organizer, author of *The Words of a Woman Who Breathes Fire* (Spinsters Ink, 1983), she has been widely anthologized and was a founding member of the Unbound Feet and Unbound Feet Three collectives. A competitive bodybuilder, she was the bronze medalist in the Women's Physique competition at Gay Games II in San Francisco in 1986. She is co-editor of *New Phoenix Rising: The Asian/Pacific Lesbian Newsletter of the San Francisco Bay Area* and of an anthology in preparation, writings by Asian/Pacific lesbians: *Breaking Ground, Making Waves, Soaring High*. She came out as a lesbian when she was twenty-one and is still a lesbian at thirty-five: "It was not a phase, as my mother told me."

A CHINESE BANQUET

for the one who was not invited

it was not a very formal affair but
all the women over twelve
wore long gowns and a corsage,
except for me.

it was not a very formal affair, just
the family getting together,
poa poa, kuw fu without *kuw mow**
(her excuse this year is a headache).

aunts and uncles and cousins,
the grandson who is a dentist,
the one who drives a mercedes benz,
sitting down for shark's fin soup.

they talk about buying a house and
taking a two week vacation in beijing.
i suck on shrimp and squab,
dreaming of the cloudscape in your eyes.

my mother, her voice beaded with sarcasm:
you're twenty six and not getting younger.
it's about time you got a decent job.
she no longer asks when i'm getting married.

you're twenty six and not getting younger.
what are you doing with your life?
you've got to make a living.
why don't you study computer programming?

kuw fu: uncle; *kuw mow*: aunt

KITTY TSUI

she no longer asks when i'm getting married.
one day, wanting desperately to
bridge the boundaries that separate us,
wanting desperately to touch her,

tell her: mother, i'm gay,
mother i'm gay and so happy with her.
but she will not listen,
she shakes her head.

she sits across from me,
emotions invading her face.
her eyes are wet but
she will not let tears fall.

mother, i say,
you love a man.
i love a woman.
it is not what she wants to hear.

aunts and uncles and cousins,
very much a family affair.
but you are not invited,
being neither my husband nor my wife.

aunts and uncles and cousins
eating longevity noodles
fragrant with ham inquire:
sold that old car of yours yet?

i want to tell them: my back is healing,
i dream of dragons and water.
my home is in her arms,
our bedroom ceiling the wide open sky.

Lisa Vice

Lisa Vice (born 1951 in Tipton, Indiana) studied writing with Audre Lorde, Cherríe Moraga, and Meredith Sue Willis. Her poetry appears in the anthologies *Early Ripening* (Pandora Press, 1988), and *Naming the Waves* (Virago, 1988). She teaches remedial writing at Hunter College and is currently at work on her first novel. She lives in New York City and has an eighteen-year-old daughter.

PANTS

I am a little girl with my pants pulled down around my ankles
soft red corduroys and thick white underpants in a tangle
somewhere below my knees
Every time my pants are down
I feel like a rubber doll
with hollow arms   eyes that never close

I am a woman standing in the thin winter sun
a headless rabbit in my hands
I run my thumb down the belly
squeeze out that last bit of pee
yank the fur down in one piece

A man who had my father's name
came to my home when my daughter was asleep
I lay on my stomach on the mattress on the floor
He unzipped his pants in the dark
Slipped mine down just far enough to fuck me in the ass
then he went away

I went to bed with a friend whose pants I pulled down
she lay on her back   waiting

for me to make love to her like a man
I did everything she expected me to
In the morning she put her t-shirt on
made coffee and toast
I put all my clothes on   even my shoes
stood at the sink smiling   nodding
But wanting to scream   put your pants on

I am a little girl with my pants pulled down around my ankles
I have to pee
A hand rubs and rubs in that place with no name
I trace every detail of the wallpaper with my eyes
Pray there is a God

I had a cat once that never got enough
no matter what he ate   never enough
I couldn't even walk towards the kitchen
without him racing to get there first
Finally I grabbed him by the neck   threw him out the door
He slammed against a boulder
bounced up and down like an electrocuted cat in some cartoon
Part of me stood aside   shocked
While the rest of me turned and walked away

There was a man who said I had to have his son
At night he liked to tie me to his bed
When he pulled my skin down in one piece
I heard rabbits screaming
saw them huddled in cages wondering
who would be next

The last woman I made love to
pulled her pants off so fast   the first time
insisting I look at her
Every time we made love   insisting I look into her eyes
All those days and nights and dinners I cooked for her
and the way she licked the bones
The only thing I could think of was that first time
when she pulled her pants off so fast
and I wanted to say   Wait

I took an art class   the teacher said
Paint your first memories

LISA VICE   377

I filled canvases with wallpaper leaves
working to get the right shade of red
Whenever I tried to paint anything else
A cock rubbed against my lips
I was a good girl   I painted the leaves

I live alone now and sleep with a cat against my back
I don't have to wait until my daughter is asleep
to bring strangers to my bed
I bring no one   I lie with a cat against my back
and look at my life as if someone else lived it

James L. White

James L. White (born 1936 in Indianapolis, died 1981) wrote four books of poetry, including *Divorce Proceedings* (1972), *A Crow's Story of Deer* (1974), *The Del Rio Hotel* (1975), and *The Salt Ecstasies* (Graywolf Press, 1982), from which the poem here is taken. After a career as a classical ballet dancer, White took two degrees in English literature and went to New Mexico and Arizona to live with and teach Navaho people. He edited two books of contemporary Native American poetry for *Dacotah Territory* and remained closely affiliated with tribal people until his death. The important national gay men's literary quarterly *The James White Review*, founded in Minneapolis in 1983, is named after him.

MAKING LOVE TO MYSELF

When I do it, I remember how it was with us.
Then my hands remember too,
and you're with me again, just the way it was.

After work when you'd come in and
turn the TV off and sit on the edge of the bed,

filling the room with gasoline smell from your overalls,
trying not to wake me which you always did.
I'd breathe out long and say,
'Hi Jess, you tired baby?'
You'd say not so bad and rub my belly,
not after me really, just being sweet,
and I always thought I'd die a little
because you smelt like burnt leaves or woodsmoke.

We were poor as Job's turkey but we lived well—
the food, a few good movies, good dope, lots of talk,
lots of you and me trying on each other's skin.

What a sweet gift this is,
done with my memory, my cock and hands.

Sometimes I'd wake up wondering if I should fix
coffee for us before work,
almost thinking you're here again, almost seeing
your work jacket on the chair.

I wonder if you remember what
we promised when you took the job in Laramie?
Our way of staying with each other.
We promised there'd always be times
when the sky was perfectly lucid,
that we could remember each other through that.
You could remember me at my worktable
or in the all-night diners,
though we'd never call or write.

I just have to stop here Jess.
I just have to stop.

John Wieners

John Wieners was born in Milton, Massachusetts, in 1934. He graduated from Boston College in 1954 and then studied at Black Mountain College under Charles Olson and Robert Duncan. In the late 50s he was co-founder of the magazine *Measure*. In a note on himself in 1960, he reports that he "worked in the Lamont Library at Harvard, until the day that *Measure #1* arrived in Boston, and then they fired me." His chapbook *The Hotel Wentley Poems* (The Auerhahn Press, San Francisco, 1958) became an underground classic, especially among other writers, and he subsequently published fourteen more books of poetry. His *Selected Poems, 1958–1984* was issued by Black Sparrow Press in 1986. In a 1973 interview with Charley Shively (*Gay Sunshine Interviews*, Vol. 2, 1982), Wieners recalls his mother as a person who "would offer aid in her mind . . . to somebody who manifested need" and "likewise feel[s] that what I'm doing is to increase those feelings in others so that they no longer have to regard themselves as tramps, deviates, guttersnipes or aberrations."

MY MOTHER

talking to strange men on the subway,

doesn't see me when she gets on,

    at Washington Street
but I hide in a booth at the side

    and watch her worried, strained face—
the few years she has got left.
    Until at South Station

I lean over and say:
I've been watching you since you got on.
    She says in an artificial
        voice: Oh, for Heaven's sake!

as if heaven cared.

But I love her in the underground
    and her gray coat and hair
sitting there, one man over from me
      talking together between the wire grates of a cage.

A POEM FOR TRAPPED THINGS

This morning with a blue flame burning
this thing wings its way in.
Wind shakes the edges of its yellow being.
Gasping for breath.
Living for the instant.
Climbing up the black border of the window.
Why do you want out.
I sit in pain.
A red robe amid debris.
You bend and climb, extending antennae.

I know the butterfly is my soul
grown weak from battle.

A Giant fan on the back of
        a beetle.
A caterpillar chrysalis that seeks
a new home apart from this room.

And will disappear from sight
at the pulling of invisible strings.
Yet so tenuous, so fine
  this thing is, I am
    sitting on the hard bed, we could
      vanish from sight like the puff
        off an invisible cigarette.
Furred chest, ragged silk under
    wings beating against the glass

    no one will open.

The blue diamonds on your back

are too beautiful to do
away with.
I watch you
all morning
long.
With my hand over my mouth.

Tennessee Williams

Tennessee Williams (born 1911 in Columbus, Mississippi, died 1983) is the celebrated American playwright whose *The Glass Menagerie* (1945), Pulitzer Prize-winning *A Streetcar Named Desire* (1947), and other writings provided touchstones for erotic and emotional reality for generations of gay people when there were few to be had elsewhere, and helped make it possible to even conceive of "gay liberation" over two decades later. In post-World War II America, many straight people were also ready to accept Williams's exposure of social and sexual hypocrisies; but no small portion of the literary establishment greeted Williams's work with possibly the most vicious—and certainly one of the most homophobic—onslaughts on works of genius in the history of English literature. Williams's fame as a playwright has overshadowed his accomplishment in verse, yet it is as a young poet that he came to New Directions publishers in the early 1940s. His two books of poems, *In the Winter of Cities* (1954; revised and expanded, 1964), and *Androgyne, Mon Amour* (1977), contain several of the best lyric poems written in America.

LIFE STORY

After you've been to bed together for the first time,
without the advantage or disadvantage of any prior
    acquaintance,
the other party very often says to you,
Tell me about yourself, I want to know all about you,
what's your story? And you think maybe they really and
    truly do

sincerely want to know your life story, and so you light up
a cigarette and begin to tell it to them, the two of you
lying together in completely relaxed positions
like a pair of rag dolls a bored child dropped on a bed.

You tell them your story, or as much of your story
as time or a fair degree of prudence allows, and they say,
    Oh, oh, oh, oh, oh,
each time a little more faintly, until the oh
is just an audible breath, and then of course

there's some interruption. Slow room service comes up
with a bowl of melting ice cubes, or one of you rises to pee
and gaze at himself with mild astonishment in the
    bathroom mirror.
And then, the first thing you know, before you've had time
to pick up where you left off with your enthralling life story,
they're telling you *their* life story, exactly as they'd intended
    to all along,

and you're saying, Oh, oh, oh, oh, oh,
each time a little more faintly, the vowel at last becoming
no more than an audible sigh,
as the elevator, halfway down the corridor and a turn to
    the left,
draws one last, long, deep breath of exhaustion
and stops breathing forever. Then?

Well, one of you falls asleep
and the other one does likewise with a lighted cigarette
    in his mouth,
and that's how people burn to death in hotel rooms.

YOU AND I

Who are you?
A surface warm to my fingers,
a solid form, an occupant of space,
a makeshift kind of enjoyment,
a pitiless being who runs away like water,
something left unfinished, out of inferior matter,

Something God thought of.
Nothing, sometimes everything,
something I cannot believe in,
a foolish argument, you, yourself, not I,
an enemy of mine. My lover.

Who am I?
A wounded man, badly bandaged,
a monster among angels or angel among monsters,
a box of questions shaken up and scattered on the floor,

A foot on the stairs, a voice on a wire,
a busy collection of thumbs that imitate fingers,
an enemy of yours. Your lover.

Heather Wishik

Heather Wishik, born 1950 in New York, is a lesbian writer and attorney living in Vermont. Her feminist legal scholarship often includes poems and has been published in the *Berkeley Women's Law Journal, Family Law Quarterly,* and the *New Mexico Law Review.* She has previously published some poetry under the pseudonym "Esther Hawk" in order to protect her rights to custody of her son. She celebrates his approaching fifteenth birthday with this, her first publication as a lesbian writer in her own name. She is now writing a novel.

VISITATION RIGHTS

1.

After fifteen months you fly in,
a day late, without a word,
and are surprised by his tears.

You have always been late,
beginning that night when I
labored until morning
and you went home to sleep.
Before dawn I called you, come,
now it is happening, and then
for two hours as the pains
scraped my back I waited, saw you,
car spun sideways on the freeway
and a crowd gathering. "Just in time,"
you laughed, scrambling
into a white gown, but you weren't.

And I hate you for teaching him
to expect so little, so young.

2.

Sometimes he does not
recognize you until you speak.

As I drive him home
in the winter dark he tells me
stories about Orion and his two dogs,
the big one, who is the Daddy,
and the little one forever falling
toward the Daddy's waiting back.

Sometimes he calls me Daddy.

Shahid

(Roosevelt Williamson)

Shahid (Roosevelt Williamson) was born in Atlanta in 1951. He is self-taught, "having read much about, and studied, while in prison for 12 years, Herbology, Comparative Religions, Yogic Philosophy, Sexology, Homosexuality in Ancient Times, Egyptology, Natural Diet, Ancient History of Various Civilizations, etc." His poems have appeared in the national gay liberation cultural journal *Fag Rag,* and he has had an article published in *Gay Community News* (Boston). Shahid is "in solidarity with the true unprejudiced gay world . . . and would love to meet some hot sexy gays, wherever/whoever you are!"

LETTERS COME TO PRISON

From the cold hands of guards
Flocks of white doves
Handed to us through the bars.
Our hands like nests hold them
As we unfold the wings
They crash upward through
Layers of ice around our hearts.
Cracking crisply
As we leave our shells
And fly over the waves of fresh words.
Gliding softly on top of the world
Flapping our wings for the last horizon,
High in the blue sky someone's Gay Love.

Brief Bibliography

Titles of works by individual poets are given in the biography for each poet.

I. ANTHOLOGIES OF GAY AND LESBIAN POETRY

Bulkin, Elly, and Joan Larkin, eds. *Lesbian Poetry: An anthology*. Watertown, Mass.: Persephone Press, 1981. Distributed by Gay Presses of New York.

Coote, Stephen, ed. *The Penguin Book of Homosexual Verse*. New York: Penguin Books, 1983.

Humphries, Martin, ed. *Not Love Alone: A Modern Gay Anthology*. London: GMP, 1985.

Larkin, Joan, and Elly Bulkin, eds. *Amazon Poetry: An anthology of lesbian poetry*. Brooklyn: Out & Out Books, 1975.

Leyland, Winston, ed. *Angels of the Lyre: A Gay Poetry Anthology*. San Francisco: Panjandrum Press/Gay Sunshine Press, 1975.

———. *Orgasms of Light: The Gay Sunshine Anthology*. San Francisco: Gay Sunshine Press, 1977.

McEwen, Christian, ed. *Naming the Waves: Contemporary Lesbian Poetry*. London: Virago, 1988.

Mohin, Lilian, ed. *Beautiful Barbarians: lesbian feminist poetry*. London: Onlywomen Press, 1986.

Winant, Fran, ed. *We Are All Lesbians*. New York: Violet Press, 1973.

Young, Ian. *The Male Muse: A Gay Anthology*. Trumansburg, N.Y.: The Crossing Press, 1973.

———. *The Son of the Male Muse: New Gay Poetry*. Trumansburg, N.Y.: The Crossing Press, 1983.

II. OTHER POETRY ANTHOLOGIES HAVING SIGNIFICANT GAY AND LESBIAN CONTENT

Allen, Donald M., ed. *The New American Poetry: 1945–1960*. New York: Grove Press, 1960.

Barba, Sharon, and Laura Chester, eds. *Rising Tides: 20th-Century American Women Poets*. New York: Washington Square Press, 1973.

Bernikow, Louise, ed. *The World Split Open: Four Centuries of Women Poets in England and America, 1552–1950*. New York: Vintage, 1974.

Canyon, and Nancy Hom, Genny Lim, Kitty Tsui, Nellie Wong, and Merle Woo, eds. *Unbound Feet*. San Francisco: Isthmus Poetry Foundation, 1981.

Cooper, Dennis, ed., assisted by Tim Dlugos. *Coming Attractions: An Anthology of American Poets in Their Twenties*. Los Angeles: Little Caesar Press, 1980.

Field, Edward, ed. *A Geography of Poets: An Anthology of the New Poetry*. New York: Bantam, 1979.

Howe, Florence, and Ellen Bass, eds. *No More Masks! An Anthology of Poems by Women*. New York: Anchor Books, 1973.

Perlman, Jim, ed. *Brother Songs: A Male Anthology of Poetry*. Minneapolis: Holy Cow! Press, 1979.

Piercy, Marge, ed. *Early Ripening: American Women's Poetry Now*. New York: Pandora Press, 1987.

III. LITERARY ANTHOLOGIES HAVING SIGNIFICANT GAY AND LESBIAN POETRY CONTENT

Beam, Joseph, ed. *In the Life: A Black Gay Anthology.* Boston: Alyson, 1986.

Beck, Evelyn Torton, ed. *Nice Jewish Girls: A Lesbian Anthology.* Watertown, Mass.: Persephone Press, 1982.

Bethel, Lorraine, and Barbara Smith, eds. *Conditions: Five; The Black Women's Issue.* Brooklyn: *Conditions* magazine, 1979.

Brant, Beth, ed. *A Gathering of Spirit: North American Indian Women's Issue.* Rockland, Maine: *Sinister Wisdom* magazine 22/23, 1983.

Cochran, Jo, and Bettina Escudero, Diane Glancy, Naomi Littlebear Morena, Kathleen Reyes, and Mary Tallmountain, eds. *Bearing Witness/Sobreviviendo: An Anthology of Native American/Latina Art and Literature.* Corvallis, Oreg.: *Calyx,* Vol. 8, No. 2, 1984.

Cochran, Jo, and J. T. Stewart and Mayumi Tsutakawa, eds. *Gathering Ground: New Writing and Art by Northwest Women of Color.* Seattle: The Seal Press, 1984.

Covina, Gina, and Laurel Galana, eds. *The Lesbian Reader: An Amazon Quarterly Anthology.* Oakland: Amazon Press, 1975.

Cruikshank, Margaret, ed. *New Lesbian Writing: An Anthology.* San Francisco: Grey Fox Press, 1984.

De Veaux, Alexis, ed. *Gap Tooth Girlfriends: An Anthology.* Bronx: KMJ, 1982.

Galloway, David, and Christian Sabisch. *Calamus: Male Homosexuality in Twentieth-Century Literature.* New York: William Morrow, 1982.

Gilbert, Sandra, and Susan Gubar, eds. *The Norton Anthology of Literature by Women: The Tradition in English.* New York: W. W. Norton & Company, Inc., 1985.

Hacker, Marilyn, guest editor. *Woman Poet. Volume Two: The East.* Reno: Women-in-Literature Incorporated, 1981.

Moraga, Cherríe, and Gloria Anzaldúa, eds. *This Bridge Called My Back: Writings by Radical Women of Color.* Watertown, Mass.: Persephone Press, 1981. Distributed by Kitchen Table: Women of Color Press.

Picano, Felice, ed. *A True Likeness: Lesbian and Gay Writing Today.* New York: The Sea Horse Press, 1980.

Ramos, Juanita, ed. *Compañeras: Latina Lesbians (An Anthology).* New York: Latina Lesbian History Project, 1987.

Roscoe, Will, coordinator. *Living the Spirit: A Gay American Indian Anthology.* Gay American Indians History Project. New York: St. Martin's Press, 1988.

Smith, Barbara, ed. *Home Girls: A Black Feminist Anthology.* New York: Kitchen Table: Women of Color Press, 1983.

Smith, Michael J., ed. *Black Men/White Men: A Gay Anthology.* San Francisco: Gay Sunshine Press, 1983.

The Women's Press Collective. *Lesbians Speak Out.* Oakland: 1974.

IV. CRITICAL WORKS ON GAY AND LESBIAN POETRY

Abbott, Steve. "The Poetry of Male Love." *Gay Sunshine* No. 24, Spring, 1975.

———. "Poetry West." *The Advocate,* May 13, 1982.

Clausen, Jan. *A Movement of Poets: Thoughts on Poetry and Feminism.* Brooklyn: Long Haul Press, 1982.

Grahn, Judy. *The Highest Apple: Sappho and the Lesbian Poetic Tradition.* San Francisco: Spinsters, Ink, 1985.

Kikel, Rudy. "After Whitman and Auden: Gay Male Sensibility in Poetry Since 1945." *Gay Sunshine* No. 44/45, Autumn/Winter 1980.

———. "Poetry East." *The Advocate*, May 13, 1982.

Martin, Robert K. *The Homosexual Tradition in American Poetry*. Austin: University of Texas Press, 1979.

Shively, Charley. "Poetry, Cocksucking and Revolution." *Fag Rag*, #10 (September, 1974).

Woods, Gregory. *Articulate Flesh: Male homo-eroticism and modern poetry*. New Haven and London: Yale University Press, 1987.

Young, Ian. "The Poetry of Male Love," in *The Male Homosexual in Literature*: A Bibliography by Ian Young. Second Edition. Metuchen, New Jersey: The Scarecrow Press, 1982.

V. OTHER CRITICAL WORKS WITH SIGNIFICANT CONTENT ON GAY AND LESBIAN POETRY

Abbott, Steve, and Rudy Kikel. "In Search of a Muse: The Politics of Gay Poetry," in *A Gift of Tongues: Critical Challenges in Contemporary American Poetry*, ed. by Marie Harris and Kathleen Aguero. Athens and London: University of Georgia Press, 1987.

Hull, Gloria T., Patricia Bell Scott, and Barbara Smith. *All the Women Are White, All the Blacks Are Men, But Some of Us Are Brave: Black Women's Studies*. Old Westbury, N.Y.: The Feminist Press, 1982.

Jordan, June. "For the Sake of a People's Poetry: Walt Whitman and the Rest of Us." Preface to *Passion: New Poems, 1977–1980*. Boston: Beacon Press, 1980.

Kalstone, David. *Five Temperaments: Elizabeth Bishop, Robert Lowell, James Merrill, Adrienne Rich, John Ashbery*. New York: Oxford University Press, 1977.

Leyland, Winston, ed. *Gay Sunshine Interviews, Volume I* (Burroughs, Ford, Genet, Ginsberg, Giorno, Harrison, Isherwood, Norse, Orlovsky, Rechy, Vidal, Tennessee Williams). San Francisco: Gay Sunshine Press, 1978.

———. *Gay Sunshine Interviews, Volume II* (Britt, Broughton, Congdon, Duberman, Duncan, Elmslie, Mead, Peters, Peyrefitte, Roditi, Rorem, Steward, Takahashi, Wieners, Jonathan Williams, Meyer). San Francisco: Gay Sunshine Press, 1982.

Peters, Robert. *The Great American Poetry Bake-off*. Metuchen, N.J.: The Scarecrow Press, 1979.

———. *The Great American Poetry Bake-off*. Second series. Metuchen, N.J.: The Scarecrow Press, 1982.

Smith, Barbara. *Towards a Black Feminist Criticism*. Brooklyn: Out & Out Books, 1980; now Crossing Press.

VI. GAY AND LESBIAN HISTORY AND CULTURE

Abbott, Franklin, ed. *New Men, New Minds: Breaking Male Tradition—How Today's Men Are Changing the Traditional Roles of Masculinity*. Freedom, Calif.: The Crossing Press, 1987.

Anzaldúa, Gloria. *Borderlands/La Frontera: The New Mestiza*. San Francisco: Spinsters/Aunt Lute Book Company, 1987.

Bronski, Michael. *Culture Clash: The Making of Gay Sensibility*. Boston: South End Press, 1984.

Bulkin, Elly, and Minnie Bruce Pratt and Barbara Smith. *Yours in Struggle: Three Feminist Perspectives on Anti-semitism and Racism*. Brooklyn: Long Haul Press, 1984; now Firebrand Books.

Cavin Susan. *Lesbian Origins*. San Francisco: Ism Press, 1985.

Core, Philip. *Camp: The Lie That Tells the Truth.* New York: Delilah Books, 1984. Distributed by The Putnam Publishing Group.

Crew, Louie, and Rictor Norton, eds. *The Homosexual Imagination—in literature—in the classroom—in criticism.* A special issue of *College English* (Vol. 36, No. 3—November 1974).

Evans, Arthur. *Witchcraft and the Gay Counterculture.* Boston: Fag Rag Books, 1978.

Faderman, Lillian. *Surpassing the Love of Men: Romantic Friendship and Love Between Women from the Renaissance to the Present.* New York: William Morrow, 1981.

Foster, Jeannette H. *Sex Variant Women in Literature.* New York: Vantage Press, 1956; also paperbound, Tallahassee: The Naiad Press, 1985.

GLARE (Gay Liberation Against the Right Everywhere). *Gay Men and Feminism: A Discussion.* Toronto: GLARE, 1982.

Grahn, Judy. *Another Mother Tongue: Gay Words, Gay Worlds.* Boston: Beacon Press, 1984.

Greif, Martin. *The Gay Book of Days: An Evocatively Illustrated Who's Who of Who Is, Was, May Have Been, Probably Was, and Almost Certainly Seems to Have Been Gay During the Past 5,000 Years.* Secaucus, N.J.: Lyle Stuart, 1982.

Griffin, Susan. *Made from This Earth: An Anthology of Writings.* New York: Harper & Row, 1982.

Heresies Collective and guests, eds. *Lesbian Art and Artists.* New York: Heresies, Vol. 1, No. 3, Issue Three, Fall 1977.

Heresies Collective, ed. *Third World Women: the politics of being other.* New York: Heresies, Vol. 2, No. 4, Issue Eight, 1979.

———. *Sex Issue.* New York: Heresies, Vol. 3, No. 4, Issue Twelve, 1981.

———. *Racism Is the Issue.* New York: Heresies, Vol. 4, No. 3, Issue Fifteen, 1982.

Jackson, Ed, and Stan Persky. *Flaunting It!: A Decade of Gay Journalism from The Body Politic.* Vancouver: New Star Books; and Toronto: Pink Triangle Press, 1982.

Katz, Jonathan. *Gay American History: Lesbians and Gay Men in the U.S.A.—A Documentary.* New York: Thomas Y. Crowell, 1976.

———. *Gay/Lesbian Almanac: A New Documentary.* New York: Harper & Row, 1983.

Lorde, Audre. *Sister Outsider: Essays & Speeches.* Trumansburg, N.Y.: The Crossing Press, 1984.

Malone, John. *Straight Women/Gay Men.* New York: The Dial Press, 1980.

Mitchell, Larry. *The Faggots & Their Friends Between Revolutions.* New York: Calamus Books, 1977.

Morgan, Robin. *Going Too Far: The Personal Chronicle of a Feminist.* New York: Random House, 1977.

Plant, Richard: *The Pink Triangle: The Nazi War Against Homosexuals.* New York: Henry Holt, 1986.

Rich, Adrienne. *Blood, Bread, and Poetry: Selected Prose, 1979–1985.* New York: W. W. Norton, 1986.

———. *On Lies, Secrets, and Silence: Selected Prose, 1966–1978.* New York: W. W. Norton, 1979.

Rowse, A. L. *Homosexuals in History: A Study of Ambivalence in Society, Literature and the Arts.* New York: Carroll & Graf, 1983.

Snodgrass, Jon, ed. *A Book of Readings: For Men Against Sexism.* Albion, Calif.: Times Change Press, 1977.

Thompson, Mark, ed. *Gay Spirit: Myth and Meaning.* New York: St. Martin's Press, 1987.

Walker, Mitch, and friends. *Visionary Love: A Spirit Book of Gay Mythology and Trans-mutational Faerie.* San Francisco: Treeroots Press, 1980.

Williams, Walter L. *The Spirit and the Flesh: Sexual Diversity in American Indian Culture.* Boston: Beacon Press, 1986.

VII. PERIODICALS OF SIGNIFICANCE FOR GAY AND LESBIAN POETRY

With few if any exceptions, no mainstream magazine in the United States has ever published *openly* gay or lesbian poetry. Nor will they now. So, beginning around 1970, gay and lesbian people founded large numbers of their own magazines and publishing operations. The Introduction describes some of this activity. Among the now defunct magazines printing openly lesbian poetry after 1970 were: *Amazon Quarterly, Azalea, Chrysalis, The Ladder,* and *Onyx*. Magazines, now defunct, that printed openly gay male poetry after 1970 include: *Bachy; Blackheart: A Journal of Writing and Graphics by Black Gay Men; Double-F: a magazine of effeminism; Gay Literature; Gay Sunshine; Little Caesar; ManRoot; Mouth of the Dragon; New Leaves Review; No Apologies; Seditious Delicious;* and *Soup*. The following publications are currently active.

I = integrated   G = gay male   L = lesbian   W = women

A.L.O.E.C. Newsletter (Asian Lesbians of the East Coast). P.O. Box 850, New York, NY 10002. *Anamika,* a newsletter for South Asian lesbians, may also be reached % A.L.O.E.C. at this address. (L)

Amethyst. Southeastern Art, Media, and Education Project, 183 Sissom Ave. N.E., Atlanta, GA 38317. (GL)

AQUA (Anarcha-Queers Undermining Authority). P.O. Box 1251, Canal Street Station, New York, NY 10013. (GL)

Bay Windows. 1515 Washington St., Boston, MA 02118. (GL)

Belles Lettres. P.O. Box 987, Arlington, VA 22216. (L)

Black/Out: The Magazine of the National Coalition of Black Lesbians and Gays. P.O. Box 2490, Washington, DC 20013. (GL)

Calyx: A Journal of Art and Literature by Women. P.O. Box B, Corvallis, OR 97339. (W)

Changing Men: Issues in Gender, Sex and Politics. 306 N. Brooks St., Madison, WI 53715. (I)

Christopher Street. P.O. Box 1475, Church Street Station, New York, NY 10008. (G)

Common Lives/Lesbian Lives. P.O. Box 1553, Iowa City, IA 52244. (L)

Conditions. P.O. Box 56, Van Brunt Station, Brooklyn, NY 11215. (W)

The Evergreen Chronicles. P.O. Box 6260, Minnehaha Station Minneapolis, MN 55406. (GL)

Fag Rag. Box 331, Kenmore Station, Boston, MA 02215. (G)

Feminary. 3543 18th St., San Francisco, CA 94110.

Focus. % Paula Bennett, Beaver Pond Rd., Lincoln, MA 01773. (L)

Hanging Loose. 231 Wyckoff St., Brooklyn, NY 11217. (I)

Heresies: A Feminist Publication on Art and Politics. P.O. Box 1306, Canal Street Station, New York, NY 10013. (W)

IKON. P.O. Box 1355, Stuyvesant Station, New York, NY 10009. (I)

The James White Review. P.O. Box 3356, Traffic Station, Minneapolis, MN 55403. (G)

Nambla Journal. 537 Jones Street, #8418, San Francisco, CA 94102. (G)

Other Countries (a literary journal by and for black gay men). P.O. Box 3142 Church Street Station, New York, NY 10008. (G)

New Phoenix Rising: The Asian/Pacific Lesbian Newsletter of the San Francisco Bay Area. P.O. Box 31631, Oakland, CA 94604. (L)

RFD: A Country Journal for Gay Men Everywhere. Route 1, Box 127-E, Bakersville, NC 28705. (G)

Sojourner: The Women's Forum. 143 Albany St., Cambridge, MA 02139. (W)

Salsa Soul Gayzette. % McCray, 533 Washington Ave., No. 4A, Brooklyn, NY 11238. (L)

Sinister Wisdom. P.O. Box 1308, Montpelier, VT 05602. (L)

13th Moon. c/o Prof. Judith Johnson, Dept. of English, SUNY, Albany, NY 12222. (W)

The Women's Review of Books. Dept. 20, Wellesley College Center for Research on Women, Wellesley, MA 02181-8255. (W)

Note: Gay Studies Newsletter, published by the Gay Caucus of the Modern Language Association, contains news and reviews of lesbian and gay literature (Michael Lynch, Editor, Department of English, 7 Kings College Circle, University of Toronto, Ontario M5S 1A1). Also, the national weekly newspaper *Gay Community News* (62 Berkeley St., Boston, MA 02116) regularly features and reviews lesbian and gay writing, and the national biweekly magazine *The Advocate* does the same for gay male and some lesbian writing. Many other local gay and lesbian newspapers and newsletters occasionally review or print gay and lesbian poetry.

VIII. BIBLIOGRAPHICAL SOURCES FOR GAY AND LESBIAN LITERATURE AND CULTURE

Bullough, Vern L., and Barrett W. Elcano, W. Dorr Legg and James Kepner. *An Annotated Bibliography of Homosexuality.* In two volumes. New York & London: Garland Publishers Inc., 1976.

Damon, Gene (Barbara Grier), Jan Watson, and Robin Jordan. *The Lesbian in Literature,* second edition, Reno: *The Ladder,* 1975. This publication lists all known books in the English language about lesbians and lesbianism in the fields of fiction, poetry, drama, biography, and autobiography, with selected non-fiction titles. Complete through 1974.

Dynes, Wayne R. *Homosexuality: A Research Guide.* New York: Garland, 1987. Lists lesbian and gay male titles in history, anthropology, art, film, theatre, and literary studies.

Kuda, Marie. *Women Loving Women.* Chicago: Womanpress, n.d. A selected and annotated bibliography of women loving women in literature.

Maggiore, Dolores J. *Lesbianism: An Annotated Bibliography and Guide to the Literature, 1976–1986.* Metuchen, New Jersey, & London: The Scarecrow Press, 1988.

Young, Ian. *The Male Homosexual in Literature.* With essays by Ian Young, Graham Jackson, and Rictor Norton. Second edition. Metuchen, New Jersey: The Scarecrow Press, 1982.

Credits

Dorothy Allison. "To the Bone," "The Women Who Hate Me," and "When I Drink I Become the Joy of Faggots" from *The Women Who Hate Me* (originally Long Haul Press, now Firebrand Books). Copyright © 1983 by Dorothy Allison. By permission of the author.

Mark Ameen. "Sonnet No 21," "Sonnet No 22," and "Monologue of a Dying Beast" from *Those of You Who Are Dying Are Very Gifted*. Copyright © 1986 by Mark Ameen. By permission of the author.

Antler. "What Every Boy Knows" (originally in *The Son of the Male Muse*, Crossing Press). Copyright © 1983. By permission of the author.

Gloria Anzaldúa. "We Call Them Greasers" and "Interface" from *Borderlands/La Frontera*. Copyright © 1987 by Gloria Anzaldúa. By permission of the author and Spinsters/Aunt Lute, San Francisco.

W. H. Auden. "Lay Your Sleeping Head, My Love," Copyright 1940 and renewed 1968 by W. H. Auden. "A Lullaby," Copyright 1973 by the Estate of W. H. Auden. Excerpt from "In Time of War," Copyright 1945 by W. H. Auden. Reprinted from *W. H. Auden: Collected Poems* by W. H. Auden, edited by Edward Mendelson, by permission of Random House, Inc. Also reprinted by permission of Faber and Faber Ltd. from *Collected Poems* and (excerpt from "In Time of War") *The English Auden: Poems, Essays and Dramatic Writings by W. H. Auden*.

Tommi Avicolli. "The Rape Poem" from *Magic Doesn't Live Here Anymore* (An Androgyny Collective Publication), Copyright © 1976 by Tommi Avicolli. By permission of the author.

James Baldwin. "Guilt, Desire and Love" and "A Lover's Question" from *Jimmy's Blues: Selected Poems* by James Baldwin. Copyright © 1983, 1985, by James Baldwin. By permission of St. Martin's Press, Inc., New York, and Michael Joseph Ltd.

Jane Barnes. "How to Dress Like a Scary Dyke," "How to Dress Like a Femmy Dyke," and "The Hot Dog Poem" from *Extremes: Poems 1971-1981* (Blue Giant Press). Copyright © 1981 by Jane Barnes. By permission of the author.

David Bergman. "Blueberry Man" from *Cracking the Code*. Copyright © 1985 by the Ohio State University Press. By permission of the author.

Frank Bidart. "Confessional, part I" and "The Sacrifice" from *The Sacrifice* by Frank Bidart, Copyright © 1979, 1980, 1981, 1983 by Frank Bidart. By permission of Frank Bidart and Random House, Inc.

Ellen Marie Bissert. "The Most Beautiful Woman at My Highschool Reunion" first appeared in *the immaculate conception of the blessed virgin dyke* by Ellen Marie Bissert © 1977 and is reprinted by permission.

Walta Borawski. "Cheers, Cheers for Old Cha Cha Ass" and "English was only a second language . . ." from *Sexually Dangerous Poet* (Good Gay Poets), Copyright © 1984 by Walta Borawski. "Invisible History" (originally in *The Son of the Male Muse*, Crossing Press), Copyright © 1983. By permission of the author.

Beth Brant. "Her Name is Helen" from *Mohawk Trail*. Copyright © 1985 by Beth Brant. By permission of the author and Firebrand Books.

James Broughton. "Wondrous the Merge" from *Ecstasies* (Syzygy Press). Copyright © 1983 by James Broughton. By permission of the author.

Olga Broumas. "She Loves" (originally printed in *Bad Attitude*, Spring, 1986). Copyright © by Olga Broumas. By permission of the author.

Charles Ortleb. "Some Boys" (appeared in *Angels of the Lyre*, 1975). By permission of the author. "Militerotics" (first printed in *Mouth of the Dragon*, June, 1975). By permission of the author. "Metaphor as Illness" and "On Finding Out That the One You Slept with the Night Before Was Murdered the Next Day" from *Three New York Poets* (GMP, London). Copyright © 1987 by Charles Ortleb. By permission of the author.

Pat Parker. "'Where Will You Be?'" from *Movement in Black* (The Crossing Press). Copyright © 1978 by Pat Parker. By permission of the author. "Prologue from 'Legacy'" and "My Brother" from *Jonestown & other madness*. Copyright © 1985 by Pat Parker. By permission of the author and Firebrand Books.

Kenneth Pitchford. "Surgery" from *Color Photos of the Atrocities* (Litle, Brown). Copyright © 1973 by Kenneth Pitchford. By permission of the author.

Ralph Pomeroy. "A Tardy Epithalamium for E. and N." Copyright © 1969 by Ralph Pomeroy. Printed by permission of Ralph Pomeroy.

Minnie Bruce Pratt. "Waulking Song: Two" from *We Say We Love Each Other* (Spinsters Ink). Copyright © 1985 by Minnie Bruce Pratt. By permission of the author. "The Child Taken from the Mother" (originally published in *Gay Community News*, Oct. 11-17, 1987). By permission of the author.

J. N. Regan. "Partial Luetic History of an Individual at Risk" (originally printed in *The James White Review*, Vol. 4, no. 3—Spring, 1987). By permission of the author.

Adrienne Rich. "Twenty-One Love Poems"—Reprinted from *The Dream of a Common Language, Poems 1974–1977*, by Adrienne Rich, by permission of the author and W. W. Norton & Company, Inc. Copyright © 1978 by W. W. Norton & Company, Inc. "Yom Kippur 1984"—Reprinted from *Your Native Land, Your Life, Poems* by Adrienne Rich, by permission of the author and W. W. Norton & Company, Inc. Copyright © 1986 by Adrienne Rich.

Muriel Rukeyser. "St. Roach" and "Then" from *The Gates* (1976), Copyright © 1976 by Muriel Rukeyser; "Looking At Each Other" from *Breaking Open* (1973), Copyright © 1973 by Muriel Rukeyser; "The Speed of Darkness" from *The Speed of Darkness* (1968), Copyright © 1968 by Muriel Rukeyser; all reprinted by permission of International Creative Management, Inc.

Michael Rumaker. "The Fairies Are Dancing All Over the World." Copyright Michael Rumaker 1975, 1977, 1983 and 1986. By permission of the author.

Kate Rushin. "The Bridge Poem" (first published in *This Bridge Called My Back: Writings by Radical Women of Color*). Copyright © 1981 by Donna Kate Rushin. By permission of the author.

Assotto Saint. "Triple Trouble: an exorcism" (first printed in *RFD*, vol. 13, no. 4—summer, 1987) Copyright © 1987 by Assotto Saint. By permission of the author.

Susan Saxe. "Questionnaire from 'Notes from the First Year'" (originally printed in *Talk Among the Womenfolk*, Common Woman Press, 1976). By permission of the author.

Ron Schreiber. "'an alarming new development'" (first printed in *Bay Windows*, September, 1983). Copyright © 1983 by Ron Schreiber. By permission of the author. "the house is old" from *Tomorrow Will Really Be Sunday* (Calamus Books). Copyright © 1984 by Ron Schreiber. By permission of the author.

James Schuyler. "Growing Dark" and "Sleep" from *The Morning of the Poem* by James Schuyler. Copyright © 1976, 1978, 1980 by James Schuyler. Reprinted by permission of Farrar, Straus and Giroux, Inc., and Maxine Groffsky Literary Agency. "Tom" from *A Few Days* by James Schuyler. Copyright © 1985 by James Schuyler. Reprinted by permission of Random House, Inc., and Maxine Groffsky Literary Agency.

Vickie Sears. "Pubescence at 39" (first published in *Gathering Ground: New Writing and Art by Northwest Women of Color*, The Seal Press, 1984). By permission of the author.

Aaron Shurin. "Exorcism of the Straight/Man/Demon" from *The Night Sun* (Gay Sunshine Press). Copyright © 1976 by Aaron Shurin. By permission of the author.

Anita Skeen. "Women Who Cook" from *Each Hand a Map*. Copyright © 1986 by Anita Skeen. By permission of the author and Naiad Press.

Linda Smukler. "The Shower" (originally published in *Conditions: 11/12*, 1985). Copyright © 1985 by Linda Smukler. By permission of the author.

May Swenson. "Poet to Tiger" by May Swenson is reprinted by permission of the author, Copyright © 1970 by May Swenson. "Four-word Lines" by May Swenson is reprinted by permission of the author, Copyright © 1965 by May Swenson.

Kitty Tsui. "A Chinese Banquet" from *The Words of a Woman Who Breathes Fire*. Copyright © Kitty Tsui, 1983. By permission of the author and Spinsters/Aunt Lute, San Francisco.

Lisa Vice. "Pants." By permission of the author.

James L. White. "Making Love to Myself" from *The Salt Ecstasies*. Copyright © 1982 The Estate of James White. Reprinted by permission of Graywolf Press.

John Wieners. "My Mother" and "A Poem for Trapped Things" Copyright © 1964 by John Wieners. Reprinted from *Selected Poems: 1958–1984* with the permission of Black Sparrow Press.

Tennessee Williams. "Life Story" from *In the Winter of Cities*. Copyright © 1956 by Tennessee Williams. Reprinted by permission of New Directions Publishing Corporation and Abner Stein, London. "You and I" from *Androgyne, Mon Amour*. Copyright © 1972 by Tennessee Williams. Reprinted by permission of New Directions Publishing Corporation and Abner Stein, London.

Heather Wishik. "Visitation Rights" (first published in *New Lesbian Writing*, 1984). By permission of the author.

Shahid (Roosevelt Williamson). "Letters Come to Prison" (originally published in *Fag Rag*). By permission of Roosevelt Williamson.

PHOTO CREDITS

Mark Ameen / © Becket Logan; Antler / photo by Jeff Poniewaz; Gloria Anzaldúa / Shelley Eisenman; W. H. Auden / Photograph © 1988 by Jill Krementz; Tommi Avicolli / © 1986 Breez Cooper; James Baldwin / Photograph © 1988 by Jill Krementz; Jane Barnes / © 1987 by Dan O'Brien; Frank Bidart / photo by Nick Capozzoli; Walta Borawski / photo by Michael Bronski; Beth Brant / © Jeffrey German; James Broughton / Chris Felver © 1988; Olga Broumas / © Ariel Jones; Susan Cavin / photo by Tee Corinne; Chrystos / Ana R. Kissed; Cheryl Clarke / Robert Giard © 1987; Jan Clausen / Colleen McKay; Dennis Cooper / photo © by Sheree Levin; tatiana de la tierra / Fabiola Barona; Alexis De Veaux / Dwight Carter; C. M. Donald / Brenda Prince, London; Robert Duncan / McDarrah Photo Collection; Jim Everhard / photo courtesy of Orry Kelly; Edward Field / Robert Giard © 1987; Beatrix Gates / Tova Green; Allen Ginsberg / Robert Giard © 1986; Jewelle Gomez / © 1984 Morgan Gwenwald; Paul Goodman / Heka; Judy Grahn / Chris Felver; Freddie Greenfield / photo by Brian Quinby; Susan Griffin / Robert Giard ©1988; Thom Gunn / Ander Gunn; Marilyn Hacker / Copyright © by Morgan Gwenwald; Joy Harjo / Paul Abdoo; Paul Harteis / Emma Rodriguez; Essex Hemphill / Daniel Cima; Richard Howard / Robert Giard © 1986; Langston Hughes / photo courtesy of Alfred A. Knopf, Publishers; Will Inman / © LaVerne Harrell Clark; June Jordan / Trudy Rosen; Maurice Kenny / Paul Rosado; Irena Klepfisz / Paula Nelson; Bill Kushner / Bernadette Mayer; Joan Larkin / Naomi Bushman; Michael Lassell / © 1986 Howard Rosenberg; Audre Lorde / Colleen McKay, All Rights Reserved © 1986; Paul Mariah / Dennis K. Hall; William Meredith / Emma Rodriguez; James Merrill / Photograph by Layle Silbert, © Copyright 1988; Honor Moore / Inge Morath; Robin Morgan / Taura; Carl Morse / © Becket Logan; Eileen Myles / © Dona Ann McAdams; Suniti Namjoshi / Brenda Prince, London; Harold Norse / © 1986 Nina Glaser; Frank O'Hara / Kenward Elmslie; Peter Orlovsky / McDarrah Photo Collection; Pat Parker / © Barbara Raboy; Kenneth Pitchford / Eva Rubinstein; Minnie Bruce Pratt / © JEB (Joan E. Biren) 1987; Adrienne Rich / Colleen McKay, All Rights Reserved © 1986; Muriel Rukeyser / © Honor Moore; Michael Rumaker / Bob Goff; Kate Rushin / Robert Giard © 1987; Assotto Saint / photo by Alcindor; Ron Schreiber / Robert Giard © 1987; James Schuyler / Photograph © 1988 by Jill Krementz; Anita Skeen / RussComm; Linda Smukler / © 1987 Maureen Seaton; May Swenson / Photograph by Layle Silbert, © Copyright 1978; Kitty Tsui / © Desiree Thompson 1987; James White / Ellen Hawley; John Wieners / photo by Brian Quinby; Tennessee Williams / Photograph © 1988 by Jill Krementz; Heather Wishik / Susan L. Donegan.

All other photographs in this book were supplied by the authors or their authorized representatives, and although no specific credit is given here, these photographs are protected under existing U.S. copyright statutes and may not be reproduced without permission.

Index of Titles

Authors are listed alphabetically in the Table of Contents.

About the Editors

Author of three books of poems, including *The Curse of the Future Fairy*, **Carl Morse** is the translator of a biography of Paul Verlaine and the essays of André Maurois. Editor with several major publishers, he was for a number of years Director of Publications for The Museum of Modern Art, New York. Morse's lyrics and speeches for theater have been performed throughout Europe and the United States. In recent years he has presented Open Lines, N.Y.—a national series of readings by profeminists, lesbians, and gay men. A selection of his poems appears in *Three New York Poets* (GMP, London, 1987). He is currently completing the full-length performance piece *Impolite to My Butchers*.

Joan Larkin's first book of poems, *Housework*, appeared in 1975; her second, *A Long Sound*, in 1986. She has taught writing at Brooklyn College since 1969. She has also taught poetry workshops in Maine, Massachusetts, Florida, and at Sarah Lawrence College. A founder of Out & Out Books, a women's independent publishing company active from 1975 to 1981, Larkin co-edited, with Elly Bulkin, the anthologies *Amazon Poetry* and *Lesbian Poetry*. She is a 1987 recipient of a National Endowment Grant as well as a New York State Foundation for the Arts Grant.